THE STRATEGY OF TRUTH

THE STRATEGY OF TRUTH

A STUDY OF SIR THOMAS BROWNE

LEONARD NATHANSON

THE UNIVERSITY OF CHICAGO PRESS
CHICAGO AND LONDON

Library of Congress Catalog Card Number: 67-18216

THE UNIVERSITY OF CHICAGO PRESS, CHICAGO & LONDON
The University of Toronto Press, Toronto 5, Canada

Published 1967

Printed in the United States of America

TO MY MOTHER AND FATHER

PREFACE

The critic who would discern the principle of unity in the writings of Sir Thomas Browne must begin by acknowledging their lack of architectonic structure. The historian of ideas is likely to conclude that Browne is deficient in elementary consistency of thought. Yet critics and intellectual historians agree with specialist students of seventeenth-century literature about the high imaginative, stylistic, and intellectual value of Browne's major prose compositions.

This book springs from interests both broader and more special than most previous studies of Browne. These have sought to define his achievement as a unique stylist and his place in the larger field of Renaissance stylistics; to explore the relation between his life and writings, his mind and art; and to examine the background and substance of his scientific and religious thought. My approach, while inevitably following some of these interests, differs in that it considers Browne's major works in the light of a multiple framework provided by literary history, the history of ideas, and modern critical theory. Thus, the study of Browne's Platonism included in this book is instrumental to demonstrating how this Platonic orientation functions as a structural and thematic principle in Browne's individual writings.

My final purpose is neither to prove a thesis in the history of ideas nor to draw a composite picture of the author's mind. Since we value Browne primarily as an artist rather than as a thinker, our focus must finally be critical, aiming at a deepened understanding and surer basis for judgment of Browne's literary works as works. Accordingly, this study involves something of a critical experiment in that it undertakes to read discursive works as if they were mimetic. Though *Religio Medici*, *Urn Burial*, and *The Garden of Cyrus* pursue discursive arguments composed of data and opinions rather than plots enacted by characters, their effects and hence their form can, I believe, be profitably examined in terms of the approximation of each, in varying degrees and ways, to an action. Not, of course, an action like that of a drama or a novel, but instead an action of ideas – resulting in what may be called a mimetic essay. For, as we will see, specific issues and the larger theme and argument of each work are subsumed within an intellectual framework which generates their interplay and their resolution.

The first three chapters are preliminary and set forth the intellectual context and critical method applied to the discussion of form and meaning in Browne's works. Chapter II deals chronologically with the development of the Platonic tradition in religion, philosophy, and science, not from the standpoint of the history of ideas as an independent discipline, but as a context selected and shaped to questions relevant to Browne. Since the content of Browne's scientific thought is outside the scope of this book, I have not included any treatment of *Vulgar Errors* except to illuminate certain facets of other works. The chronology of Browne's life and literary career is appended for convenience of reference.

All quotations from Browne are from Sir Geoffrey Keynes's revised edition, *The Works of Sir Thomas Browne*, 4 vols. (Chicago: University of Chicago Press, 1964), referred to as *Works*. This takes full account of bibliographical and textual work done since Keynes's six-volume edition (London: Faber and Faber, 1928–31) and reprints the text of *Religio Medici* by Vittoria Sanna (University of Cagliari, 1958).

References to the three works upon which this study concentrates have been incorporated as follows: *Religio Medici*, first or second part followed by the number of the section, as (I, 16); *Urn Burial* and *The Garden of Cyrus*, chapter of the work followed by page number in Volume I of Keynes, *Works*, as (III, 152).

It is a pleasure to record my gratitude to those who have

contributed to the making of this book. I consider myself fortunate to have been introduced to the serious study of seventeenth-century literature in the seminar of the late Professor Ruth Wallerstein at the University of Wisconsin. The dissertation from which this book grew was written under the direction of Professor Merritt Y. Hughes, who allowed the freest possible rein to my thoughts and critical interests while attending to them with all the discriminating thoroughness for which this eminent scholar is known. In their earliest form, parts of this study were read by my good friend Professor William Rosen of the University of Connecticut. I owe a very special debt to Professor J. Leeds Barroll of the University of Cincinnati for the personal support of his friendship and the stimulus of his true and open conversation during the half-dozen years this book took shape. Professor Austin M. Wright, my office-mate at Cincinnati, was an intellectual companion and most instructive sounding board against whom some of the basic assumptions in this study were tested. Professor Frank L. Huntley of the University of Michigan, to whom anyone writing on Browne is indebted for the wisest and most comprehensive account of the author's life and works, read the entire book and offered many helpful suggestions. I especially appreciate the generosity of mind with which he was willing to entertain an approach to *Urn Burial* and *The Garden of Cyrus* quite different from his own. I wish also to thank Mrs. Virginia Mueller for her careful preparation of the typescript; the Committee of the Taft Memorial Fund at the University of Cincinnati for a research grant for the summer of 1962; the Graduate School of the same institution for a grant to pay for preparation of the typescript; and finally the staffs of the various libraries where my research was carried on for their many favors and courtesies – the Universities of Wisconsin and Cincinnati, the Newberry Library, the Sir Thomas Browne Institute at Leyden, and the British Museum.

Vanderbilt University

LEONARD NATHANSON

CONTENTS

PART ONE

CONTEXTS AND METHOD

PART TWO

SIR THOMAS BROWNE AND THE STRATEGY OF TRUTH

PART ONE

CONTEXTS AND METHOD

CHAPTER I

BROWNE AS LITERARY ARTIST

"KNOWLEDGE is pleasure as well as power," said William Hazlitt, amending and humanizing Bacon's apothegm.[1] And though Hazlitt found more to censure than to admire in Sir Thomas Browne, his phrase remains a fitting epigraph for the distinguished physician of Norwich. For Browne, as for the youthful Milton declaiming before his fellow scholars at Christ's College, Cambridge, "the delights that are the secret of study and learning as such easily surpass all others." Milton praised the pleasures of comprehending the physical universe and of knowing human history as manifested in the institutions of all times and places. "To take our flight over all history and regions of the world . . . is the way to live in all the epochs of history . . . and to be a contemporary of time itself."[2] Sir Thomas Browne pursued knowledge throughout his long life with as wide an interest and as fresh a pleasure as Milton endorsed. If for Donne an idea was an emotion, for Browne an idea – though when false, a challenge – was always a positive delight. Bacon's pulse quickens in the *Novum organum* as he reflects that there is "much ground for hoping that there are still laid up in the womb

[1] "On Imitation," *The Round Table: The Complete Works of William Hazlitt*, ed. P. P. Howe, 21 vols. (London, 1930–33), IV, 75.

[2] Prolusion VII, "Learning Makes Men Happier Than Does Ignorance," *John Milton: Complete Poems and Major Prose*, ed. Merritt Y. Hughes (New York, 1957), p. 625.

of nature many secrets of excellent use."[3] Browne, on the other hand, looks less eagerly to the practical application of unrevealed truths than to their enjoyment. Toward the close of *The Garden of Cyrus*, he notes with happy anticipation that "a large field is yet left unto sharper discerners" and that "the whole volume of nature" – human, natural, and mysterious, which his own quest for knowledge encompassed – is still capable of "affording delightful truths."[4]

Montaigne, who turned to literature after he had retired to his tower study, sought those truths useful to man as a moral being in the wise conduct of life. Bacon was interested primarily in the truths useful to man as governor of society and inhabiter and would-be controller of the physical world. Browne, by vocation a scientist who composed his massive *Vulgar Errors* "by snatches of time" wrested from his professional duties, was less absorbed than either Montaigne or Bacon in the utilitarian value of truth. Even in his most practical and subliterary efforts – the *Miscellany Tracts*, his correspondence and note books, and long stretches of *Vulgar Errors* – he threads his way through the "Labyrinth of Truth" and the swamps of mere fact with eager curiosity, but in a disinterested spirit and with little immediate concern for application. Only in the posthumously published *Christian Morals* does he reveal what James Joyce would call a kinetic motive, the exhortation to traditional Christian-Stoic ethics, an area in which he offered few fresh insights. Where Browne is exploring the world of nature, his mind, and his books, he seeks truth primarily as something affording pleasure to man while offering greater glory to God, and only secondarily, and in some areas, to be valued for its power to improve the human condition.

In Browne's attitude toward the search for truth lies an important clue to his position as a writer. That he should be regarded as a philosopher even in the loose sense Montaigne and Emerson sometimes are has never been seriously

[3] Bk. I, Aphorism CIX (*Bacon*, ed. R. F. Jones [New York, 1937], p. 320).

[4] *Works*, I, 225–26.

entertained. While anyone who would understand Browne well must know something of the science of his age, those interested in the methods and contributions of science in the seventeenth century can evidently afford to ignore him. Professor Lynn Thorndike, in the two large volumes (1958) devoted to the seventeenth century in his *History of Magic and Experimental Science*, mentions Browne only twice, and then very briefly.[5] To the student of the history of ideas, in its modern sense of the interrelation of philosophy, science, religion, and art, Browne is of greater importance. Because of his wide interests and sensitivity to many currents of thought, he has frequently been regarded as typical of the intellectual inclusiveness and complexity of his age. While we can profitably read Browne for illustration of his age, we more often read him for himself and the appreciation of his unique literary quality. It is primarily as an artist that we value Sir Thomas Browne.

As an artist, however, he is a difficult figure to approach. The appreciation of personality or of style as a detachable element is no longer consonant with the practice of serious literary criticism. Though the individual reader remains as free as Lamb or Saintsbury to respond to the charm of Browne's personality or to the music of his prose, the critic must define his grounds more rigorously. Nor will it do to group Browne with writers like Gibbon and Burke. The man whose imaginative power and depth of insight transcend his immediate subject and who in addition to producing superb history or brilliant political theory writes with high artistic merit is still, at bottom, a historian or a political theorist. Browne can hardly be considered a scientist or philosopher or religious writer who happened also to be endowed with great literary talent. Writers like Marcus Aurelius and Montaigne, whom we regard as essayists and

[5] But it should be noted that Thorndike's slighting of Browne's scientific importance is not necessarily the final estimate. In her review of these volumes, Marjorie Nicolson – *Philological Quarterly*, 38 (July, 1959): 282–85 – singles out this neglect of Browne as a particular weakness of Thorndike's study.

value for their revelation of personality, were, it can never be forgotten, spokesmen for important and well-defined intellectual positions, Stoicism and Skepticism, upon which their literary stature heavily depends. While modern criticism has raised our estimation of Browne's intellectual attainments, or at least stressed them favorably, he can claim no such niche as Aurelius' or Montaigne's in intellectual history.

There remain those essayists whom we associate not with any particular intellectual discipline or position but simply with themselves – writers like Lamb and De Quincey. It is no accident that the Romantic essayists read and admired Browne so much, for the nature of his discourse is apparently very like theirs. However, to approach him as an unusual and gifted practitioner of the personal essay is inadequate. Unlike his admirers of the early nineteenth century, Browne did not take the purpose of his writing to be entertainment or the projection of his personality. The problem of intention is basic to appraising Browne's writing as imaginative literature. The *Religio Medici* was written as an exercise in faith, a personal meditation, by a conscious man of science. The *Pseudodoxia Epidemica,* or, as it is more often called, *Vulgar Errors,* was his serious contribution to that clearing away of error and determination of truth so vital to thinking men of his age. The companion pieces, *Hydriotaphia,* or *Urn Burial,* and *The Garden of Cyrus,* may well have been conscious artistic efforts, as suggested by their dedicatory epistles and, even more, by their premeditated structure and use of symbol. Yet the bulk of even these pieces is devoted to antiquarian and scientific fact and speculation. His chief works provide, then, no single or clear-cut answer to the question of literary intention. And the issue is further complicated by Browne's explicit distrust of imaginative literature and his continual inveighing in *Vulgar Errors* against metaphorical language as one of the deadly enemies of truth.[6]

[6] Egon S. Merton, in *Science and Imagination in Sir Thomas Browne* (New York, 1949), says of the author's literary and scientific intents:

It is possible, however, even without recourse to the theory of the intentional fallacy, to dispel this issue, since generations of readers and critics have appreciated Browne for the potency of his imagination. In any case, we return inevitably to the conclusion that Browne is an artist. Still, we cannot be sure how the actual works he produced may be submitted to critical examination. For example, can the greatness of *Urn Burial* best be shown by a Longinian method which isolates and analyzes touchstones of the poetic spirit? Or should one seek an Aristotelian method to demonstrate a structural unity, a shapeliness, in this apparently formless and digressive work? Or would a New Critical approach that traces imagery and symbols best establish its status as a genuine and integrated work of art as distinct from the product of an artistic temperament? Of these methods the first has been most generally applied in the past; the second, hardly at all; and the third, though only recently used, has provided many illuminating insights.

No longer tenable is the older view of Browne: that he was at once a dusty antiquarian and a man of remarkable poetic gifts interested in everything, but mainly in dull things, who somehow stumbled into art in those few golden passages which regularly find their way into the anthologies. We now realize, for example, that he was as conscious in his discrimination of the three levels of style as were Milton and Dryden.[7] To say that in the fifth chapter of *Urn Burial* Browne unwittingly ascends high above this tract's pedestrian subject on the wings of poetry is of a piece with the naïveté that wonders why Dryden lapses in *The Hind and the Panther* after so magnificent a beginning or why Milton does not sustain his sublimity in the middle books of *Paradise Lost*. The answer, of course, is that Browne was as sensi-

"Browne's ambition conflicted with his gift; his ambition was to be thorough and professional, his gift to be discursive and lyrical." Browne's literary imagination, Merton declares, "came gratuitously . . . he never cultivated it, or never admitted cultivating it, for its own sake" (p. 7).

[7] See Austin Warren, "The Style of Sir Thomas Browne," *Kenyon Review*, 13 (1951): 674–87.

tive to the requirements of decorum, to the need for suiting level of style to his subject, as were Milton and Dryden. When he mounts to the high style of his most celebrated passages, he does so not by accident or "transport" but because his theme demands all the resources of rich cadence and ardent thought. Particularly in *Urn Burial* the proper thematic occasion leads Browne to take up the gorgeous mantle of the high style with the full deliberation of the Renaissance artist. This would suggest, too, that those informational parts that are frequently only tolerated for their quaintness do contribute to his total effect, just as the angel Raphael's lessons and instructions have their essential place in Milton's design. It implies that a neo-Aristotelian approach might be applied to Browne with profit.

While Browne is a prose writer whose deepest significance cannot be defined in terms appropriate for a Montaigne or a Gibbon, he is an artist of a very high order. His value is akin to that of the poet. Certainly the convergent feelings of readers and critics for three centuries would confirm that judgment. In recent decades Browne has shared in the honors bestowed upon the metaphysical poets and has been admired, like Donne, as a man whose various levels of intellectual perception and emotional response were constantly crossing in the attempt to achieve a unified whole. He provides us not with intellectual proofs or even coherent positions, but with the experience of ideas and of ideas and emotions mingled or in conflict in a unique sensibility. Thus while there are good reasons for setting Browne, with his calm adherence to Anglicanism, in the great rational tradition of Hooker, to mark him as an Anglican apologist is to misplace the emphasis. For Browne argues hardly at all for the rightness of his religious position; instead, he communicates what it is like for a man of his interests and temper to be of the Anglican persuasion. In other words, as a religious writer he is closer to a devotional poet than to a theologian, and his is a kind of discourse more akin to George Herbert's than to Hooker's.

Browne qualifies, then, as a poet. He does not offer propositions for our consent; rather, imaginative embodiments of his experiences – both intellectual and emotional – which we are invited to share and for which the criteria of assent and dissent carry little immediate weight. Yet this in no way means that we can dismiss Browne's ideas and interests as irrelevant to our appreciation of him. Critics who find the greatness of Dante or Milton attested by the fact that we need not accept their beliefs to enjoy their poetry are missing a point as important as the one they are making. Such a view and the approach it implies are unsatisfactory and misleading for at least two reasons. First of all, great imaginative literature cannot be apprehended without sympathetic attention to what the imagination is embodying, which is, after all, inseparable from what the imagination creates. Second, and more important, the very workings of imagination are influenced by the ideas and materials that appeal most powerfully to it at a particular moment in a particular culture. For example, the experience that Spenser felt impelled to recreate in poetry, together with his ideas and attitudes, did more than provide thematic material for his art to work upon. They contributed directly to his mode of experiencing that material and to his allegorical method for embodying that experience in *The Faerie Queene*. Consequently, the critic who seeks to convey as much of the wholeness of the creative work as possible must attend to the ideas within the work and in the milieu of the artist as more than mere subject matter or mere background.

Happily, it is not so pressing to argue this position now as it was a decade or more ago, when the dogma all but prevailed that a mind clinically free of historical aesthetic and intellectual presuppositions, dextrous in the manipulation of certain scalpel-sharp tools of analysis (themselves the product of sweepingly asserted presuppositions) was the only objective instrument to apply to a literary work. A great irony of the New Criticism as a whole is that its salutary stress upon the verbal texture of literature (perhaps inadequate as a *theory* of literature, as the Chicago Aristotelians insist, but certainly indispensable to some of the most useful *techniques* of analysis) has been so often betrayed by lack of historical perceptivity into blunders of interpretation at once far-fetched and literal-minded. On the other hand, a criticism essentially historical in its assumptions and methods, as practiced, for example, by Rosemond Tuve and Louis Martz, has made some of the most valuable contributions to our understanding of particular works of Renaissance literature as well as of the literary art of the period in general.

While evaluation is by definition an absolute from which historical considerations should be eliminated, most students of literature, outside as well as within Academe, spend the greatest part of their effort on the less ultimate activities of analysis and elucidation, without which no just evaluation is possible. In so far as these two functions are addressed to specifically aesthetic issues, as they increasingly are, they cannot be exercised apart from an historical method. Since principles and traditions of artistic representation are aspects of history, one must at some fairly early point in the examination of a writer seek to view the formal qualities of his work within its intellectual and cultural context.

CHAPTER II

THE PLATONIC CONTEXT

If three readers unacquainted with Sir Thomas Browne were each given a different one of his major works and asked to compare impressions, they might well find the resulting conference perplexing. The man who had read *Vulgar Errors* (the first book with careful attention, the later ones only skimmed and sampled) would probably report that Browne was a man with a great zest for facts, especially out-of-the-way facts about natural and human history, and must also have been, in his day, a champion of direct observation rather than hearsay as the true method of science. The second reader, limited to *Urn Burial*, might have found the author somewhat baffling. He could discover no clear-cut purpose in this short work, but had noted that while most of *Urn Burial* deals with curious antiquarian fact, the final chapter rises to the most sublime heights of imagination. He had been so impressed that he would have reread it and would like to read it a third time, though preferring to forego the rest. The third man, having read the *Religio Medici*, would not understand his fellows' implication that Browne was an uneven writer. The *Religio*, he would assure them, though rambling, sustains a high level of interest throughout. Its author is concerned with religion in a distinctly personal way and is remarkably genial and tolerant. He prefers to delight in the mysteries of religion rather than argue about them and becomes positively incandescent about the great mysteries of faith.

Having each rendered their separate impressions, our

three readers might then attempt to synthesize these into a composite picture of the writer. The reader of *Vulgar Errors* would insist that Browne, though fond of old books and prone to whimsical speculations, was primarily an empirical scientist, or was at least trying hard to be one, interested especially in biology, but hardly excluding any subject, scientific or learned, from his compass. The man who had so enjoyed the last chapter of *Urn Burial* would admit that Browne was unquestionably a man of science and learning, but one who must have missed his true calling: that of poet. "Poet, nonsense," our first reader would interrupt, "you should see what he says about poetry and figures of speech in *Vulgar Errors*. He thinks they're a menace." At this point, the reader of the *Religio* might enter the affray in support of the man who had reread the final chapter of *Urn Burial*. "That may be, but in thinking about religion Browne says he prefers easy metaphors to rigid definitions. And he certainly takes some poetical flights in the *Religio*." If, to keep this discussion from becoming too lively, we should now introduce a literary critic, he would doubtless restore order by saying, "Gentlemen, all three of you are right. Browne, you see, was an eclectic. He is at once all the things you say, and more. He is of paradox compact."

Though no such experiment is likely to be performed, the individual reader who proceeds from one to another of Browne's works, or even from one part to another of the same work, is apt to set off a comparable tug of war within his own mind. The wide scope of Browne's interests and the range of his attitudes have earned him such various labels as epistemological pluralist and seeker of the One, Anglican apologist and Latitudinarian, spokesman for religious toleration and devotee of Anglo-Catholic ritual, Baconian scientist and Cartesian rationalist, mystic and humorist, skeptic and occultist, antiquary and poet. And a large measure of justification can readily be demonstrated for any of these. Many of these differing roles are, of course, perfectly compatible; but there are enough real contradictions to substantiate the usual charge of eclecticism and to cast a dubious light upon the man who could live so comfortably with all these positions.[1]

Some central paradoxes in Browne might be stated as follows. How can a man who professedly believes in the unity of truth be a pluralist in epistemology? How is it possible to hold that truth is fully visible not to the senses, but only to faith and intuition, and yet to devote so much of one's life and energy to painstaking observation and study of the physical world? How, in short, can one be an empiricist and a Platonist at once? The answer to this and to many other puzzles about Browne lies in the complex and eclectic nature of his Platonic outlook. The Platonism of Sir Thomas Browne, hardly recognizable as the beliefs of Plato himself, was capable of reconciling the empirical study of nature, the exercise of discursive reason, and the practice of faith. The reconciliation was not a philosophic system, but a personal and poetic method linked to the long tradition of Platonism Browne shared with other writers of his age.

In this chapter we will try to define the broad development of Platonic thought on the complicated questions of the natural world and human knowledge. The long procession of pagan and Christian thinkers relevant to the Neoplatonism and the Platonizing science and theology of the Renaissance were widely known to educated Englishmen. It is worth stressing at the outset that these authors, like others, ancient or modern, were regarded first of all as "authorities" to be cited or borrowed from. Writers of the period often invoke a Platonic thinker with no intention of implying his Platonism nor anything of that leaning in themselves.[2] Their uncritically ravenous appetite for citations from revered ancients and learned moderns allowed Renaissance

[1] Studies of Browne's thought, as positive and sympathetic as the following, still admit or even stress his eclecticism and inconsistency: Basil Willey, *The Seventeenth Century Background* (London, 1934); William P. Dunn, *Sir Thomas Browne: A Study in Religious Philosophy* (Minneapolis, 1950); Frank L. Huntley, *Sir Thomas Browne: A Biographical and Critical Study* (Ann Arbor, 1962).

[2] See Sears Jayne, "Ficino and the Platonism of the English Renaissance," *Comparative Literature*, 4 (1952): 214–38.

writers to be quite comfortable about quoting authorities whose general positions might differ radically from their own. At the same time there existed an awareness of the line of spokesmen whose doctrines, beliefs, and values constituted the Platonic tradition and of authors who were conscious descendants of Plato. Ficino, especially, we will see, insisted upon this sense of a living tradition, all of whose members were equally "present."[3]

The shaping influence of Platonism on Sir Thomas Browne has long been recognized by those attracted to the intangible atmosphere of his mind. Emphasis upon his Platonism has continued as critical interest has shifted to the furniture of Browne's mind and the arrangement of that furniture. In this study I will attempt to show the specific relevance of Platonic epistemology for the material substance of his writings and for their thematic and structural principles. This will involve a detailed application of the Platonic paradigm of knowledge – Idea, nature, custom, to be elaborated in these preliminary chapters – to Browne's major works.

At this point, we may suggest in more general terms that his Platonism accounts for the fact that he exercised his reason in two apparently antithetical ways that encompass at least three distinct modes of thought. First, he employs reason according to the Aristotelian and scholastic method which allowed for the derivation of general ideas from the data of sensation as well as the inference of inevitable particular truths from given assumptions. In *Vulgar Errors* inductive and deductive strategies are often employed side by side on the same problem. Second, Browne uses reason in its Platonic and Augustinian sense, the strategy of faith and intuition which enables the individual to grasp ultimate truths. Such epistemological pluralism is perhaps the favorite evidence adduced to support the charge of irresponsible eclecticism leveled at Browne even by some of his staunchest

[3] Raymond Klibansky, in *The Continuity of the Platonic Tradition during the Middle Ages* (London, 1939), pp. 45–47, has made available a key document which illuminates this attitude – Ficino's letter to his friend Martin Prenninger, who had "sought instruction about Platonic Philosophy and its Latin exponents."

admirers. If so, it is a charge to which most of his contemporaries would also stand guilty. We will see, however, that these ways of knowing cannot be interpreted simply as supplementary to one another or as interchangeable. Rather, they are hierarchical; and for Browne the Christian and Platonic way is clearly the highest strategy of truth.

1

At first consideration, the attempt to combine empiricism and Platonism, as personal leanings as well as philosophical positions, appears a logical and temperamental contradiction. If truth inheres solely in intelligibles unknowable to the senses, the study of particulars becomes fruitless. Socrates, in the *Theaetetus,* had shown sense perception to be a deceptive instrument for reaching truth. In place of the atomism of earlier Greek philosophers, to whom reality inhered in matter, Plato substituted the reality of immaterial Ideas. Because the Ideas were rational they could not be apprehended through the senses, but only through the faculty and power of dialectic.[4] Ideas or Forms have an objective existence; though man's knowledge of them is conceptual, as all real knowledge is, they are not the creations of human thought, nor even of divine thought. Rather, they are eternal epistemological and ethical absolutes: the final aim of knowledge and the basis for the good life.[5] Whatever disparate notions have been incorporated into the Platonic tradition, the assumption of ontological and moral absolutes along with an unalterable opposition to any type of relativism has been constant down through the centuries.

It is a commonplace that Plato's own thought, as recovered by modern scholars like Jowett, Paul Shorey, A. E. Taylor, and F. M. Cornford, is not a very useful or even dependable guide to seventeenth-century writers acknowledging in-

[4] *Republic* 532 ff.

[5] The theory of Forms in this sense is presented especially in *Phaedo* and *Republic.* The concept appears in various guises and stages of development also in *Parmenides, Theaetetus,* and *Timaeus.* See Paul Shorey, *What Plato Said* (Chicago, 1933); Francis M. Cornford, *Plato's Theory of Knowledge* (London, 1935).

debtedness to him or expressing explicitly Platonic ideas. In most of the twenty centuries between Plato and Sir Thomas Browne, few of Plato's own writings were known at first hand.[6] Even after the revival, from the East, of Greek studies in fifteenth-century Italy and the recovery and dissemination of Plato's works through Ficino's translations, Cicero and the Church Fathers remained Platonic sources of the first importance.[7] Indeed, Ficino himself had written about Plato prior to his serious work on the texts, while he still knew little Greek; and the patristic and classical sources upon which he had depended continued to exercise an independent influence alongside the commentaries, compendiums, translations, and learned or popular expositions that were the products of the humanistic revival of Plato. Also, Plato's doctrines had, from his own time, been interpreted and modified in the light of other philosophies and thus fused with and adapted to them. It is hardly necessary to stress the extreme complexity of the intellectual history – both pagan and Christian – in which Plato's thought figured. What must be emphasized is that in the Renaissance Platonism meant a body of tradition and not the writings or the ideas of a single thinker.

This condition was not "unconscious" or merely the result of uncritical presuppositions. Rather, the Renaissance quite consciously and deliberately did not think of Platonism as a system of thought found in or derived solely from the writings of Plato. Instead, this period considered the whole line of thinkers, including Hermes Trismegistus, Zoroaster, and Pythagoras, though their attributed writings were mistakenly assumed to antedate Plato, as Platonists. The aim

[6] For the survival and transmission of Plato's text see Klibansky, *Continuity of the Platonic Tradition.*

[7] A standard account of the Platonic tradition from the viewpoint that seeks Plato himself is Paul Shorey, *Platonism Ancient and Modern* (Berkeley, 1938). For students of literature the approach in Paul O. Kristeller's survey, *Renaissance Thought* (New York, 1961), pp. 48–69, is more valuable. On a larger scale of intellectual and literary contextualism is E. R. Curtius, *European Literature and the Latin Middle Ages*, trans. W. Trask (New York, 1953), *passim.*

was not to recover or restate the exact doctrines of the dialogues, but to combine some fundamental belief such as the idea of permanence, the immortality of the soul, or spiritual love with ideas derived from other sources.[8] Such an approach was supported by the superstition, long enjoying wide credence, that Plato's philosophy was a continuation of esoteric knowledge received by him from the East, which he had in turn passed on in a deliberately veiled form comprehensible only to the chosen.[9] An important corollary of this view (aside from allegorical interpretation) is that the problem of knowledge and of the right use of reason involves the ethical purity of the soul's direction as much as correct intellection. This attitude, prominent among both Christian and pagan idealists, appears of course in Plato's own writings and also in Scripture, so that its occurrence in Browne's period among the Cambridge Platonists involves a fusion for which it is all but impossible to determine a precise source. The main point to be borne in mind, however, is that Plato was regarded as the pivotal agent in the formulation and dissemination of a great body of scientific, philosophic, and religious knowledge, rather than as an originator in the strict sense. Moreover, the diversity of his own writings, along with their oblique and often inconclusive presentation, fostered even wider divergences among Platonists already separated by their own differences of selection and emphasis. And there are still other major reasons for the eclecticism and diffuseness of this tradition.

Long before the great revival and consolidation of Platonic philosophy in Alexandria during the third century, marking the beginning of true Neoplatonism, the writings of Plato had undergone irrevocable changes at the hands of his successors in the Athenian Academy. The most important of his immediate followers was, of course, Aristotle, who quarreled with his teacher's notion of how unchanging universals

[8] Kristeller, *Renaissance Thought*, pp. 48 ff.

[9] For the tradition of religious knowledge as concealed and esoteric, see Edgar Wind, *Pagan Mysteries in the Renaissance* (New Haven, 1958), esp. pp. 13–30, 176–88.

caused the existence of particular sensibles. Or, to be more exact, Aristotle pointed out that Plato never really described how the universals caused the existence of sensibles; instead of giving an explanation, he had employed a metaphor—that of pattern and copy—to define the relationship.[10] Aristotle conceived of substance as deriving its identity from form and from final cause (or function). According to his teleology, the final cause does more than direct a process towards its preconceived end. It is also the source of energy, stimulating the object toward its own realization in material form.[11] In other words, the final cause is an efficient cause as well, though not in the sense of an agent or maker, but of an immaterial motive which tends toward the growth or development into the material shape, without which the object has only an ideal existence.[12] This notion of teleology, concerned with the manifestation of substance potentially and actually, is related to Aristotle's biological interests and method.

As for the concept of Forms, Aristotle is often distinguished from Plato in thinking of them as inherent in material objects, thereby determining their kind or species, rather than as transcendent. Actually, Aristotle was not opposed to the concept of Forms (he makes constant use of them in the *Metaphysics* and elsewhere), nor did he explicitly deny their transcendent existence apart from matter. Where Aristotle splits with Plato is over the question of the *objectivity* of the Forms, which is a different question from their transcendence.[13] And even here Aristotle, in effect, rejects the theory of Forms found, say, in the *Phaedo* in favor of a reinterpretation of that found in the *Timaeus*, the most important of the dialogues for the ancient and medieval

[10] *Metaphysics* 991 ff. (W. D. Ross, trans. and ed., *The Works of Aristotle*, 11 vols. [Oxford, 1908–31], vol. VIII). See Werner Jaeger, *Aristotle: Fundamentals of the History of His Development*, trans. R. Robinson (Oxford, 1934), pp. 125 ff.

[11] *Metaphysics* 1072^{b}.

[12] *Metaphysics* 1043^{ab}.

[13] See the discussion by R. G. Collingwood, *The Idea of Nature* (New York, 1960), pp. 80–92.

world. In the *Timaeus*, the notion of the Forms as eternal immaterial entities, propounded earlier in the *Phaedo*, is juxtaposed to and yet kept sharply distinct from the idea of God as eternal thinker and mind. While God thinks the Forms, divine thought does not actually create or support them. Forms are as independent of the mind of God, though only the divine mind knows them perfectly, as they are divorced from the activity of human thought, which can never enjoy perfect knowledge of them, just as material objects can never do more than approximate intelligibles.

As Plato's only scientific work, the *Timaeus*, widely known through the translation of Chalcidius, was the foremost influence in the tradition of Platonic cosmology and empirical studies.[14] Its comprehensive scheme of the creation and the nature of things is expounded with enthusiastic fervor by the Pythagorean philosopher for whom the dialogue is named. The heavens, planets, earth, elements, mineral and vegetable bodies, animals, and man himself were all created according to purposeful design. "The world came into being — a living creature truly endowed with soul and intelligence by the providence of God."[15] The world of nature, however, the result of a willed, creative act by God, is modelled after something which is a priori both to nature and to God's will: the world of intelligibles. This seniority of abstract and rational Forms to the divine will, despite reinterpretation by later pagan Platonists and despite the attempts of Christian Platonists to modify it in accordance with basic dogma, remained a stubborn obstacle to a truly philosophic

[14] Chalcidius' translation of *Timaeus* 17A–53C and his commentary on this fragment have been sumptuously edited with full apparatus as Volume IV in *Corpus Platonicum medii aevi*, the editorial project under the direction of Raymond Klibansky, sponsored by The Warburg Institute: *Timaeus a Calcidio translatus commentarioque instructus*, ed. J. H. Waszink (London, 1962). The evidence as to Chalcidius' religious position and the likelihood of his having been a Christian are examined by Waszink (pp. xi–xvii).

[15] *Timaeus* 30[b], (B. Jowett, trans., *The Dialogues of Plato*, 4 vols. [Oxford, 1953], III, 717). The corresponding passage in Chalcidius reads: "Ex quo apparet sensibilem mundum animal intellegens esse diuinae prouidentiae sanctione" (Waszink, p. 23).

synthesis of Christian and Platonic thought. The *Timaeus*, however, is extraordinary in that its influence often worked in precisely the opposite direction than its doctrine, as we now understand it, might lead us to expect. To some extent this may be the result of the assumption that Plato was presenting strongly held views of his own, when he may, as A. E. Taylor has attempted to show, have been summarizing the scientific opinion of his day.[16] But the great range of un-Platonic ideas derived from the *Timaeus* may be attributed as much to the ambiguous suggestiveness of the dialogue itself as to the misconstructions and eclecticism of later writers. Its wealth of ideas propounded with poetic and moral ardor inevitably elicited richly diverse elaborations from others.

The priority, and therefore superiority, of the intelligible Forms to the mind and will of God had to be shunned as a terrible heresy by the Fathers of the Church.[17] Yet they could take over many details of the creation as given in the *Timaeus*, using them as a scientific support and expansion of Genesis. The outstanding example of this is the answer to the question of why God created the world: because his goodness, being without jealousy, wished to communicate itself.[18] The very appealing idea that God in his goodness bestowed that goodness upon the design of the world and that the plenitude of Ideas as known to the mind of God caused the plenitude of the creation, was the source for the orthodox world view expressed in the great chain of being.[19] The parts of the *Timaeus* translated into Latin by Chalcidius, along with his influential commentary, was almost all that the early Middle Ages had of Plato's own writ-

[16] *A Commentary on Plato's Timaeus* (Oxford, 1928), pp. 18 ff.

[17] See Étienne Gilson, for example, on the crucial difference between Augustine's identification of the One with Being (HE WHO IS) as opposed to the Plotinian view of the One as the absolutely first principle to which being is subordinated, in *History of Christian Philosophy in the Middle Ages* (New York, 1955), p. 70 f.

[18] *Timaeus* 29^{d}–30^{c}.

[19] The subject, of course, of A. O. Lovejoy's classic study in the history of ideas, *The Great Chain of Being* (Cambridge, Mass., 1936).

ings, and the Neoplatonic cosmology of the period was based upon it. The dependence of nature, composed of matter (or space) and time, upon the intelligible world, eternal and without matter, gave rise to a dual view of the gulf between the two realms. The separation of being and non-being fostered distrust of the study of nature as a vain concern with the world of ceaseless change. However, an emphasis upon the other side of the dichotomy, the relatedness of visibles to invisibles, encouraged natural studies, justifying them as a way of apprehending God through the creation.

Space is presumed in the *Timaeus*, and also by Aristotle, to have existed before the act of creation, as the inchoate matter shaped in imitation of the pattern of intelligibles. Time, on the other hand, came into existence as a part of the creation itself and therefore paralleled in all its elements the intelligible world after which it was modelled. One of the most famous statements in the *Timaeus* expresses just this relationship: "Time is the moving image of eternity."[20] The vehicle for expression of the time-eternity relation is itself the very concept of metaphor. This perhaps is why the line of thinkers descending from the *Timaeus*, despite their aim of expatiating a scientific account of the universe and the systematic or even encyclopedic organization of their writings, characteristically produced discourse more closely allied to poetry than to dialectic in its relation of referents to language and of objects to concepts.[21] In terms of the ethics of knowledge, however, if all things in time are likenesses of eternal entities, the world of phenomena becomes a philosophically, and later a theologically, valid object of

[20] 37^{d} (Jowett, III, 723). Chalcidius' version: "Quapropter imaginem eius mobilem numeroque serpentem factae a se machinae deus sociabat eam quae tempus dicitur, aeuo intacto et in singularitate perseuerante" (Waszink, p. 30).

[21] Edgar Wind, in *Pagan Mysteries*, p. 176, offers this explanation: "But because the ultimate One is thus invisible, His visible manifestations must be manifold. Poetic pluralism is the necessary corollary to the radical mysticism of the One. To Renaissance Platonists, as to Plato himself, a generous and varied use of metaphor was essential to the proper worship of the ineffable god."

study, provided of course that such studies are pursued for the sake of their proper end and not out of vain curiosity or, still worse, the impious desire to assert human power over the world. A predominant focus of post-Classical and medieval Platonism, the attempt to work out scientifically the detailed relation between matter and spirit, the transitory and the permanent, has usually been regarded by modern students as a lamentable aberration. Nevertheless, the Timaean tradition along with certain less respectable infusions has enjoyed right up to our own day an underground life in various types of occultism and theosophy. And though, strictly speaking, the *Timaeus* is free of pantheism, it has always exercised a powerful appeal for the pantheistically inclined.

The *Timaeus'* long history of interpretation and accretion cannot be traced here in anything like the fullness required for an understanding of the dialogue's precise significance in the seventeenth century. But certain shifts of meaning and fusions with other streams of thought must be noted. Plato distinguished the beneficent craftsman who willed the creation of the universe from the Ideas, patterns, or standards according to which the universe was constructed. Aristotle, departing from Plato on the objectivity of the Forms, identified the Creator completely with the Forms; they are the modes of his thought.[22] By denying the antecedent and independent existence of the Forms apart from the divine mind, he filled the crucial gap in Plato's ontology.[23] Instead of static, objective Forms, which are the final cause of nature, and the will of God, operating as efficient cause, Aristotle conceives of a single unmoved mover in whom final and efficient cause coalesce. In his theology, then, as in his theory of nature, efficient and final cause are inseparable.

[22] See Jaeger, *Aristotle*, pp. 382 ff.

[23] From a critical standpoint, Plato's whole theory of Forms is a posteriori his epistemology and may, indeed, be considered an ontologizing of his theory of knowledge. It is therefore not surprising that he does not consider the question of causality: "*How* do the Forms cause the existence of sensibles?" but only the question "*Why* did sensibles come into being?"

The Forms are the categories of God's thought; God's knowledge of himself and of all that truly is thus becomes identical. The belief in later mystical Platonism that all knowledge is really a kind of self-knowledge may be viewed as a microcosmic corollary of this position as much perhaps as it is a product of the doctrine of recollection.

The *Timaeus* as modified by Aristotle was of key importance in shaping the tradition of Christian Platonism. Aristotle elaborated the moral purposiveness implicit in the *Timaeus* into the detailed teleological system which was the groundwork for the prevailing philosophy of nature until the seventeenth-century revolution of thought. On one side, the Platonic-Aristotelian synthesis was worked by a thinker like Proclus, the last major figure in the Athenian school, into a comprehensive science of being. On the other side, Plotinus, the great filter through whom the Renaissance collected its Platonism, saw the beauty of the Forms encompassing their ethical and cognitive value and built his system upon the doctrine of the *eros*, the longing of the imperfect soul to ascend through *nous* (intelligence) to the original source of its emanation.

2

After Aristotle, Platonic thought ramified into an intricate pattern of cross branches. The Athenian Academy turned from the search for knowledge and the determination of the life lived according to the Idea of the Good toward skepticism. They abandoned as unattainable the quest for rational knowledge and dismissed the issue of justice, since they considered any laws humans might devise as mere convention. Meanwhile, the Stoics—as free from doubt as the Skeptics were obsessed by it—evinced a strong interest in Plato.[24] The dialogues exercised an influence upon them destined to play an important role in the later development of the tradition. It was Stoic ethics that appealed most powerfully to future generations: the stress upon submission to natural

[24] For a general account of this period and of Stoicism, see Wilhelm Windelband, *A History of Philosophy*, trans. James H. Tufts, 2d ed. (New York, 1958), pt. 2, chap. 1.

law, upon the imperturbability won through control of the passions, and upon the sense of duty that paradoxically makes the individual fulfill his social responsibilities in a world from which—even though he may govern it—he has won a detached independence. The Stoics' lack of real intellectual penetration and their patent question-begging have justly earned them the contempt of modern students of philosophy. But to the Hellenistic world and to many later troubled periods in search of practical wisdom the Stoic answers were more satisfying than those of any other pagan school. Then too the combined literary and personal distinction of such spokesmen as Seneca and Marcus Aurelius assured Stoicism its great popularity. Moreover, though seemingly incompatible with Christian feeling, Stoicism, with its rigorous self-sufficiency once reinterpreted, served later Christian centuries as well as Boethius in the ancient world as the common personal consolation and the instructor in public duty. The man shaped by the ethical ideals of a Platonically leavened Stoicism came to be something very like a normative figure for the Renaissance.[25]

The Stoic view of nature derived from Heraclitus' doctrine of the nature *logos* and accordingly saw the primal and dynamic power directing the universe as a divine force eternally moving everything as a single connected whole.[26] Certainly teleological and antimechanistic, the Stoics were nevertheless sharply opposed to Aristotle in their doctrine of the unceasing change of particular things not because they are inspired toward universals, but because the divine power informing them is in a state of perpetual activity. This biological emphasis of Stoic rationalism ran even more counter to Plato's view that intelligence is the faculty whereby men go beyond the fleeting relationships discernible in particulars to an understanding of the eternal and mathematically expressible relations of beings. To the Stoics, intelligence was

[25] Herschel Baker, "Sixteenth-Century Ethics and the Development of Neo-Stoicism," *The Dignity of Man* (Cambridge, Mass., 1947), chap. 18.

[26] See Windelband, pp. 178 ff.

a living, self-contained force in which the complete source and law of its determinations inhered. They thus embraced a pantheism which broke down the dualistic opposition between material necessity and divine rational activity. This position explains why the Stoics, however popular as ethical teachers, had to be firmly rejected for their physics by Christians, since this point was quite unadaptable to orthodox thought.[27]

Nonetheless, this physics was the underpinning for the Stoic ethical position. The assurance that the design of the universe and the order of its processes were established for the welfare of creatures endowed with reason had as its ethical counterpart the injunction that man adapt himself to the cosmic order. That order is defined in the key Stoic doctrine of an eternal natural law written by divine reason into the universe and upon the mind of man. In the Golden Age, man had lived in perfect concord with the law of nature; in the present evil world he can live wisely and happily in so far as his existence conforms to natural law. The assumed universality of natural law results in a procedure of ethical discovery which is an exact reversal of skeptical suspension of belief in the face of a bewildering human variability. The Stoics chose to focus their gaze upon the appearance of more or less identical ideas among men widely separated in time and place. According to the adherents of natural law, ideas such as moral right and wrong, the existence of God, and the immortality of the soul are most cogently proven universal truth by the consent of all men.

Cicero was the sturdiest proponent of the concept of natural law among the ancients. His eloquent embodiment of the Stoic and Platonic commonplaces in a style that was the mark of cultivated learning for the High Renaissance gave this assumption a currency so great as to define one whole side of Renaissance humanism. Indeed, the habit of mind that

[27] Augustine considers and angrily rejects the Stoic view of God as the soul of the world and the world as the body of God in *The City of God* 4. 12 (trans. John Healey [1610], 3 vols. [London: Temple Classics, 1903]).

saw in the *consensus communis* the surest authority (except for revealed religion, which it confirmed) persisted long after the close of the Renaissance among most writers who may be labeled classicists in the broadest sense – from Pope and Dr. Johnson down to T. E. Hulme and Irving Babbitt. For the Renaissance in England, the fullest statement of natural law and the firmest dedication to it is to be found in Hooker, who built the intellectual structure of his *Laws of Ecclesiastical Polity* upon its principles. "The general and perpetual voice of men is as the sentence of God himself. For that which all men have at all times learned, Nature herself must needs have taught; and God being the author of Nature, her voice is but his instrument."[28] Innate rational knowledge, especially of God and of the absolutes which best govern man's private and civil life, is the cornerstone of Stoic ethics. That this idea bears very close resemblance to the Platonic doctrine of recollection is not surprising,[29] since Stoicism in the ancient world and Christian Neo-Stoicism in the Renaissance usually appear in intimate connection with Platonism.

By the beginning of the Christian era, a highly eclectic philosophy compounded of Plato, Aristotle, and Stoicism (but hardly resolving the differences among them) was very widely known in the Hellenistic world, with Alexandria its leading center. At about this time, the development of Platonism, already so greatly modified from the dialogues, became interwoven with a variety of specifically religious strands of thought. This juncture marks more certainly than any other the point in the history of Platonism accounting for the extreme heterogeneity of the tradition in the seventeenth century. I can do no more here than list some of the movements and thinkers that availed themselves of Plato and of Greek

[28] Bk. I, chap. 8, par. 3.

[29] While Christians had to reject Plato's belief in cognitions recalled from an earlier life, since this would be to accept the heresy of the pre-existence of the soul, the fact that intelligible truths could not be attained through the senses meant that Christians, as well as Platonists, recognized them to be inner and accessible only to a contemplative process.

philosophy in general to produce the interincorporation known as Middle Platonism.

Pythagorean mathematics, an important ingredient of Plato's own thought, was revived and combined anew with the Platonism current in the Mediterranean world. A strongly occult flavor was added by the interpreters of the philosophy attributed to the supermythical Graeco-Egyptian god Hermes Trismegistus. Hermeticism had roots going back to the mingling in the third century B.C. of the Greek scientific impetus with Egyptian religiosity. Hence the characteristic focus upon the physical world, but pursued in the spirit of mystical religion. Fathoming the profoundest secrets of the universe did not depend upon empirical or rational enquiry, but upon the explication by elite practitioners of the sacred texts revealed to the thrice-great Hermes.[30]

The first figure in the Platonic tradition who, strictly speaking, was of great *theological* importance was Philo Judaeus. In order to answer the challenge raised to the Hebrew scriptures by Hellenized Jews, Philo undertook a synthesis of revealed and natural religion. His attempt to discover the truth common to a theology based upon the historically revealed Law of Moses and also upon Greek philosophy, while insisting upon the superior authority of the Word of God, represents the earliest grappling in the Judeo-Christian tradition with the perennial problems of religion and science, faith and natural reason.[31] One of Philo's most influential contributions lay in drawing a distinction between the literal meaning of Scripture, the base for the positive religion or dogma needed by the man of ordinary understanding, and the eternal philosophic and spiritual meaning which is the object of the man of trained intelligence and high ethical character.[32] This distinction was a fundamental premise of

[30] See A. J. Festugière, *La Révélation d'Hermès Trismégiste*, vol. I, *L'Astrologie et les sciences occultes* (Paris, 1944).

[31] Harry A. Wolfson, *Philo: Foundations of Religious Philosophy in Judaism, Christianity, and Islam*, rev. printing, 2 vols., (Cambridge, Mass., 1948), I, 143–54.

[32] *Ibid.*, I, 55–73.

patristic thought and is of particular relevance to the questions we are tracing since this philosophical allegorizing implies an identification of the "scientific" and spiritual sense.

Admittedly, the proponents of scientific or philosophical interpretation of religious documents always faced an opposition party. Clement of Alexandria and Origen [33] both urged Christians to read Plato, but after them willingness to make use of humanistic learning along with the felt need to do so declined. The stubborn anti-intellectualism of Tertullian and Jerome's notorious refusal to admit the relevancy of the classical heritage he so fully possessed represented an attitude which persisted despite Augustine's attack upon pious ignorance and his insistence that men consider the rational basis of their faith. And even the alleged dominance centuries later of scholastic philosophy was accompanied by a continuing tradition of antirational pietism.[34]

Yet it would be accurate to say that from the period of Hellenistic Christianity down to the Renaissance, the scientific approach to truth did not necessarily appear to the orthodox as opposed or irrelevant to the spiritual. The ethics of knowledge which Augustine worked out in which *scientia* is vain unless it leads to *sapientia* nevertheless stressed that without understanding there is no proper faith in Christian doctrine, just as faith is necessary for knowledge. What I am getting at is that the equation of science with materialism (or secularism) and the resultant perplexity assumed for, say, Victorian religion is invalid and often misleading when applied to earlier periods. One can trace a constant thread of materialism running from the pre-Socratics to Hobbes (materialism was what was meant by atheism), but it was by no means the strand of thought peculiarly or exclusively associated with the scientific quest. Indeed, Platonic idealism was

[33] Like Plotinus, Origen was born in Egypt and studied under Ammonius Saccas, traditionally regarded as the founder of Neoplatonism.

[34] Ruth Wallerstein has traced the tradition of anti-intellectual pietism in relation to Marvell and other seventeenth-century English writers in *Studies in Seventeenth-Century Poetic* (Madison, Wisc. 1950), pp. 231–54, *et passim*.

indispensable for the growth of medieval science.[35] The confusion is one of terms. When we speak of "science" we mean a specifically narrowed object of study – the natural world – and also a certain method of study, which since the time of Bacon and Descartes has entailed a complete split between spirit, faith, and religion on one side, and matter, natural reason, and science on the other. To put it another way, we can hardly conceive of "science" apart from a nominalist world view and a purely empirical method. But for the Christian Fathers, the possibility of reaching a true understanding of the physical universe and of spelling out its order rests upon the Platonic theory that universal mathematical Forms constitute the nature of things.

Two kinds of interest in the created world fit within this framework of philosophical realism: the scientific endeavor to discover the logical structure of things, as in Aquinas, and the habit of symbolic interpretation especially associated with Platonically oriented thinkers like Augustine and Bonaventura. While the former may properly be labelled Aristotelian, it stems ultimately from the *Timaeus*. For the line of Neoplatonic thinkers from Plotinus to Ficino, however, the tendency to symbolic interpretation of natural data is unquestionably the more important. The term "Neoplatonic," it should be noted, was coined by modern students to distinguish the Alexandrians from Plato's own thought. More specifically, it is applied to the Alexandrians of the third century of our era who consciously identified themselves with Plato, taking his writings as a supreme authority in a way unlike his earlier followers, and sought to build a synthesis that would harmonize Aristotle and the Stoics with Plato's dialogues.[36] Plotinus was the leading exponent of this syncretism and the founder of the Neoplatonic school. Born in Egypt and educated under Ammonius Saccus in

[35] This is the subject of an article by Paul Shorey, "Platonism and the History of Science," *Proceedings of the American Philosophical Society*, 66 (1927): 159–82.

[36] A standard account of the movement is Thomas Whittaker, *The Neo-Platonists: A Study in the History of Hellenism*, 2d ed. (Cambridge, 1918).

Alexandria, after travels in the East he went to Italy where he established his great reputation as a teacher. These biographical facts, when coupled with the striking resemblance between many of Plotinus' key doctrines and the Hermetic writings worthiest of serious attention, suggest the likelihood of a link going back to Middle Platonism. While no direct relation between Plotinus and Hermetic thought has been definitely established, both represent attitudes of Timaean derivation received through independent channels and passed on by each into medieval Platonism.

The basic and often-repeated ideas of the *Corpus Hermeticum*[37] recall Plato, the Stoics, and Philo, while prefiguring much of what is intellectually most important and religiously exalted in Plotinus. The concept of God as the One (*monas*) in a specifically mathematical sense is presented in Treatise IV. "Being then the source, the One contains every number, without being contained in any of them. And it generates every number, without being generated by any other number."[38] The tendency of medieval Platonism to equate the created and the eternal simply with the visible and the invisible is strongly marked, along with the epistemological corollary that "thought alone can see what is hidden from sight, since it is itself hidden from sight."[39] Hermes explains to his son Tat how God can make Himself manifest to his bodily eyes even though the thought within Tat is concealed from his own sight: through study of "the sun, the course of the moon, the arrangement of the stars"[40] and consideration

[37] The standard modern edition is by A. D. Nock, who established the Greek text, and A. -J. Festugière, who provided a French translation and the commentary. *Corpus Hermeticum,* 4 vols. (Paris, 1945–54). I have translated Festugière's French for quotations incorporated into my discussion and given the French in the note for passages either translated or referred to.

[38] *Corpus Hermeticum* 1. 53. "Etant donc principe, la monade comprend tout nombre, sans être comprise en aucun d'eux. Et elle engendre tout nombre, sans être engendrée par aucun autre nombre."

[39] *Ibid.* 1. 61 (Treatise V). "Seule . . . la pensée voit l'inapparent, puisqu'elle est elle-meme inapparente."

[40] *Ibid.*, "Si donc tu veux voir Dieu, considère le soleil, considère le cours de la lune, considère l'ordonnance des astres."

of the marvellous Providence of the Creator in shaping the heavens and everything on earth, including the body and faculties of man.[41] And *Nous* itself, acting as a character in a dialogue, elsewhere instructs Hermes: "Mind makes itself visible in the act of thinking, God in the act of creating."[42] Hermes distinguishes between the ever-living world and the eternal God, denying that they are coeval.[43] The Timaean double view of the value of the physical world is prominent; but Plato's willed creation at a particular moment has been modified into a world that is ever being made.[44]

It is only a short step from these doctrines of the *Corpus Hermeticum* to Plotinus' divided attitude toward the condition of the soul in the sensible world. Plato's idea of imitation is altogether absent from the *Enneads*.[45] With Plotinus the relation between eternal ideas and mutable particulars shifts from pattern and copy to absolute and emanation. The result is a sharpening of the opposition between the soul's role as the ordering agent in matter and as exile seeking to return to its home. Plotinus, a vehement critic of the Gnostics,[46] was tireless in his praise of the beauty of the world. He held that nature was not evil, but only put to bad use when fastened on for its own sake rather than employed as a step lead-

[41] *Ibid.* 1. 62.

[42] *Ibid.*, 1. 157 (Treatise XI). "L'intellect se rend visible dans l'acte de penser, Dieu dans l'acte de créer."

[43] *Ibid.*, 1. [87] (Treatise VIII). "En tête réelement de tous les êtres vient Dieu, éternel, inengendré, créateur de l'univers; en second vient celui qui a été fait par le Premier à son image et qui est par lui conservé, nourri, et doué d'immortalité en tant qu'issu d'un père éternel, vivant sans fin en tant qu'immortel. Car le *vivant sans fin* diffère de l'*éternel*."

[44] *Ibid.*, 1. 118 (Treatise X). "Quel est donc le dieu matériel que voici? – C'est le monde qui est beau, mais qui n'est pas bon. Car il est fait de matière et il est aisément affecté; le premier parmi tous les passibles, il ne vient qu'en second dans la série des êtres et il est en lui-même incomplet; ayant lui-meme commencé d'être, mais subsistant toujours, il subsiste dans le devenir; et ainsi toujours en devenir, il est le devenir des qualités et des quantités: car il est en mouvement, et tout mouvement de la matière est devenir."

[45] I have used Plotinus, *The Enneads*, trans. Stephen MacKenna, 2d ed., rev. B. S. Page (London, 1956).

[46] *Enneads* 2. 9.

ing to the One. The individual soul in body and the world soul in nature are imprisoned only if they willingly surrender to the narrowness of matter instead of striving to transcend it and rise to *nous*. Nonetheless, students of Plotinus acknowledge that his conclusion is essentially that of the Gnostics: the sensible world is to be rejected.[47] Plotinus himself was not unaware that his position was contradictory, as he pointed out in regard to Plato:

> We have to fall back on the illustrious Plato, who uttered many noble sayings about the Soul, and has in many places dwelt upon its entry into body so that we may well hope to get some light from him.
>
> What do we learn from this philosopher?
>
> We will not find him so consistent throughout that it is easy to discover his mind.
>
> Everywhere, no doubt, he expresses contempt for all that is of sense, blames the commerce of soul with body as an enchainment, an entombment, and upholds as a great truth the saying of the Mysteries that the Soul is here a prisoner. . . .
>
> In the Phaedrus he makes a failing of the wings the cause of the entry to this realm . . .
>
> In all these explanations he finds guilt in the arrival of the Soul at body. But treating, in the Timaeus, of our universe he exalts the Cosmos and entitles it a blessed god, and holds that the Soul was given by the goodness of the Creator to the end that the total of things might be possessed of intellect, for thus intellectual it was planned to be, and thus it cannot be except through soul. There is a reason, then, why the Soul of this All should be sent into it from God: in the same way the Soul of each single one of us is sent, that the universe may be complete; it was necesary that all beings of the Intellectual should be tallied by just so many forms of living creatures here in the realm of sense.[48]

[47] William R. Inge, *The Philosophy of Plotinus*, 2 vols. (London, 1918); Emile Bréhier, *The Philosophy of Plotinus*, trans. J. Thomas (Chicago, 1958).

[48] *Enneads*, 4. 8. 1.

Plotinus grasped the essential optimism about nature in the Timaean explanation of the plenitude of the creatures and was responsive to the beauty radiated into sensibles from intelligibles. Yet he definitely preferred the side of the Platonic coin which pictures All-Love as the ineffable One in withdrawn contemplation.

Plotinus fused his version of Plato's metaphysic with the doctrine of the *eros* from the *Symposium* and predicated upon it a life of complete detachment of soul from body. He thus inferred a substantially Gnostic attitude, though explicitly opposing it. For the Stoics and for Platonists influenced primarily by the *Timaeus*, the soul is the animating and organizing power which gives matter its importance. Thinkers drawing more upon the earlier, Socratic dialogues and influenced as well by the Orphic and Pythagorean traditions were inclined to view the soul's entry into the world as an indication of its impurity. Bréhier has noted "the state of tension to which the image of the sensible world gives rise in Plotinus" and stresses how "this double appraisal" contributes to the richness and enduring interest of his thought.[49] "The admiration for its beauty arises from the fact that we see in it the intelligible beings whose radiation has produced it. The disparagement of the world, on the contrary, arises because, in referring these beings to the intelligible world of which they are members, Plotinus considers only the equivocal and incomplete way in which this radiation has been received and the ugliness of matter which has obscured its brilliance."[50] This wavering between a positive and negative valuation of the world is implicit in all idealistic thought which depends upon both the distinctness and relatedness of matter and spirit, body and soul. There is no more familiar attitude in the literary Platonism of the Italian Renaissance and of the sixteenth and seventeenth centuries in England than the dualism which celebrates the superiority of the abstract and eternal Ideas to the sensible and transitory phenomena and which yet finds great value in the physical

[49] Bréhier, p. 170.
[50] *Ibid.*, p. 170 f.

through its correspondences – scientific, ethical, aesthetic – with the spiritual in the world soul, the intermediate essence posited by Plato in the *Timaeus.*

The problem of assigning value to the material within this idealistic framework took on an added dimension among Christian thinkers because of the doctrine of the Incarnation. From the standpoint of Orphic or Gnostic thought, for God to assume a body of corruptible flesh was metaphysically impossible and ethically repugnant. It was therefore necessary for Augustine to refute the Manichaean identification of matter with evil, so that evil derives not from the body but from the apostasy of the will.[51] To assert otherwise is to blaspheme against the goodness of the creation and, more seriously, to dishonor Christ's body and his Incarnation. This consideration must be counted an underlying factor in Augustine's psychologically subtle conception of human personality as the soul in the body, a complex integration, rather than as body and soul, a simple dualism.

Nevertheless, the image of man's body as a prison-house, with all that it implies for his ethical and epistemological status, we need hardly remind ourselves, is extremely common among Christian writers. Disgust with the world of sensibles and with man's body can often verge upon heresy among Christians exercising their pessimism on the favorite Stoic theme *contemptus mundi.* There is no need to invoke Gnosticism to account for the persistent survival of this habit of feeling among Christian thinkers, even after the apparent triumph of rational theology. St. Paul's distrust of human faculties and his emphasis upon sin and upon the need for the transforming conversion through grace are, of course, more proximate and more authoritative sources for Augustine and the pattern of thought that was to be revived in the Reformation. But it is important to distinguish the distrust of matter based upon its uncertainty as an object of knowledge, characteristic of both naturalistic and idealistic Greek philosophy and of such different later thinkers as Montaigne and Des-

[51] *City of God* 14. 3.

cartes, from that of religious thinkers like Plotinus or Augustine. With the specifically religious Platonists and with the Christian Fathers the grounds of this traditional distrust were extended with a peculiar ethical force. Plotinus employs the figure of initiation into the mysteries to express how the Good is obtained by those "who will divest themselves of all that we have put on in our descent." [52]

The worshipful praise of the goodness and beauty of the world could not be harmonized with this attitude. To escape from this dilemma Plotinus denied the reality of matter and hence of evil.[53] Everything that *is* partakes to some extent of the goodness overflowing from the One into *nous*, soul, and the sensible world.[54] Evil is merely the negative condition of non-inclusion in the hierarchy of emanation; it is therefore meaningless.[55] To climb the ladder of emanation so as to proceed from objects less illumined by the One to those more illumined entails detachment of the soul from the sensible world beneath it. The final destination is union, or rather re-union, with the One.[56] The experience is precisely that of mysticism wherein the individual achieves full illumination through direct contact with the Deity, and thus *identity* and *unity* with Him.

Plotinus' infusion of mysticism into the Platonic tradition was of decisive importance for the subsequent Christian centuries, since it qualified the role of intellectual and spiritual endeavors.[57] Mysticism is radically unlike Plato's own dialectical method and humanistic concern and is directly contrary to the historical Revelation conceived by the primitive Church. Plato envisioned the world of intelligibles as attainable through a dialectical process, a continuous act of contemplation that eschews sensibles for mathematicals and ends in the Idea of the Good, the realization of justice in man

[52] *Enneads* 1. 6. 7.
[53] *Enneads* 2. 5. 4, 5.
[54] *Enneads* 1. 7.
[55] *Enneads* 1. 8. 3.
[56] *Enneads* 6. 9.
[57] See J. Guitton, *Le Temps et L'Éternité chez Plotin et Saint Augustin* (Paris, 1933).

and in the state.[58] For Plotinus the longed-for release of the soul and its return to the One are achieved through an ecstasy, a mystical vision beyond the boundary of dialectics. Historically, this shift was of the utmost importance, since the tone of Platonism from Augustine to the monks of St. Victor, Bonaventura, Ficino, Henry More and the other Cambridge men in England was to be essentially Plotinian on the crucial point of the nature of contemplation.

3

The Neoplatonic transformation of the problem of knowledge from rational inquiry to mystical illumination was the foundation for Augustine's epistemology.[59] Augustine held the Platonists in ambivalent esteem. He warmly acknowledged in Book X of *The City of God* his personal indebtedness to them and that of Christian theology in general. At one point in his youth he had been a follower of Pyrrhic skepticism, believing that all knowledge was tied to sense perception and therefore hopelessly subjective. The Platonists had rescued him from the dismal conclusion that the real nature of things is unknowable by introducing him to a class of non-sensory realities independent of the mind's invention and exempt from the flux of time and the mutability of matter. But the crux of Augustine's comparative examination of Christian worship and Platonic theology is the disparity between their fundamental assumptions. He opposes the Platonist belief that "that which has not been for ever cannot be for ever" with the view expressed in the *Timaeus* "that both the world, and the gods, made by that great God in the world, had a beginning, but shall have no end, but by the will of the Creator endure for ever." [60] This distinction, already observed in the Hermetic writings, ren-

[58] See A. -J. Festugière, *Contemplation et Vie Contemplative selon Platon* (Paris, 1950), pp. 157–209.

[59] For my general view of Augustine I have depended chiefly upon Étienne Gilson, *The Christian Philosophy of Saint Augustine*, trans. L. E. M. Lynch (New York, 1960).

[60] *City of God* 10. 31.

ders the Plato of the *Timaeus* compatible with Christian orthodoxy.

Though Platonism had extricated Augustine from materialism and epistemological nihilism it was still inimical to his purpose. The impetus of Augustine's controversial and dogmatic writings, one should never forget, was toward giving the Church of his time a firm doctrinal shape. The choice and direction of his philosophic speculations were guided by this pragmatic motive and the problem of knowledge therefore took on dimensions for him unknown to previous thinkers in the Platonic tradition. His polemics were successively aimed at two chief targets: Manichaeism and Pelagianism. Both of these heresies challenged the supremacy of the divine will. The identity of good, Augustine maintained, derives from its having been willed by God, not from any prior or inherent relation to what is good. Similarly, human knowledge of what is true can be born only through an act of divine grace. Only that knowledge is certain which God reveals of himself; it cannot be won by the endeavors of human understanding but is attainable through grace alone to those possessing faith. The sensible world is not an object of valid knowledge but merely of belief. While the comprehension of physical objects necessary for practical life is a genuine concern of Augustine, he distinguishes this from the knowledge of the eternal structure of the world inaccessible to reason. For all his insistence upon man's depravity and his Pauline distrust of human faculties, Augustine is, of course, no obscurantist. The mathematical forms, the Platonists had taught him, provided the natural objects of our understanding with a substantial being. But these forms are themselves types derived from the supreme source and object of all knowledge, into whose nature we have insight only through grace.

The ethics of knowledge that grows from these presuppositions is in essential agreement with Plotinus. For Augustine the Plotinian *nous* and the *logos* of St. John as interpreted by Origen are one and the same. It is therefore very difficult to mark off the Plotinian from the Pauline tension in this eloquent statement of the ethics of knowledge:

> Non enim frustra et inaniter intueri opportet pulchritudinem coeli, ordinem siderum, candorem lucis, dierum et noctium vicissitudines, lunae menstrua curricula, anni quadrifariam temperationem, quadripartitis elementis congruentum, tantam vim seminum species numerosque gignentium, et omnia in suo genere modum proprium naturamque servantia. In quorum consideratione non vana et peritura curiositas exercenda est, sed gradus ad immortalia et semper manentia faciendus.[61]

The sense of the mathematical structure of the universe and of the procession of the seasons is, as we might expect, charged with the Timaean spirit of science and of poetry fused under the pressure of religious optimism. Augustine's discussion of cosmology and natural phenomena depended upon Platonic theories no less than did the principal pagan authorities Chalcidius and Macrobius, whose influence dominated until the Aristotelian revival of the twelfth century. His scientific thought stemmed from and added the immense authority of his own name to the sacramental view of nature implicit in the chain of being.

In almost every department of seventeenth-century thought Augustine played, through direct impact and his influence as transmitted through others, a role of incalculable importance. Even if one puts aside his special role in Calvinist theology, before any other thinker he is the one who most profoundly defines what we mean by Christian ortho-

[61] *De Vera religione*, 1. 29 (Migne, *Patrologia Latina*, XXXIV [Paris, 1845], col. 145). "For we should not idly and vainly observe the beauty of the sky, the order of the stars, the brightness of light, the alternation of days and nights, the monthly courses of the moon, the fourfold seasons of the year, congruent with its fourfold elements, such power of germinal seeds giving birth to species and numbers, and everything preserving in its own class its own way and nature. In the consideration of these things one must not exercise a vain and fleeting curiosity, but must make an approach to what is immortal and abides forever."

doxy in the English Renaissance.[62] Augustine's was the accepted view of human history: a plan willed and completed in the mind of God and guided by his providence toward the end revealed in Scripture. The doctrine of history in *The City of God* was the working assumption for Raleigh's *History of the World* and was embodied in epic poetry in Books XI and XII of *Paradise Lost.* It is not too much to say that even without the Florentines' editing the works and spreading the thought of Plato and the Platonists, this philosophical tradition would have been familiar to seventeenth-century writers, and respected by them, through the agency of Augustine alone.

We have come to appreciate that the Aristotelianism advanced by Aquinas never dominated later medieval philosophy to so full an extent as had been assumed. The Platonism of Augustine flourished among the Franciscans and fed a kind of piety at once mystical and popular that persisted alongside scholastic rationalism. The greatest of the Franciscan Platonists was Saint Bonaventura, who was an exact thirteenth-century contemporary of Aquinas.[63] He placed especial stress on the link between the knowledge of sensibles and affective piety. In the *Itinerarium mentis ad Deum*, Bonaventura likens man's five senses to five doors "through which enters into his soul the cognition of all that is in the sensible world." Moreover, "since by sense we perceive not only these particular sensibles, which are light, sound, odor, savor, and the four primary qualities which touch apprehends, but also the common sensibles, which are number, magnitude, figure, rest, and motion, and since everything which is moved is moved by something, and some are self-moved and remain at rest, as the animals, it follows that

[62] Of particular interest to the student of seventeenth-century literature is the recent study by Louis L. Martz, *The Paradise Within* (New Haven and London, 1964), in which Augustine's "concept of interior 'illumination'" (p. xiii), intimately bound up with his Platonism, is applied to Vaughan, Traherne, and Milton.

[63] The fullest and most valuable study is Étienne Gilson, *The Philosophy of St. Bonaventure*, trans. I. Trethowan and F. J. Sheed (New York, 1938).

when through these five senses we apprehend the motion of bodies, we are led to the cognition of spiritual movers, as through an effect we are led to a knowledge of its causes." [64] In the seventeenth century Bonaventura served as model for the popular treatise by Cardinal Bellarmine, *De ascensione mentis in Deum per scalas rerum creatarum opusculum* (1615); this manual sought to awaken and focus religious feeling through meditation on God's works, the book of the creatures.[65]

4

In the fifteenth century, with the aid of a fresh cultural and textual infusion from the East, the tradition we have been following became the renewed possession and the life purpose of Marsilio Ficino (1433–99). Translator and commentator of Plato and Plotinus, central figure of the famous Platonic Academy of Florence, author of *Theologia Platonica* and other theological and philosophical works, Ficino not only made Plato and the Platonists accessible in Latin but, by shaping the reading and interpretation of them, pervaded, directly or indirectly, almost every department of Renaissance thought, culture, and art.[66] His aims and

[64] Quoted from the translation by George Boas, *The Mind's Road to God* (New York: The Library of Liberal Arts, 1953), p. 15.

[65] Ruth Wallerstein, in *Seventeenth-Century Poetic*, pp. 213–16, discusses Bellarmine's book, which had an English translation (1616) at Douay. In this same study Miss Wallerstein has extensively traced the Christian and Platonic background of the book of the creatures and has sought to demonstrate its relevance to Marvell's poetry and to much of the writing of the age: "the book of the creatures [was] the most immediate expression of the sense of the unity of all experience and of the dependence of the visible and momentary world upon the divine, which in some one of its forms entered into all currents of sixteenth- and seventeenth-century thought which were in any way brought into the religious stream" (pp. 253–54).

Mr. Martz, in *The Paradise Within*, pp. 55–102, offers a very discriminating analysis of Traherne's *Centuries* in relation to Bonaventura.

[66] The standard work is Paul O. Kristeller, *The Philosophy of Marsilio Ficino*, trans. Virginia Conant (New York, 1943); Nesca A. Robb, *Neoplatonism of the Italian Renaissance* (London, 1935), deals with the broader cultural context as well as the thought of Ficino. More specialized studies include A. Chastel, *Marsile Ficin et l'art* (Paris,

methods were not those of disinterested scholarship; a student of this philosophy because a believer in it, he was, like the Alexandrian Neoplatonists, a deliberate eclectic.

Ficino's purpose was to organize the entire body of Platonic writings and doctrine as a viable philosophical system harmonious with Christian faith, as he believed it to be, and even to show its consonance with truths discoverable in other religions.[67] His inclusion within this tradition of the *Corpus Hermeticum* (which he translated before he set to work on Plato's dialogues), the writings erroneously attributed to "forerunners" of Plato like Zoroaster, Orpheus, and Pythagoras, and later followers of Plato and Plotinus among the Church Fathers and the medieval schoolmen, while based on mistaken scholarship, cannot be dismissed as a failure of historical discrimination. It is better understood in terms of the motivation of Ficino's life-long labors with the Platonists: to determine and consolidate their commonly shared truths as the basis for the fullest possible philosophic comprehension of the one true God of Christianity. The significant resemblance, for example, of the Plotinian three hypostases of the Divine-Being to the triune God of Christian doctrine attested, for Ficino, to the ultimate identity of the truths in all religious systems.[68] This is not the same as saying that all doctrines of other religions participate equally in truth; Christian doctrine is the absolute norm and other systems offer some veiled or imperfect intimations. But, at the

1954) and John C. Nelson, *Renaissance Theory of Love* (New York, 1958), for the best-known aspect of Ficino's influence.

[67] This kind of syncretism was carried still further by Ficino's glamorous disciple Giovanni Pico della Mirandola, who sought to synthesize Platonism and Aristotelianism and to demonstrate the harmony of the Cabala with Christan theology. See Eugenio Garin, *Giovanni Pico della Miandola* (Florence, 1937); Ernst Cassirer, "Giovanni Pico della Mirandola," *Journal of the History of Ideas*, 3 (1942): 123–44, 319–46; Joseph L. Blau, *The Christian Interpretation of the Cabala in the Renaissance* (New York, 1944); F. Secret, *Les Kabbalistes Chrétiens de la Renaissance* (Paris, 1964).

[68] Sears Jayne, *John Colet and Marsilio Ficino* (Oxford, 1963), p. 44. The philosophical basis of Ficino's concept of the doctrine of the Trinity is noted by Kristeller, *Ficino*, pp. 168, 249.

same time, this approach suggests that questions not treated or not entirely clear in Christian faith can be filled in and illuminated from other sources. It leads inevitably, as we will see, to an attitude of toleration both of intrinsic-doctrinal and of external-institutional differences.

No habit of mind is more characteristic of Ficino than this syncretism of likenesses, at once humanistically broad and scholastically detailed. Nor is his descent from the ancient Neoplatonists (Ficino regarded himself as re-establishing the continuity broken after Proclus and the end of the Athenian Academy) more significantly indicated than by his quest to advance truth by a process of synthesis that ever extends itself through the discovery of correspondences in the world of thought and in the universe rather than through analytic differentiation. Herein lies much of the appeal of Florentine Platonism to the poetic imagination, for such a system lends itself quite naturally to that mythologizing of doctrine and philosophizing of myth best witnessed by Ficino's own mode of expression.[69] If a fatal philosophical weakness derives from this syncretism, so does a liberating spirit that tends to dispel the exclusiveness of religious authority.

Philo, we saw, admitted philosophy as the handmaiden of religion; Ficino raised her to the rank of a younger sister with practically equal rights in the heritage of truth. With Professor Kristeller's study, the nineteenth-century view of Ficino as devoid of original importance, as a rather turgid exponent of the thought of others, has given way to a new respect for him as an independent thinker. He transformed the traditional Platonic attitude that man's knowledge of the world and of God originates from his knowledge of himself. The contemplative act involves, as in all Platonic thinkers, the soul's transcendence of the world, but Ficino goes be-

[69] The most impressive exploration of this aspect of Renaissance Platonism has been carried on by the art historians, notably Erwin Panofsky in his seminal *Studies in Iconology: Humanistic Themes in the Art of the Renaissance* (New York, 1939).

yond this to assert that the soul can never transcend itself.[70] Positions such as these encourage a humanism which, however different from that of Plato, measures Ficino's distance from the mystery-cult strain of the Alexandrians.

Ficino's humanistic emphasis upon the goodness of man and the world is implicit in the two major theories he gave widest currency in the Renaissance: the immortality of the soul and Platonic love. He read Plato's doctrine of the *eros* (essentially the same for him as Christian *caritas*), like everything else, through a Plotinian lens. But he filtered out the ascetic implications, discarding in effect the essentially Gnostic side of Plotinus' dualism for a monism which optimistically stresses the continuity of experience from the lowest to the highest level and finds the unity of matter and spirit manifested in their beauty. We have seen again and again the potential reversibility of Platonic dualism which allows for a positive interpretation of matter. In Ficino this tendency develops so far as to jettison altogether the underlying burden of Gnosticism of Platonists and Christians alike. This key passage from his commentary on Plato's *Symposium* may be profitably set against Plotinus' treatment of the same question, considered above:

> . . . Venus is two-fold: one is clearly that intelligence which we said was in the Angelic Mind; the other is the power of generation with which the World-Soul is endowed. Each has as consort a similar Love. The first, by innate love is stimulated to

[70] Professor Kristeller notes in his analysis of "internal experience" (*Ficino*, chap. xi), which he calls the "living center" of Ficino's thought, that herein "we touch, perhaps, on the most important point at which Ficino's philosophy differs from that of Plotinus. For Plotinus there is in each contemplative act the distinction between the objective substance and the consciousness striving inward. This contrast is overcome only by a wholly new, transcendent act of consciousness, in which the last cause of existing things is experienced as being also the source and origin of internal life itself, and this is really the true reason for the ontological distinction between the One and the Mind. For Ficino the contemplative attitude cannot be transcended at all, but can only be perfected within itself" (p. 229).

> know the beauty of God; the second, by its love, to procreate the same beauty in bodies. The former Venus first embraces the Glory of God in herself, and then translates it to the second Venus. This latter Venus translates sparks of that divine glory into earthly matter. It is because of the presence of sparks of this kind that an individual body seems beautiful to us, in proportion to its merits. The human soul perceives the beauty of these bodies through the eyes.[71]

Ficino identifies divine love, mythologized as the two Venuses, with both the Plotinian emanation down through the hierarchy of beings and man's desire to ascend and reunite with God. Under this aesthetic definition of love as the first principle of the universe, generated beings tend to assume, ethically and imaginatively, a status closer to intelligibles. The application of such doctrine through the ancient macrocosm-microcosm parallel encourages an exalted, indeed, religious view of human love; the soul's attraction to generated beauty becomes a proof of its immortality. The natural powers of the soul become capable of reaching the highest good. Joined with a Petrarchan sensuous idealism and popularized in works like Castiglione's *Cortigiano*, these doctrines exerted an immense influence on the literature of the high Renaissance, most notably on the love poetry of France and England.[72]

Certain broader implications of Ficino's thought are particularly relevant to the interests we have been following. While he cited with sincerity as well as strategy Augustine's

[71] *Commentary on Plato's Symposium*, ed. and trans. Sears Jayne, University of Missouri Studies, Vol. XIX, No. 1 (Columbia, 1944), p. 142.

[72] The ubiquitous presence of literary Platonism is, of course, assumed by students of Renaissance literature. The following standard works may nonetheless be cited: John Smith Harrison, *Platonism in English Poetry of the Sixteenth and Seventeenth Centuries* (New York, 1903); Robert Ellrodt, *Neoplatonism in the Poetry of Spenser* (Geneva, 1960); A. -J. Festugière, *La Philosophie de l'amour de Marsile Ficin et son influence sur la littérature Française au XVIe siècle* (Paris, 1941).

approval of Plato, Ficino's own use of Plato and of the tradition was quite different from that of Augustine and the other Fathers. It represented a cultural and intellectual innovation of the first importance. Augustine chose those elements of Platonic philosophy that could help construct and support the framework of Christian theology, while rejecting the value of Platonism as a whole. Ficino, on the other hand, attempted to synthesize the entire substance of this system of natural and mystical knowledge, derived from the vast Platonic *corpus* itself, with the theological formulations Christianity had determined centuries before. The dominant medieval attitude had been Augustine's: only what God revealed was real knowledge, as opposed to uncertain opinion, and this knowledge was unattainable by man's natural faculties. Ficino, by fusing the whole system of Platonic thought, which he regarded as divinely inspired, with a theology often fundamentally at odds with it, inaugurated adjustments and reinterpretations on both sides that redressed the inferior role assigned to philosophy. As in the abandonment of Plotinian asceticism, to which it is obviously related, this break with Augustinianism tended to create a new balance in which the knowledge of God reached through natural reason became as authoritative as inferences about the world from revealed knowledge. This renewed belief in man's natural access to divine truth was to have an enormous impact upon epistemology and upon religious attitudes in general. From the other direction, Ficino's stress upon the sparks of divine glory in earthly matter accounts in considerable part for the specifically spiritualistic and theosophical character of much Renaissance science.[73]

The very title of Ficino's major work—*Theologia Platonica*—challenges orthodox assumptions and indicates his

[73] It is not always possible, however, to separate this less respectable aspect of Renaissance Platonism from its important contributions to the development of modern science, especially through its mathematical emphasis, widely recognized in our own century through such works as E. A. Burtt, *The Metaphysical Foundations of Modern Physical Science*, rev. ed. (London, 1932).

awareness of the originality and difficulty of his task. Sir Thomas Browne's central title—*Religio Medici*—poses in its time a much less audacious oxymoron, and this work is a great deal less bold and difficult an intellectual undertaking. The reason is not only that Browne is writing in a loosely personal manner, without a formal philosophic purpose. Rather, Ficino's humanistic synthesis of faith and philosophy as Christian Platonism had come long before Browne's time to lie at the heart of the body of beliefs and attitudes which define the conservative world view of the age. The commonplaces of Christian Platonism could be mobilized, as in Hooker, against an anti-intellectual orthodoxy which dismissed the role of reason in religion and also, as in the Cambridge Platonists, against a materialist philosophy that dispensed with divine spirit in the world of nature.

5

There is probably no English writer of the seventeenth century who more habitually avows and exhibits attachment to the Platonic tradition than Sir Thomas Browne. Though it is impossible to define the Platonic context of the period with great precision, since it included so much (excluding perhaps only outright materialism and relativism) and often gathered a single doctrine from several different, and otherwise unrelated, sources, there is little doubt as to its essential role for an understanding of Browne. His critics tend to agree that Christian Platonism was the framework in which his temper was formed, as it was also the context of knowledge and belief appealing most powerfully to his mind and imagination.[74] As with Ficino, Browne's sense of the

[74] W. P. Dunn says: "Obviously, among the complex elements of Christian philosophy, the ones which Browne finds most congenial are the Platonic, and these he seems to absorb for the most part from Cabbalist and Hermetical sources" (*Sir Thomas Browne*, p. 120). Frank L. Huntley considers Browne's Neoplatonism, along with his Stoicism and Skepticism, as one of the three philosophies that figure importantly in his writing (*Sir Thomas Browne*, chap. 11). Douglas Bush, *English Literature in the Earlier Seventeenth Century*, rev. ed. (Oxford, 1962),

contemporaneity of this body of literature is of more than methodological relevance. It is of substantial interest as well, since it attests to a belief in the continuous revelation of truth, not through one thinker or at some particular moment in history, but throughout the entire historical process. This attitude, given an emphatic and explicit weight, ultimately undermined the special authority of revealed Christianity as conceived by Augustine, subordinating dogma to a universal, Platonic religiousness. Browne, we will see, was seemingly untroubled by this profound split, if indeed at all aware of it, and was able to commit himself to both attitudes with equanimity.

It is the Timaean strand of the Platonic tradition that is especially obvious in Browne. He warmly subscribes to the belief we have traced that in addition to the Revelation of the Bible, God reveals himself through "his servant Nature, that universall and publik Manuscript, that lies expans'd unto the eyes of all" (*Religio Medici*, I, 16). The continual application of this idea is fundamental to his characteristic harmonizing of the man of faith with the man of science. A central theme of the *Religio* is that the study of nature leads to the conclusions of religion. So far from driving him into atheism, his scientific pursuits provide another route to faith and an additional support for it; he therefore respects the natural religion of "the Heathens [who] knew better how to joyne and reade these mysticall letters, than wee Christians, who cast a more careless eye on these common Hieroglyphicks, and disdain to suck Divinity from the flowers of nature" (I, 16). His stress upon Timaean teleology, summed up in Aristotle's *Natura nihil agit frustra*, which he asserts in the *Religio* "is the onely indisputable axiome in Philosophy" (I, 15), recurs in *Vulgar Errors* and wherever he is considering the phenomena of nature. And his feeling

pp. 348–58, approaches Browne as a Platonist above all else and notes that "however much he owes to Stoicism, scholasticism, and other sources, and to his study of comparative religion, it is the Platonic strain (with all its 'impurity') that broadens, deepens, and sweetens his religious thought and feeling" (p. 352).

for the *anima mundi*, for nature as a living creature, pervades much of what he writes. His interest in Hermeticism, the Cabala, and various exotic bypaths of Timaean Platonism is perhaps all too well known and, though shared with Ficino and Pico and English contemporaries like Henry More, has doubtlessly detracted from his reputation for some readers. He likes to entertain the notion of nature as an alphabet by which the learned can read eternity and makes both serious and fanciful use of it, along with the Pythagorean symbolism of numbers, in *The Garden of Cyrus*, his most fully Timaean work. He acknowledges his favor for the allegorical description of God attributed in the seventeenth century to Hermes Trismegistus, *Sphaera cuius centrum ubique, circumferentia nullibi*, and is inclined to credit allegorical interpretations of Scripture and "the mysticall method of *Moses* bred up in the Hieroglyphicall Schooles of the Egyptians" (*Religio*, I, 34).

But while Browne "admired the mysticall way of Pythagoras, and the secret Magicke of numbers" (I, 12), elsewhere the critical scientific investigator was prone to withhold his credence. The man who in *The Garden of Cyrus* was to hunt down every example of the number five in this world and the next could nonetheless criticize in *Vulgar Errors* those who had overconsidered the numbers seven, nine, and sixty-three:

> The Philosophy of Plato, and most of the Platonists, abounds in numeral considerations: above all, Philo the learned Jew, hath acted this part even to superstition: bestowing divers pages in summing up every thing, which might advantage this number. Which notwithstanding, when a serious Reader shall perpend, he will hardly find any thing that may convince his judgment, or any further perswade, then the lenity of his belief, or prejudgment of reason inclineth.[75]

Such discrepancies between works with different purposes may, however, be expected and seem quite minor compared to Browne's habit in the *Religio* of now entertaining habits

[75] Bk. IV, chap. 12 (*Works*, II, 307–308).

of occult thought with hearty approval and now casting a very skeptical eye upon them.

The manner of diffusion of Platonic doctrines makes firm attributions of Browne's "sources" practically impossible. Since the history of a particular idea in the Platonic tradition and even its exact stage of development as represented by a given thinker may be a very different thing from the actual source of derivation for a writer, only the very closest verbal parallels, and fairly extended ones, can establish a definite relation. And even then a passage of Plato or Plotinus is likely to have been picked up secondhand from another author who quoted it. The evidence points to this being very much the case with Sir Thomas Browne.[76]

We are fortunate to have a record of Browne's personal library, the catalogue printed at the time of the public auction of his books and those of his son Dr. Edward Browne.[77] Though a very valuable document for the study of Browne, this catalogue must, for obvious reasons, be used with caution. It can by no means be taken as a certain index to the books Browne owned, let alone to those he read or did not read, simply on the basis of their being listed or not. It is nevertheless interesting that only one work of Plato appears in the catalogue and this, significantly, is Chalcidius' version of the *Timaeus*, in the edition of 1617 with notes by Meursius.[78] Plotinus is not listed at all. For Proclus there is only a Latin translation of the *Paraphrase to Ptolemy's Tetrabiblos* in an edition (1654) [79] too late to have counted in the

[76] The researches of Robert R. Cawley ("Sir Thomas Browne and His Reading," *PMLA*, 48 [1933]: 426–70) and Jeremiah S. Finch ("Sir Thomas Browne and the Quincunx," *Studies in Philology*, 37 [1940]: 274–82) demonstrate how fully Browne shared in the tendency to quote or cite learned authorities at second hand.

[77] *Catalogue of the Libraries of the Learned Sir Thomas Brown, and Dr. Edward Brown, his son* (London, 1710–11). I wish to thank the Yale University Library for generously allowing me to examine in Cincinnati their copy of this very rare catalogue. Dean Jeremiah S. Finch of Princeton University is presently engaged on an edition.

[78] *Catalogue*, p. 11, No. 106.

[79] *Catalogue*, p. 30, No. 1. Though Browne evidently did not own the more important works of Proclus – *Elements of Theology, The*

Religio and in the early editions of *Vulgar Errors*. Browne's numerous quotations, allusions, and paraphrases of Plato[80] almost require us to assume some direct knowledge of the dialogues, though it is impossible to be sure how much of this was at firsthand.

The problem can be solved, at least in part, by the fact that Browne owned Ficino's *Theologia Platonica* (Paris edition, 1559)[81] which, while addressed to "The Immortality of the Soul" (its subtitle), reproduces the important statements and doctrines of Plato, Plotinus, and the other Platonists on most philosophic questions. A notable direct use of Ficino is probably the famous account of man's status in *Religio Medici*:

> . . . we are onely that amphibious piece betweene a corporall and spirituall essence, that middle frame that linkes those two together, and makes good the method of God and nature, that jumps not from extreames, but unites the incompatible distances by some middle and participating natures; that wee are the breath and similitude of God, it is indisputable, and upon record of holy Scripture; but to call ourselves a Microcosme, or little world, I thought it onely a pleasant trope of Rhetorick, till my nearer judgement and second thoughts told me there was

Platonic Theology, and the very extensive *Commentary on Timaeus* — he may well have been acquainted with the larger aspects of his thought. Dr. Thomas Lushington, Browne's tutor at Oxford and later a close friend who persuaded him to settle in Norwich after he himself had gone to Norfolk in the service of Bishop Corbet, was interested in Platonism and left notes (never published) on Proclus' theology. See Browne's letter to the Oxford antiquary John Aubrey, dated 14 March 1672/3, in *Works*, IV, 375–76. For a comprehensive account of Proclus, see Laurence J. Rosán, *The Philosophy of Proclus* (New York, 1949).

[80] These have been collected by Paul Shorey (*Platonism Ancient and Modern*, pp. 192–98), who introduces his inventory with this very curious statement: "Sir Thomas Browne can hardly be classed as a Platonist either in temperament or in scholarship" (p. 192).

[81] *Catalogue*, p. 15, No. 95.

> a reall truth therein: for first wee are a rude masse, and in the ranke of creatures, which only are, and have a dull kinde of being, not yet priviledged with life, or preferred to sense or reason; next we live the life of plants, the life of animals, the life of men, and at last the life of spirits, running on in one mysterious nature those five kinds of existences, which comprehend the creatures not of the world, onely, but of the Universe; thus is man that great and true *Amphibium*, whose nature is disposed to live not onely like other creatures in divers elements, but in divided and distinguished worlds. (I, 34)

This passage is a typical attempt to consolidate a number of hierarchical schemes and to achieve the kind of synthesis of truth dear to the heart of Renaissance Platonists. The five steps of the "Scale of creatures" – presented in the preceding section of the *Religio* (I, 33) – those with existence but no life (minerals), those with life but no sense (plants), those with sense but no reason (animals), those with rational understanding (man), and those with pure intelligential being (angels), correspond, Browne suggests, to the five stages of the individual's progress from embryo, to infant at birth, to child, to man, to soul in glory. This microcosm-macrocosm parallel, based upon the Timaean and Aristotelian commonplace, is introduced by a close imitation of Ficino's concept of the human soul as "the third or intermediate essence" of the five degrees of Being, as expressed in *Theologia Platonica*:

> Finally, to come to the point, we again collect all Being into five degrees, putting God and Angel in nature's highest place, Body and Quality in the lowest, and Soul right in the middle between these highest and lowest degrees. We rightly call it, in Platonic fashion, the third or intermediate essence, since it is both intermediate between the others and in every sense third. In descending from God, Soul is found in the third grade of the descent; and in ascending from Body it is also found in the third

> grade of the ascent. In our opinion it is exceedingly necessary for there to be an essence of this kind in nature, since Angel indeed, as the Platonists say, possesses true Being, that is, remains at all times unchanged; whereas Quality is Becoming, that is, changes from time to time. Clearly Quality is completely different from Angel. While Quality changes, Angel remains unchanged; and while Quality comes into being from time to time, Angel exists at all times. There must therefore be something intermediate (medium) which may agree partly with Angel, and partly with Quality.[82]

While Ficino's own scheme is indebted, of course, to the *Timaeus* and to Plotinus, it has enough distinctive features so that we can see Browne following him rather than the ancient Platonists.

Another work from which Browne could have reaped a rich harvest of Platonic opinions is John Healey's translation of *The City of God* (second edition, 1620),[83] containing not only Augustine's influential discussion of the Platonists in relation to Christian thought but also Vives' detailed chapter-by-chapter commentary with its extensive citations from the entire tradition. Browne's library, very strong in theology, included Philo[84] and the Christian Fathers, in addition to Augustine, who incorporated Platonism in one form or another as a substructure for their own thought—Clement of Alexandria,[85] Dionysius the Areopagite,[86] and Origen.[87] The

[82] Marsilio Ficino, *Platonic Theology*, Bk. III, chap. 2 (trans. in part by Josephine L. Burroughs, *Journal of the History of Ideas*, 5 [1944]: 227).

[83] *Catalogue*, p. 45, No. 74.

[84] *Opera* in 1613 Folio. *Catalogue*, p. 1, No. 12.

[85] *Opera* in 1629 Folio. *Catalogue*, p. 1, No. 15.

[86] *Opera omnia*, 2 vols., in Folios of 1644. *Catalogue*, p. 1, No. 16. The identity of pseudo-Dionysius remains a matter of controversy, but in the seventeenth century this father of Christian mysticism, whose works were not written before the middle of the fifth century, was taken to be the disciple of St. Paul mentioned in Acts 17: 34.

[87] *Opera omnia*, 2 vols., in Folios of 1571. *Catalogue*, p. 1, No. 17.

devotional side of medieval Platonism is represented by Bonaventura's *Meditationes* (Rome edition, 1638)[88] and there is also Cardinal Bellarmine's *De ascensione mentis in Deum* (1615).[89] Too late to have exerted direct influence upon the *Religio* but indicative of Browne's continuity of interest is Henry More's *Immortality of the Soul* (1659),[90] probably closer to Ficino, by virtue of its Plotinianism and its scholastic complexity, as well as its subject, than any other original work of an English Platonist. The exotic side of the tradition is represented by a little book of Thomas Vaughan, twin brother of the poet and arch-Hermeticist of seventeenth-century England, *Hermetical Banquet drest by a Spagyrical Cook* (1652),[91] a fantastic mixture of theosophy and alchemy. In a soberly analytic and mathematical vein is Louis de Morainvillier's *Examen philosophiae Platonicae* (St. Malo, 1656),[92] now an extremely rare book. Finally, Browne owned the authors from whom the Middle Ages had derived a fragmentary knowledge of Plato (besides Chalcidius and, of course, Cicero) and who continued to figure in Renaissance Platonism – Apuleius' *De Deo Socratis* (1625)[93] and Macrobius' commentary on *Somnium Scipionis*, with its comparison of Plato's and Cicero's philosophies.[94]

Browne's citations of Plato in *Vulgar Errors* (vastly outnumbered by those from Aristotle) and in his other works of scientific investigation refer most often to cosmology and phenomena rather than to broader Platonic attitudes. As such they are more likely to have come from his numerous medical books and volumes on natural philosophy than from the Platonists in his library. We may assume, however, that the thinkers considered in this chapter played a more direct

[88] *Catalogue*, p. 58, No. 56.
[89] *Catalogue*, p. 4, No. 11.
[90] *Catalogue*, p. 49, No. 22.
[91] *Catalogue*, p. 51, No. 113.
[92] *Catalogue*, p. 15, No. 94. I have not been able to locate this work in any American library but was able to examine a copy of an earlier edition (1650) in the British Museum.
[93] *Catalogue*, p. 17, No. 208.
[94] *Opera*, 8° edition of 1556. *Catalogue*, p. 13, No. 34.

and decisive part in his mystical Platonism, which permeates the *Religio* and *The Garden of Cyrus* in a way that specific references can scarcely begin to measure. Ethical Platonism, known to the Renaissance more through Cicero than the Florentines, and mingled with neo-Stoicism, is a mainstay of Browne's reflections on the human condition, while the Florentine ideal of friendship as a sign and path toward the love of God informs Browne's glowing tribute in the *Religio* (II, 5).

And to return to our primary concern with Browne's epistemology, we can see from this survey of the tradition which was his preferred context of thought why the question of knowledge could not be confined merely to a specialized rational activity. The soul, according to Ficino, "knows by 'intellection' or pure thought . . . In ourselves we see perfectly that knowledge is nothing else than a spiritual union with some spiritual form."[95] While the man of faith takes precedence over the man of science, within the framework of his Platonism, Browne can be confident of their essential agreement. For this hierarchy composes a continuum, not an opposition. Or, as Ficino said of the soul in relation to the hierarchy of beings: "And in ascending it does not forsake the inferior, and in descending it does not relinquish the sublime."[96] Thus if we cannot look to Browne's Platonism to reconcile all the positions suggested at the outset of this chapter as relevant to him, we can at least account for their often confusing variety and even comprehend them in orderly ranks.

Finally, one may ascribe to the kind of pluralism associated with Platonism one of Browne's most attractive features – his spirit of toleration. For while he believed in the ultimate unity of all truth, he recognized that for man truth is accessible on divided levels. God comprehends all at once, and Browne would assent to John Donne's statement that in

[95] *Platonic Theology*, Bk. III, chap. 2 (*Journal of the History of Ideas*, 5: 232).

[96] *Ibid.*, p. 228.

heaven "God shall Create us all Doctors in a minute."[97] In his fallen state in this world, however, man can at best reconstruct the dismembered body of truth and discern the relatedness between the phenomenal and the noumenous, the noumenous and the divine, through laborious observation and study crowned by rare moments of intuition.

[97] From "A Sermon Preached at the Spittle, Upon Easter-Munday, 1622," *The Sermons of John Donne*, ed. G. R. Potter and E. M. Simpson, 10 vols. (Berkeley, 1953–62), IV, 128.

CHAPTER III

AN APPROACH TO BROWNE

1

THE PRECEDING rehearsal of certain issues in the Platonic tradition provides the context for the approach I wish to pursue in this study of Sir Thomas Browne. Even a slight acquaintance with Browne makes it evident that his mind, for all its diverse and divergent tendencies, or, better still, because of them, was firmly centered in his Platonism. No other current of thought was sufficiently broad and eclectic to encompass him as man of religion, science, and philosophy. Just as Plato's doctrines along with Aristotle's reinterpretations were amalgamated historically with Pythagorean mathematics, Stoic ethics, Plotinian and Christian mysticism, Hermeticism, Philonic and Patristic cosmology and theology, Franciscan empiricism and pietism, Florentine humanism and idealism, and several types of occult symbolism, to name only the most important elements that make up seventeenth-century Platonism, so, many facets of this heterogeneous tradition are reflected with varying degrees of intensity in Sir Thomas Browne.

It is precisely this all-pervasive influence of Christian Platonism that makes a significant treatment of it so difficult: one cannot pin down something that is everywhere, nor even make attributions for Browne's ideas when parallels among Platonists can be so readily multiplied as to become meaningless. The problem is much the same for Vaughan, Marvell, Traherne, and the Cambridge Platonists, since the same context can serve, in general, for one as well as for another. This is not to say that these writers do not have their distinct emphasis and tone, the result of differing selections from the Platonic tradition and of the impact of other interests as well as of individual sensibility. Obviously, Browne, Marvell, and Vaughan, even if we limit our view of them solely to their Platonism, possess distinctive traits of thought, feeling, and expression.

Approaching a writer through the history of ideas cannot, I think, be critically fruitful unless the method goes beyond pointing out resemblances between attitudes and beliefs expressed by the writer and the background against which they may properly be viewed. Such a procedure is indispensable for many kinds of elucidation, and this study, like previous studies of Browne, makes considerable use of it. But for the purpose of analysis it may indicate less of special application to the works under scrutiny than is often assumed. Assigning the attitudes of an author to corresponding niches in the intellectual background or projecting aspects of that background upon the author suffers from obvious weaknesses. As I have suggested, interchanging the author with other writers of the period can often produce similar identifications. Second, since the aim of this procedure is to discover similarities, it may, for the sake of more "findings," neglect the context of particular ideas and fail to discriminate between an attitude asserted only for some strategic reason, and therefore not substantially relevant, and one carrying the main burden of a man's position. I can recall a sophomore insisting to me (with the supporting passages underlined and cross-referenced in his textbook) that the religious outlook of Calvinists and Deists was basically the same since Jonathan Edwards and Benjamin Franklin alike expressed belief in an almighty God and in rewards and punishment in an afterlife. It is not surprising that an immature student, with only anthology snippets to work from, should yoke similar general statements in such entirely different thinkers without questioning whether the motives and dialectical roles of these statements were the same for each writer. However, in a recent study in the history of ideas, as proportionately inaccurate a conclusion is reached by a professional scholar in dealing with Calvin, Montaigne, and Bacon on the efficacy of human reason. The author of that study, by tracing similar attitudes and arguments, links all three figures as reactionary and antihumanistic because they sought to undermine faith in man's rational capacity. The incompleteness of such demonstrations can be very misleading.

But even when such a study proceeds with proper methodological safeguards, its direct value to the student of literature is often dubious. For the literary work ceases to be the object of real interest and is reduced to a document which illustrates or supports a thesis in the history of ideas. A desirable method for applying an author's controlling philosophic orientation to his literary compositions would be one capable of relating that orientation to the larger elements of theme and structure in entire works, considered as works. If we wish to treat Browne's writings as artistic entities we must do more than explain particular attitudes in terms of their appropriate referents outside the work. We must seek as our critical purpose to define the wholeness of the work which determines the significance of its parts. This means that however essential our understanding of Browne's Platonism in passages where he is thinking about or averring belief in Platonic doctrines, such understanding is only a preliminary step. It must be followed by the attempt to see how Browne thinks with and relies upon Platonic doctrine in those elements which hardly appear as actual statements — theme and structure.

2

The function of Browne's Platonism beyond the level of general attitude and explicit assertion has received scant attention. His assurance that "this visible world is but a Picture of the Invisible" and his insistence everywhere upon the universe as living, coherent, and teleologically governed have been employed most often to define the temper of the man or the spirit of his writings as a composite. I should like to demonstrate a closer relevance for Browne's Platonic orientation by showing how it can be adapted into an analytical instrument for increasing our understanding of the intention, form, and theme of his individual works. In the major literary works — *Religio Medici*, *Urn Burial*, and *The Garden of Cyrus* — Browne's Platonic epistemology functions, I would suggest, as a thematic and structural principle.

The problem of truth absorbs Browne's attention more than any other issue. His sensitivity to the seventeenth-century crisis of truth marks him, above any other feature, as a representative man of his age. As a Platonist, Browne assumes that the truths man can discover originate from three different realms of experience. The first comprises the works, activities, and institutions of man; the second is the physical universe, the entire scale of creatures from the sublunary world to the heavens; the third is the supersensuous realm of intelligibles, comprehending both the Platonists' world of Ideas and the domain of grace and revealed truth, which, we have seen, were fused in Christian thought. The relation between the first and second of these sources of experience and knowledge is defined by the concepts of *nomos* (custom or convention) and *physis* (nature), which from the time of fifth-century Athens implied not only the distinction between physical phenomena and human invention but also the opposition between what is objective and according to universal natural law and what is subjective and according to particular and erroneous opinion.[1] As the middle term, created nature, along with the natural reason through which it is approached, is epistemologically inferior to the supersensuous realm which is reached intuitively. But nature is superior to the authority of custom, which only opinion and human tradition support. We must envisage, then, not three sectors which — placed one beside another — complete the circle of knowledge, but three hierarchical planes representing in ascending order the Platonic and Christian movement toward truth: custom, nature, and Idea.

[1] The development of the idea of "nature as norm" has been studied and documented by Arthur O. Lovejoy and George Boas, *Primitivism and Related Ideas in Antiquity* (Baltimore, 1935), pp. 103–16.

The Platonic *locus classicus* for these epistemological categories is the unequally divided line, or the four stages of knowledge, in Book VI, 509d–511e, of the *Republic*. The line is first divided into a shorter portion, the changing world of *visibilia* known through the senses with the aid of the sun, and into a longer portion, the eternal world of intelligibles known to the mind through the aid of the Idea of the Good. Each of these two realms, coinciding with the basic Platonic dualism, is in turn divided according to the ratio of the first division: the visible world into the segments of man-made objects (works of art, social conventions, laws, as well as tables and chairs) and of natural phenomena; the two segments of the line of invisibles are objects of mathematics known through abstract thought and involving axiomatic hypotheses and the Ideas intuitively perceived through a higher reason without benefit of discursive thought.

From the preceding chapter of this study it is evident that the two middle stages of knowledge – natural phenomena and the mathematical forms which support them – were fused in the Platonic tradition to become the ambiguous realm of natural knowledge. We have already examined the relation of this middle stage to the Forms or Ideas, and have seen that only knowledge derived from the realm of supernature (for Plato himself through dialectic, for most of the ancient and Christian thinkers descending from him, through revelation) is absolute truth. But man must nevertheless employ his natural reason to come to a knowledge of God as well as direct it to the data of sense, the one indeed providing the justification for the other. These assumptions were common to all thinkers, whether of primarily Platonic orientation or not, who might be called "orthodox" from the standpoint of Renaissance epistemology. Aquinas, no less than Bonaventura, had taken it for granted that "man cannot obtain the knowledge of God by natural reason except from creatures."[2]

[2] *Summa theologica* 1. 32. 1 (trans. Fathers of the English Dominican Province, 2d ed., 22 vols. [London, 1921], II, 61 [hereafter cited as "Dominican translation"]).

We have noted the complexity of stance adopted to the Platonic distinctiveness-relatedness view of matter and spirit, sensibles and intelligibles. While this is the real crux of the problem of truth in the seventeenth century, it takes account of only two of the three sources of knowledge. In order to approach Browne's writings through his Platonic epistemology we must also consider the third element of the triad: human custom. Theoretically, the question is very simple. Human custom is the least valuable area of experience; its lack of authority, its invalidity as an index to truth, is undisputed. Man can gain neither eternal truth nor knowledge of the nature of things from custom; for it is at once the source and the crystallization of opinion—and opinion is wayward and unstable, varying sharply among men according to differences of time and place. Accordingly, custom and its relation to its two epistemological superiors should play no such role in the problem of knowledge for the Christian Platonist as does the relation of nature to Idea. But the fact that custom in actuality exerts the most powerful influence over human thought and behavior raises difficulties that cannot be readily settled. The practical conduct of life could be of as acute concern to Platonic thinkers as the quest for knowledge; and the former, they held, should depend upon the latter. While guidance should come from the highest source of wisdom and virtue, men unfortunately rely most often on custom to regulate their behavior. Rather than deriving their ethic from universal absolutes, they turn to the peculiar practices of their own sect or nation; and the usurped authority of custom extends even to the realms of learning. Such are the complaints levelled against custom by serious Renaissance authors. Meric Casaubon, one of Browne's most learned contemporaries and a traditional humanist, published *A Treatise of Use and Custome* in 1638 in which he brought together under the headings of the various departments of practical and intellectual activity all that the ancient authors, the Fathers, and the learned of his own age had to say on this obvious but intractable issue. The relative unreliability of custom as a source of knowledge, the obedience that wise men should or should not render its authority, along with a host of allied questions, could be the subject of a long monograph in the history of ideas. Our concern with custom must be limited to its nature and function as the third assumption in Browne's Platonic strategy of truth.

3

Man is the measure of all things, Protagoras insisted, and his disciples, the Sophists, seized upon this motto. Plato's greatest dialogues record the battle Socrates waged against this notion. In the *Republic* Socrates argues that mere agreement among men, custom, cannot determine justice, since justice does not depend upon opinion. As material nature is less real than the supersensuous Ideas, so true justice cannot be determined by how man actually behaves, but only by the universal pattern for justice which tells him, through reason, how he ought to behave. Renaissance Christians were to a very large degree ethical descendants of Plato. While believing in the dignity of man and avouching a faith in his capacity for growth that required the constant check of reminders of the Fall, they did not believe that man was the measure of all things. Indeed any possibilities for improvement were bound to miscarry if man identified his natural desires or particular customs with virtue and abandoned the search for ethical absolutes. The problem of custom thus ramified into fundamental questions of ethics and practical applications of epistemology.

Agreement with Plato was easy enough so far as the relation of custom to truth was concerned, for custom can readily be shown to disobey the law of contradiction. Only the kind of skeptic who denies the possibility of the mind's possessing ideas that accord with reality could regard custom as a source of real knowledge, since the notion of real knowledge was to him a flattering delusion and custom was therefore as valid (i.e., no less valid) as any other authority. In practice, though, such skepticism was likely to spurn adherence to law and ethical principles because they *are* reducible to custom (the libertine position) as well as to abandon the search for truth. This kind of libertine naturalism was assumed by Montaigne at one point in his career, though the thoroughly conservative French aristocrat never suggested that the consequences of this attitude should be put into practice.

Aristotle, too, had attacked the position of Protagoras. His defense of the absoluteness of truth against the relativism of the skeptic took the form of a limited and common sense criticism. "For in pursuing the truth one must start from the things that are always in the same state and suffer no change. Such are the heavenly bodies; for these do not appear to be now of one nature and again of another, but are manifestly always the same and share no change."[3] However ironic this cosmological example becomes in view of the seventeenth-century discoveries which helped to loosen the traditional epistemological moorings, Aristotle's general position remained irreproachable to most men in Browne's time, since they still believed that there were "things that are always in the same state," if not the same things that Aristotle and the medieval world assumed.

The distinction between natural and posited law, between universally operative principles and varying human customs, is a commonplace of Western thought. In the ancient world the great spokesman for this idea is Cicero, the entire body of whose writings is permeated by it. The classic philosophic treatment is to be found in Aquinas for whom divine and natural laws (with the first including but transcending the second) proceed from the reasonable will of God and are therefore absolutes. Human law proceeds from the will of man and carries authority in so far as it is regulated by reason. Though "custom has the force of law" in human affairs, "abolishes law, and is the interpreter of law," it may be far removed from the truth.[4] "The first rule of reason is the law of nature. . . . Consequently every human law has just so much of the nature of law, as it is derived from the

[3] *Metaphysics* 11. 6. 1063ᵃ.

[4] *Summa theologica* 2. 97. 3 (Dominican translation, VIII, 80).

law of nature. But if in any point it deflects from the law of nature, it is no longer a law but a perversion of law."[5]

Hooker fully agreed with Aquinas' position on the limits of custom and of all humanly framed institutions. "In laws, that which is natural bindeth universally, that which is positive not so."[6] Nothing could be more clear-cut than this distinction. But when the abstraction was brought down to the practical authority of custom in religion, the issue, as we will see, became so fierce that no solution acceptable to both Puritans and Anglicans was possible. One can almost say that the religious differences kindled in Elizabeth's time, raging during the 1630's, and finally exploding into civil war in 1642, resolve themselves to the proper sphere and extent of the authority of custom, with the Laudian party making very large claims for custom, the Puritans disallowing it entirely, and certain liberal Anglicans delicately mediating an attitude of toleration between the two extremes. The accommodation of truth to custom for the sake of maintaining visible order in religion is an important issue in the *Religio Medici*. It is also part of a larger ethical question which provides the context for Browne's treatment of custom in all his writings.

Aristotle had noted that an argument based on human law could always be answered by one based on nature and that this tactic could be reversed.[7] The Platonic position that knowledge of the Good is something man can discover but not devise can lead to an absolutist-idealist approach that is always prepared to scrap existing institutions to undertake a radical reconstruction of society. Arguments based on nature are obviously strategic in gaining acceptance for reform, and men outside the circle of constituted power find in the absolutes of reason, nature, or truth their most suasive arguments against the reigning customs of the establishment.

[5] *Summa theologica* 2. 95. 2 (Dominican translation, VIII, 57).

[6] *Of the Laws of Ecclesiastical Polity* 1. 10. 7 (2 vols. [London, 1907], I, 193).

[7] *De sophisticis elenchis* 12. 173[a] (trans. W. A. Pickard-Cambridge, in *Works of Aristotle* [Ross ed.], Vol. I).

Accordingly, appeal to nature, attack on custom, and a general minimizing of the value of institutional continuity figured as prominent arguments in the championing of reforms in Church and State that absorbed John Milton for twenty years. In the first of his antiprelatical tracts, *Of Reformation in England* (1641), Milton insisted that custom should not be allowed to hinder truth from prevailing, "for Custome without Truth is but agednesse of Error."[8] This attitude, so intimately connected with his firmest beliefs, was skillfully used as a controversial tactic in Milton's later polemical writings.[9]

However, it was more generally assumed in the Renaissance that men capable of the disinterested pursuit of absolute justice were very rare. The accumulated wisdom of man as enshrined in custom was therefore considered an indispensable safeguard for individual liberty as well as for the order of society. Meric Casaubon, when speaking of philosophic and religious principle, notes that the ancient philosophers and the Fathers of the Church warned those who "seeke the *truth*, to beware of *custome*: and to this purpose *Tertullian* would haue us to remember, that *Christ* called himselfe *veritatem, non consuetudinem*: *truth*, not *custome*, be it never so generall, or so ancient."[10] Yet, in the framework of practical civil considerations, the conservative Casaubon points out that laws "grounded upon *custome*, are thought by many as the most acceptable, so the most naturall and obligatorie Lawes that are: as being not the invention of any single man, but of long Time and experience."[11] The realization that a particular custom does not carry the sanc-

[8] *Complete Prose Works of John Milton*, ed. Don M. Wolfe *et al.*, 8 vols. (New Haven, 1953–), I, 561.

[9] Notably in *The Doctrine and Discipline of Divorce* (1643), in the dedication addressed to Parliament, where Milton fashions an allegory in which custom "accorporate[s] herself with error"; in *The Tenure of Kings and Magistrates* (1649), which opens with an attack upon custom, which alone sanctifies the person of a king against violence; and in the Preface to *Eikonoklastes* (1649).

[10] *A Treatise of Use and Custome* (London, 1638), p. 20.

[11] *Ibid.*, p. 108.

tion of natural law may result in a conclusion altogether different from Milton's. The Platonic ideal of truth appealed to Montaigne, as an ideal, as much as to Milton. "*Truth ought to have a like and universall visage throughout the world.* Law and justice, if man knew any, that had a body and true essence, he would not fasten it to the condition of this or that countries customes." [12] Montaigne's skepticism derives from his appreciation of the complexity of the issue. At the same time that he perceives how seldom human practice reflects truth, he recognizes the danger of attempting to take truths laid up in heaven and establish them on earth with a radical disregard for custom. Governments observe human rather than natural laws, though every people regards its own form of government as natural, all others as monstrous. While the variability of government from nation to nation should preclude the condemnation of foreign customs and the claim of natural law for one's own, there is excellent reason for adhering to the customs of one's own nation, since those of others are probably no closer to the truth.

The relativism of the would-be absolutist, for whom absolutism has been put out of the question by skepticism, leads Montaigne not to political or moral anarchism, but to a conservatism that can at times foreshadow Burke. "*Lawes take their authoritie from possession and custome*: It is dangerous to reduce them to their beginning: In rowling on, they swell, and grow greater and greater, as doe our rivers: follow them upward, unto their source, and you shall find them but a bubble of water, scarse to be discerned, which in gliding on swelleth so proud, and gathers so much strength." [13] Montaigne's attitude is characteristically ambivalent. He values custom and shrinks from change, but is free from the illusions that can render a conservative of Burke's stamp blind to fundamental issues. Montaigne's skeptical realism is capable of striking at assumptions about morality so as to threaten

[12] *An Apologie of Raymond Sebond*, in *The Essayes of Michael Lord of Montaigne*, trans. John Florio (1603), 3 vols. (London, 1928), II, 296.

[13] *Ibid.*, II, 301.

the traditional religious view of man. "The lawes of conscience, which we say to proceed from nature, rise and proceed of custome: every man holding in special regard, and inward veneration the opinions approved, and customes received about him, cannot without remorse leave them."[14] While this statement is potentially subversive, Montaigne's heresies remain purely speculative. The perception of such unsettling ideas was a pleasure of the secular mind; their candid expression was the delight of the skeptical essayist. But the possibility of their application to the life of man or to society was unthinkable to the worldly man of affairs. Montaigne's antiprovincialism was a great contribution to the freeing of the human spirit in his age; for us liberalism and toleration seem inevitable consequences of this position. Nevertheless, the practical reach of his toleration did not extend as far as has sometimes been thought.

The difficulties raised by custom were acutely present to Pascal, who boldly framed the dilemma of choice between the authority of variable human notions and the quest for ungraspable universals. "On what shall man found the order of the world which he would govern? Shall it be on the caprice of each individual: What confusion! Shall it be on justice? Man is ignorant of it."[15] Pascal's genius lay precisely in stating this issue as insoluble. These questions yield no answer so long as man, because he is man, seeks Platonic absolutes while the Platonic theory of knowledge is feasible only for pure intelligences for whom ethical and epistemological conflicts do not exist.

If this perennial issue appears to advance not at all toward any resolution, its consequences for the conduct of men have been of more than speculative interest. The range of positions that can be taken toward custom and the fact of its limits and the assurance of its value has played a major role in history. The question figured prominently in the religious controversies that rent England in the seventeenth century.

[14] "Of Custome, and How a Received Law Should Not Easily Be Changed," *Essayes of Montaigne*, I, 114.

[15] *Pensées*, V, 294 (trans. W. F. Trotter [New York, 1958], p. 83).

And while Browne's own attitude of religious toleration is consistent with his temperament, it can be more profitably examined in the intellectual framework of his position on custom. Moreover, custom appears in many other guises in the various departments of human thought and activity treated in his writings.

4

Browne's loosely associative conduct of discourse is notorious. His individual works are often innocent of apparent organization and can fall into an almost medieval digressiveness. For example, in Part II of the *Religio*, after disclosing his natural disposition to charity, he goes on to declare that alms should be given to satisfy the command of God and not merely to relieve one's feelings of compassion. This leads him to observe that experienced beggars can select a merciful person by his aspect, "for there are mystically in our faces certaine characters which carry in them the motto of our Soules." The skill of "Master Mendicants" in reading men's natures takes Browne directly to the Hermetic idea of signatures in plants: "in every one of them, some outward figures which hang as signes and bushes of their inward formes" (II, 2). Such examples of the tangential movement of Browne's discourse abound. For this reason the unity of his writings cannot be located in their organization. It lies rather in patterns emerging from the epistemological stance toward a given question.

The great diversity of topics Browne treats in any work all belong to one or another of the three realms defined in the traditional Platonic and Christian epistemology we have traced in these preliminary chapters. That his intellectual and moral valuation of the choices comprising particular issues should depend upon their identification with custom, or nature, or the realm of intelligibles and faith is hardly a startling hypothesis. Indeed, once this implicit consideration of Renaissance epistemology is consciously thought about, it may seem almost too basic an assumption to be critically useful. Yet, however clearly demarcated and orthodox this hierarchy of knowledge, it was, we have seen, shot through with ambiguities which preclude automatic answers, available simply by measuring questions against the theoretic scheme. Instead, the tensions inherent to this habit of thought allow for endless possibilities for individual speculation. The traditional aspects of Browne's assumptions about the problem of truth account as much as the impact of new currents of thought for the rich complexity of his writings and for their achievement of veritable actions of ideas.

While the usual stress on Browne as a representative figure of his age is generally correct, it is finally more important (to define this "representativeness" with greater precision as well as to appreciate his individuality) that we recognize how Browne's thought and art produce in each of his major works a separate coherence and an effect peculiar to each. The context of thought I have described is, I believe, essential to a full and accurate grasp of the material components of Browne's thought and of his individual writings. But, in the last analysis, Browne's works are not demonstrations of his philosophic outlook. In *Religio Medici, Urn Burial,* and *The Garden of Cyrus,* as in all major art, the work is not a medium for a set of ideas, for something else, but the uniquely valuable thing itself.

PART TWO

SIR THOMAS BROWNE AND THE STRATEGY OF TRUTH

CHAPTER IV

RELIGIO MEDICI: GENRE, STRUCTURE, TEMPER

1

IN THE Preface to *Religio Medici* Sir Thomas Browne announces that what is to follow is a private exercise directed to himself. Since so much of the *Religio* is about faith, and since its original audience was supposedly limited to its author, the reader is cued to expect a dialogue of self and soul. This expectation is partially fulfilled. Yet one cannot read beyond the opening paragraphs without sensing that from the outset Browne abandoned the avowed audience of his own mind and turned to address the world.[1] Whatever his intention, the world has for three centuries chosen to listen to the words Sir Thomas Browne wrote as a "memorial" to himself, and men of quite diverse leanings have responded to his voice — a voice which, when we regard ourselves most benignly, can seem so like our own.

A great essayist attracts us through his power to make us feel that what he believes and says we have ourselves believed and at least wished to say. Because he can impart this sense of identification to men with convictions different from his own, indeed to men who might argue strenuously against the very ideas he expresses if presented in another form, he shares with the poet and the dramatist the potency

[1] Frank L. Huntley has challenged Simon Wilkin's long-accepted opinion (in the latter's edition of Browne's *Works,* 1835–36) that Browne wrote the *Religio* in Halifax, Yorkshire; he argues that "Browne, while practicing physic at Oxfordshire, wrote *Religio Medici* for someone dear to him in Halifax" (*Sir Thomas Browne,* p. 95).

of art. However, his readers, especially those of his own day, do not all grant him the necessary allowance of the poet: a willing suspension of disbelief accompanied by the realization that their beliefs must also be temporarily suspended. As a result, a writer like Browne tends to evoke one of two reactions from his contemporaries. First, there are those who succumb to his art and, having been won to him, assume that he must have been won over to them. After the publication of the authorized edition of the *Religio* in 1643, members of religious sects ranging from Roman Catholics at one end of the doctrinal spectrum to Quakers at the other wrote admiring letters to Browne.[2] That both could discern a latent adherent in the sturdily Anglican physician is at once a tribute to his literary power and breadth of sympathy and a measure of the narrowness of most religious writing in the harsh decade of the 1640's.

But while many admired this candid little volume, and some who approved it were flattered to think that its author approved them, there were those who fell into the opposite and more deadly snare of an inflexibly literal reading. If the Norwich Quaker Samuel Duncon had too hastily confounded Browne's imaginative flights and his capacity for individual religious feeling with a penchant for the inner light, Alexander Ross was guilty of a grosser misapprehension. This learned Scotsman insisted upon submitting every statement in the *Religio* to the test of his rigid Presbyterian and Aristotelian orthodoxy.[3] Since he was the sort of pedant incapable of reading anything in a "soft and flexible sense," he found much that deserved his self-righteous vituperation. With an uncanny instinct and real flair for attacking men far greater than himself and ideas larger than he could under-

[2] For the contemporary reception of the *Religio*, see Jeremiah S. Finch, *Sir Thomas Browne: A Doctor's Life of Science and Faith* (New York, 1950), pp. 107–18, and Frank L. Huntley, "The Publication and Immediate Reception of *Religio Medici*," *The Library Quarterly*, 25 (1955): 203–18.

[3] *Medicus medicatus: or the physician's religion cured, by a lenitive or gentle potion: With some animadversions upon Sir Kenelme Digbie's Observations on Religio Medici* (London, 1645).

stand, Ross was predestined in the seventeenth century to wield a busy pen. His diatribes against Bacon, Hobbes, Galileo, and William Harvey, to name only his more notable targets, have won him a place in English thought and letters that most men would gladly exchange for oblivion. Without firing more ammunition at so riddled a reputation, it is worth noting that his failure with Browne stems less from lack of intellectual grasp than from insensitivity coupled with bigotry. Ross represents pre-eminently those qualities of dogmatism and pedestrianism that disable one for reading Browne with sympathy or even fairness.

Sir Kenelm Digby, himself a victim of Ross,[4] and the most intelligent, as well as celebrated, of the early commentators on the *Religio*, also misjudged Browne's method and intention. Digby's *Observations*[5] were instrumental, along with John Merryweather's Latin translation (1644), in gaining an immediate and European reputation for the *Religio* and its author. His remarks reveal, too, the fullest contemporary recognition of its literary merit. Yet the long stretches of captious criticism which now seem so gratuitous indicate his failure to perceive Browne's object. Coleridge remarked on Digby's failure to consider "the Religio Medici in a *dramatic* & not in a metaphysical View — as a sweet Exhibition of character & passion, & not as an Expression or Investigation of positive Truth."[6] While a twentieth-century reader may balk at "a sweet Exhibition of character" with its suggestion that Browne's aims were no different from a nineteenth-century essayist's, he will certainly agree that it is futile to measure the *Religio* with the gauge of a theological, scientific, or philosophic treatise.

For all our advantage of historical perspective, the work remains difficult to assign to a particular genre of literature. This has not proved an obstacle to appreciation; admirers

[4] In *The Philosophicall Touch-Stone* (London, 1645), as well as in *Medicus medicatus*.

[5] *Observations upon Religio Medici* (London, 1643).

[6] *Coleridge on the Seventeenth Century*, ed. Roberta F. Brinkley (Durham, N.C., 1955), p. 438.

of Sir Thomas Browne have been content to place the *Religio* with the large number of famous books that criticism shrugs off as *sui generis*. Yet the misconstructions of purpose and interpretation to which the book was subject in its own time raise questions which the serious student cannot ignore. Religious books were the chief products of the press in seventeenth-century England.[7] If the *Religio* seemed "strange" in its own day, as it evidently did, it was not because of the subjects included or the conclusions reached, but because of the way religious and other issues were handled. Still, no work, however strange or baffling at first sight, is utterly without relationship to existing books. Seventeenth-century readers of the *Religio* encountered much that was familiar from their reading of the most popular books of the day. To show this, one need only rehearse the type of religious writing that flourished in the seventeenth century and dealt with material like that of the *Religio.*

Studies of the interior life are as old as the Christian tradition itself. Protestantism further encouraged self-examination, as did the whole drift of society and civilization in the earlier seventeenth century. For as the visible Church became more and more fragmented by controversy and schism, with the conflict between Roman Catholic and Protestant Europe and between Anglican and Puritan Englishmen growing ever more bitter, men turned increasingly inward to find religious certainty. The medieval saint's life, charting the individual path of penitence and conversion, was confessional and exemplary in purpose. This genre had Puritan successors and counterparts issuing from habits of introspection about the inner state of grace and the spiritual crisis of conversion. Such personal chronicles were numerous in the seventeenth century and reached a notable climax in Bunyan's *Grace Abounding* (1666).

The Counter-Reformation produced a large body of liter-

[7] Douglas Bush points out: "More than two-fifths of the books printed in England from 1480 to 1640 were religious, and for the years 1600–40 the percentage is still higher" (*English Literature in the Earlier Seventeenth Century*, rev. ed. [Oxford, 1962], p. 310).

ature intended to encourage and instruct the practice of meditation.[8] Manuals of spiritual exercise were widely used by recusants, by Anglicans, and even by some Puritans. These were meant to aid the devout in following a regular pattern of meditation on the mysteries of Christian faith and to instill the habit of pious thought. Louis Martz has demonstrated the importance of these manuals and their devotional methods for the poetry of Donne and Herbert, and goes so far as to suggest "poetry of meditation" as a more meaningful label than "metaphysical poetry."[9] Ethical treatises, essentially exhortations to the way of life indicative of salvation, were enormously popular; their aim of Christian edification figured heavily in almost all religious writing of the time. Here the primary impetus was didactic rather than devotional.

As the century wore on, and impatience and even a certain distrust grew of lofty meditation on mysteries, emphasis on the pragmatic results of the good Christian life was strengthened.[10] At least two such works of ethical religiosity, Thomas Fuller's *Holy State* (1642) and Jeremy Taylor's *Holy Living* (1650), have endured because of their stylistic merits and broad humanistic interest. To this type belongs Browne's

[8] See Helen C. White, *English Devotional Literature* [*Prose*] *1600–1640* (Madison, Wisc., 1931); *The Tudor Books of Private Devotion* (Madison, Wisc., 1951).

[9] *The Poetry of Meditation* (New Haven, 1954), p. 4.

[10] This is a regular theme of Jeremy Taylor, who qualifies his endorsement of the practice of meditation with this warning: "True it is that everything we see or can consider represents some perfections of God; but this I mean, that no man should consider too much, and meditate too frequently, upon the immediate perfections of God, as it were by way of intuition, but as they are manifested in the creatures and in the ministries of virtue: and also whenever God's perfections be the matter of meditation, we should not ascend upwards into Him, but descend upon ourselves, like fruitful vapours drawn up into a cloud, descending speedily into a shower, that the effect of the consideration be a design of good life; and that our love to God be not spent in abstractions, but in good works and humble obedience. The other kind of love may deceive us; and therefore so may such kind of considerations which are its instruments." *Works*, ed. R. Heber and C. P. Eden (London, 1847–54), II, 139.

Christian Morals, a sequel to the *Religio* probably written a good many years later, a handbook of applied ethics which unhappily draws more on platitude than on felt experience; it is characteristic of its type in touching religious instruction on one side and the Christian courtesy or conduct book on the other. Throughout the seventeenth century, the sermon was a pervasive force in the lives of Englishmen of all social classes and nearly all doctrinal persuasions. Along with the Bible, the pulpit was the unmatched source of edification and instruction. Though a ministry devoted wholeheartedly to preaching was the shibboleth of the Puritans, it was at the hands of great Anglican preachers like Andrewes, Donne, and Taylor that the sermon attained an intellectual distinction and imaginative grandeur never to be surpassed.[11] Finally, there were innumerable polemical volumes and pamphlets, cast like so many ponderous boulders and sharp pebbles down the barren slopes of doctrinal and ecclesiastical controversy, building by the time of the Civil War into an avalanche that all but buried other kinds of prose. It is evident even to the most cursory reader that *Religio Medici* includes one aspect or another of all these forms of religious discourse.

The *Religio* has, too, important affinities with books of non-religious character. Today it is most generally and loosely classed with the essay, whose greatest practitioners in the Renaissance were, of course, Montaigne and Bacon. Two distinct forms of the essay may be traced to them. Montaigne's essays had grown from the pages of his commonplace book – a collection of quotations and aphorisms that was a record of his reading.[12] Some quotation or incident of history frequently evoked a personal comment, and

[11] The standard account is W. Fraser Mitchell, *English Pulpit Oratory from Andrewes to Tillotson* (London, 1932). Joan Webber's *Contrary Music* (Madison, Wis., 1963), on Donne's prose style, carries the literary and intellectual study of the seventeenth-century sermon to a new level of critical maturity.

[12] The fullest account of Montaigne's reading, method of composition, and intellectual development is Pierre Villey, *Les Sources & l'évolution des essais de Montaigne*, 2d ed. 2 vols. (Paris, 1933).

as such comments grew longer than the copied material the product became an essay. The ideas and reflections of others collided with the self and the self responded with ideas and reflections of its own. His method was quite literally a self-testing, a trial or *essai* of his own convictions. Though Montaigne was never to abandon the common Renaissance practice of expanding and applying his thought through allusion and comparison to classical life and letters, his writing was, almost from the first, no mere humanistic commentary on ethical and public matters, but a personal revelation of the man. Whatever his subject, self-scrutiny was important, sometimes more important than the matter under consideration. This meditative attitude became increasingly prominent over the years. It is therefore not surprising that after first rejecting Stoicism and then dwelling briefly in the epistemological dead end of the skepticism represented by the *Apology for Raymond Sebond*, Montaigne finally settled upon self-knowledge derived from experience as the most valuable and trustworthy knowledge available to man.[13]

The aim and temper of Bacon's essays were quite different.[14] Bacon was not concerned with self-exploration but with epitomizing in aphoristic form those instructions most

[13] A conclusion that explains in large measure the esteem in which Gide and other twentieth-century existentialists hold Montaigne.

[14] A comparative examination of the two essayists, still valid in many respects and minimizing the influence of Montaigne on Bacon, is Jacob Zeitlin, "Development of Bacon's Essays," *Journal of English and Germanic Philology*, 27 (1928): 496–519. The close interrelation of the development of the essay with the Senecan movement in prose is a commonplace of modern criticism, stemming from the important studies by Morris Croll, "Attic Prose in the Seventeenth Century," *Studies in Philology*, 18 (1921): 79–128; "Attic Prose: Lipsius, Montaigne, Bacon," *Schelling Anniversary Papers* (New York, 1923) pp. 117–50; "The Baroque Style in Prose," *Studies in English Philology: A Miscellany in Honor of Frederick Klaeber*, ed. K. Malone and M. B. Ruud (Minneapolis, 1929), pp. 427–56. The interest of these and other articles by Croll is carried further by George Williamson, in *The Senecan Amble* (Chicago, 1951), who traces the shift, both in theory and practice, from Ciceronian, to Senecan, to the "plain" style of the Restoration.

useful for the conduct of public life and affairs. One of the best measures of the differing aims and methods of the two is their styles. In Montaigne, discursive self-exploration finds expression in the loose Senecan style with its suggestion of tentative probing. Bacon, less interested in the curve and process of mental exploration than in the hits a discovering mind could score, cultivated the form of Senecan prose that goes under the label "curt style."

The meditative and speculative temper of the *Religio* suggests, then, many possible resemblances between it and some of the other religious books of the age, and also relates it to the essay. Its subject matter links it in places to books of science and pseudoscience. Browne's excursion carries him into such far-ranging subjects as religious belief, Biblical exegesis, the composition of the soul, providence and fortune, witches and spirits, the creation and regulation of the world, and the scientific quest of truth. Yet the book does not seem primarily an inclusive commentary on the main topics of religious and philosophic interest of the day. Indeed, encyclopedic scope, or, still less, solidity, is the last quality we associate with the *Religio*; that is the province of *Vulgar Errors.* Its freedom from bookishness, too rarely encountered in the serious prose of the Renaissance, may be partially explained by the conditions under which Browne tells us he wrote. "It was penned in such a place and with such disadvantage, that (I protest) from the first setting of pen unto paper, I had not the assistance of any good booke, whereby to promote my invention or relieve my memory." [15] While this disclaimer should probably not be taken literally, one can only wish that more Renaissance authors had journeyed to places remote from their libraries to compose their books. But the absence of excessive quotations and decorative learning cannot go far in accounting for the extraordinary success of the *Religio.*

In broad outline *Religio Medici* is a meditative essay on the Christian virtues of faith and charity. As such, its stance is not that of an objective disquisition, but reflects a partic-

[15] *Works,* I, 10.

ular man's contours of response. Browne sets forth in his opening paragraph the position from which he speaks. A physician by vocation, he is by intellectual bent a man of science and by religious conviction a firm Anglican. From one point of view, all that follows can be regarded as an attempt to qualify this twin assertion: to show that while he is a scientist he is no atheist, and that while "there is no Church wherein every point so squares unto [his] conscience" as the Church of England (I, 5), he claims no exclusive power of salvation for it; nor is he blind to the truth possessed by other Christian Churches. In short, faith and charity, which serve as the headings for the two parts of his meditation, are put to the test of the practice of science and of sectarian membership, then as now potentially at odds with these virtues. In this *essai* Browne displays his own character and his inclination on these issues, and also redefines atheism and belief, belief and toleration, so as to resolve, at least to his own satisfaction, the conflict between them. He does not handle these two strands separately, but knits them along with other related matters into the rich fabric of his discourse. Ethics illuminated by revelation, the place of reason in religion and of God's design in nature, the wisdom and eternity of God, the nobility and power of friendship, and examination of his own mental and spiritual life are some of the public and private channels through which Sir Thomas Browne's meditation on faith and charity flows. The reconciliation of science with faith and of his religion with toleration creates drama and tension. These two major reconciliations are reached through the Platonic epistemological hierarchy — defined in the previous chapter — of custom, discursive reason, and intuitive knowledge. The result is a work that conveys a comprehending spirit of wonder and an informing tone of liberal intelligence.

2

The opening of *Religio Medici* conveys a sense of opposition and of resolution typical of the entire work.

> For my Religion, though there be severall circumstances that might perswade the world I have none at all, as the generall scandall of my profession, the naturall course of my studies, the indifferency of my behaviour, and discourse in matters of Religion, neither violently defending one, nor with the common ardour of contention opposing another; yet in despight hereof I dare, without usurpation, assume the honourable stile of a Christian: not that I meerely owe this title to the Font, my education, or [the] Clime wherein I was borne, as being bred up either to confirme those principles my Parents instilled into my unwary understanding; or by a generall consent proceed in the Religion of my Countrey: But [that] having in my riper yeares, and confirmed judgement, seene and examined all, I finde my selfe obliged by the principles of Grace, and the law of mine owne reason, to embrace no other name but this; neither doth herein my zeale so farre make me forget the generall charitie I owe unto humanity, as rather to hate then pity Turkes, Infidels, and (what is worse) [the] Jewes, rather contenting my selfe to enjoy that happy stile, then maligning those who refuse so glorious a title. (I, 1)

The man of science is also a firm Christian, but one whose religious convictions were reached through individual effort. The man who maintains a placid attitude amid religious controversies is warm in his faith, yet has a charitable spirit of toleration instead of distemper toward those who think or feel otherwise. Habits of mind ordinarily considered antithetical are harmonized without losing their distinctive character and without upsetting the inner poise of the man. All this is encompassed within a single paragraph, indeed, within a single period, if we follow the conventions of the seventeenth-century punctuation. The conciliation of these diverse tendencies is shown as well as stated, and the reader can feel Browne's equilibrium before he knows the terms in which that equilibrium is worked out.

The themes to be elaborated later are limned in miniature in the first section. Though Browne's style is calculatedly different from the public, the rhetorical, or the epic, the initial paragraph of the *Religio* serves its function in a manner similar to the opening of *Paradise Lost.*

> Of Man's First Disobedience, and the Fruit
> Of that Forbidden Tree, whose mortal taste
> Brought Death into the World, and all our woe,
> With loss of *Eden*, till one greater Man
> Restore us, and regain the blissful Seat,
> Sing Heav'nly Muse, that on the secret top
> Of *Oreb*, or of *Sinai*, didst inspire
> That Shepherd, who first taught the chosen Seed,
> In the Beginning how the Heav'ns and Earth
> Rose out of *Chaos*. . . .

Not until Milton has stated his entire theme, which is both the tragic Fall of Man and his joyful restoration, does the first independent predication appear, marking the invocation ("Sing Heav'nly Muse"). Unlike other treatments of the Fall, Milton's is to present not only the destruction of human innocence and the introduction of death into the world, but also the greater counteraction of divine grace. The negative, downward action, embodying the results of Satanic pride, hatred, and sterility and paralleling human disobedience and loss of Eden, is balanced throughout the poem by the upward, constructive movement of divine providential love forever bringing greater good from evil.

Similarly, in the opening section of the *Religio*, Browne indicates the entire scope of what is to follow. This section epitomizes under their broad headings the innumerable specific issues the author is about to treat and distills his complex attitudes toward them down to their essence. Like Milton, Browne begins with a lengthy suspension, setting forth the opposed elements which make up his central theme. The suspended structure running until the first semicolon may be analyzed thematically and syntactically as follows. The opening phrase ("For my Religion") introduces the matter to be considered; this is immediately subjected to the pressure of a clause that tends to deny the validity of Browne's talking about his religion ("though there be severall circumstances that might perswade the world I have none at all"). The "severall circumstances" are then specified in a parallel series as:

(1) "the generall scandall of my profession"
(2) "the naturall course of my studies"
(3) "the indifferency of my behaviour, and discourse in matters of Religion"

Because the third element in the series is asymmetrical to the preceding two it receives an additional emphasis, underscored by a further development: "neither violently defending one, nor with the common ardour of contention opposing another." (It will be to this third circumstance that Browne will first direct his attention.)

Before predicating his religious position Browne notes the apparent two-fold contradiction to his having one. First, he is a physician, a profession by a long-standing tradition notoriously prone to "materialism" and to atheism. Moreover, his studies, so it seems to the world, are aimed at natural phenomena rather than toward divinity. In such a man faith would appear likely to have been corroded by too great a dependence upon natural reason. For the purposes of Browne's discussion these first two circumstances fuse into one. Second, his attitude toward theological issues and points of church practice and government is free of dogmatic certitude. Here again reason takes precedence, in this case over the narrow claims of custom to sole possession of truth. Running through this opening is a strong vein of irony aimed at those who could be persuaded of a man's lack of faith because he is a scientist and is imbued with the spirit of charity. When, after declaring the circumstances of his religious position, Browne asserts "yet in despight hereof I dare, without usurpation, assume the honourable stile of a Christian," he is not only setting down "the paradox of one man's mind," as Professor Huntley [16] has well described the

[16] *Sir Thomas Browne*, p. 104.

Religio as a whole, but is also suggesting that to those who view these matters rightly no contradictions are entailed. Browne aims at more than a reconciliation of a religious commitment with charity toward those of different doctrinal position and of the pursuit of natural studies with orthodox belief. The *Religio* seeks to demonstrate for each of these issues the interdependence of their opposed tendencies.

The remainder of the opening section, following the first colon, sets forth the rational basis for Browne's position. The stress upon reason in his assent to Christian principles and to the Church of his country is characteristically Anglican. His religion is not held in mere conformity to his countrymen or as the result of the education instilled in him by his parents. The law of his own reason, not custom (which we would here gloss "environment"), has led him to embrace the name of Christian. This name is rightfully his even though he shows a certain indifference to polemical discourse, "neither violently defending one, nor with the common ardour of contention opposing another." Christian faith kindles warm emotion in Browne, but not the fire of disputatious zeal which might make him "forget the generall charitie [he] owe[s] unto humanity." He is satisfied to enjoy the "happy stile" of a Christian without "maligning those who refuse so glorious a title."

Stylistically, the first section opens in a kind of rhetorical *medias res*: "For my Religion, though there be severall circumstances that might perswade the world I have none at all." As many readers have noted, this conveys the impression not of a beginning but of a sudden transition. Having finished with some other matters, the author will now speak, so it seems, about his religion. Though by ordinary standards of discourse this is a disconcerting start, the abrupt plunge into the very center of the writer's mind cues the reader to attend to the unfolding of that mind as well as to the exposition of a subject. From the outset one is certain of the presence of the whole shape and substance of a man's mind as distinct from simply the presentation or arguing of views on particular topics. This is the appropriate effect sought by the essayist as opposed to the orator, by the writer for whom deliberative rhetoric is more a search for truth than a convincing of his audience.[17]

The next seven sections (2–8) develop the religious issue which receives the chief stress in the opening section: the relative authority of reason and custom in matters of doctrine and worship. Browne asserts the usual Anglican identification of his "reformed new-cast Religion" with the Church of the true apostolic succession "so decaied, impaired, and fallen from its native beauty, that it required the carefull and charitable hand of these times to restore it to its primitive integrity" (I, 2). He defends his Church against Rome by defining the points of difference and agreement between the two and also the proper attitude of an Anglican toward the beliefs and practices of Rome. The extreme claims of both Rome and Geneva must be denied by a loyal son of the English Church. But where does the individual look for authority to determine religious truth? To his own Church, of course; but he can find no such exclusive or entire answers as are available to the Puritan or the "papist." Browne's Church, since it posits but few absolutes, raises more questions for its adherents than it provides answers: on many points where its rivals have their respective firm positions, the English Church holds that one must instead apply reason to distinguish among absolutes, matters of custom requiring uniform settlement, and matters left to individual determination. Therefore, as "a sworne subject" to the Church of England, Browne "subscribe[s] unto her Articles,

[17] Morris Croll's famous remark that the characteristic asymmetry and appearance of improvisation in baroque style had as its purpose "to portray, not a thought, but a mind thinking" clearly applies to the effect Brown produces here and elsewhere in the *Religio* ("The Baroque Style in Prose," p. 430). A thesis of Rosemond Tuve is relevant in broader terms: that deliberative rhetoric becomes in metaphysical poetry (generally acknowledged a counterpart of anti-Ciceronian prose) a process of "examining, meditating, pursuing differences and essences and causes" instead of proving by disputation the truth or falsity of a proposition. *Elizabethan and Metaphysical Imagery* (Chicago, 1947), p. 352.

and endeavour[s] to observe her Constitutions," yet reserves to his reason a large measure of freedom, a freedom implicit in the make-up of his Church (I, 5). From the exercise of personal choice and his charity toward the choices of others in the sphere of sectarian differences Browne moves in Section 6 to the broader question of the proper strategy of truth in philosophical matters. Here, too, the claims of opposed authorities and of warring philosophical schools encourage private speculation which further intensifies the sense of uncertainty.

Browne's posture vis-à-vis these issues and the associated religious and intellectual currents of the time will be more fully delineated in the next chapter of this study. For the moment our interest lies in the broad structure of his discussion. Sections 2–8 may be viewed as an elaboration of one side of the dual concern set forth in Section 1. The opening of each section marks the stages of the development and analysis of his "discourse in matters of Religion": "But because the name of a Christian is become too generall to expresse our faith . . ." (I, 2) "Yet have I not so shaken hands with those desperate Resolutions . . ." (I, 3) "As there were many Reformers, so likewise many reformations; every Countrey proceeding in a peculiar Method . . ." (I, 4) "But to difference my self neerer, & draw into a lesser circle . . ." (I, 5) "I could never divide my selfe from any man upon the difference of an opinion . . ." (I, 6) "Now the first of mine [i.e. heresies] was that of the Arabians, that the soules of men perished with their bodies, but should yet bee raised againe at the last day . . ." (I, 7) "That Heresies should arise we have the prophecy of Christ, but that old ones should be abolished we hold no prediction . . ." (I, 8).

Then, having touched upon various facets of sectarian differences, Browne abruptly makes a new departure with Section 9: "As for those wingy mysteries in Divinity. . . ." As Section 1 begins with a seemingly arbitrary transition from some other matters, Section 9 hastily moves on to a new question with no logical transition from what immediately precedes. It does, however, refer back to Section 1, to the question of basic religious beliefs and the difficulties they raise for natural reason. Browne also returns to the deeply personal note struck at the opening of the *Religio*. Section 9 and what follows will, we expect, be co-ordinate to Sections 2–8, both stemming from the two basic issues announced in the first section. The first half of 9 is the best-known passage in the *Religio* and is frequently cited as the quintessence of Browne's religious thought and feeling. Critics, however, have drawn sharply varying pictures of Browne on the basis of this passage: mystic, contemplative adept, fideist, doctrinal relativist—all these, and others, have been suggested. Because there is little agreement about this passage, though all readers regard it as crucial, we shall want to consider it later with some fullness. For the present it is enough to see how it serves to introduce the primary action of the *Religio*, the way in which a man can be both a scientist and an orthodox Christian.

In Section 10 Browne acknowledges his Platonic orientation as the key to his assent to religious mysteries. From here he moves on to partition his religious contemplations into two categories corresponding to those two mighty attributes of God: "his wisedome and eternitie." The orthodox Augustinian Christian expatiates on the second of these through Section 11, and in 12 he poses the hard problem of the Trinity and other contradictions of philosophy and divinity. His solution is recourse to "Saint *Pauls* Sanctuary," as already represented in the *o altitudo* of Section 9. The reflections on God's eternity end suitably with the most famous of his avowals of Platonism: "The severe Schooles shall never laugh me out of the Philosophy of *Hermes*, that this visible World is but a picture of the invisible, wherein as in a pourtract, things are not truely, but in equivocall shapes, and as they counterfeit some more reall substance in that invisible fabrick" (I, 12).

Section 13 refers back to "that other attribute . . . his wisedome" and thus initiates the discussion co-ordinate to 11 and 12. Though it is in the role of man of science that Browne contemplates God's wisdom, the Platonic outlook again provides the key to true understanding, as it does for the Christian believer. What we have seen earlier about the development of what I have called the Platonic context should keep us from being surprised or confused because in Sections 14 and 15 Browne invokes Aristotelian teleology as the assumption and aim of his scientific investigation. This group of three sections, showing how the study of nature is a religious activity, is brought to a glowing close as Browne fuses the two Platonic commonplaces of man as the little world shining forth the entire universe and that of all knowledge as a kind of self-knowledge: "wee carry with us the wonders, wee seeke without us: There is all *Africa*, and her prodigies in us; we are that bold and adventurous piece of nature, which he that studies wisely learnes in a *compendium*, what others labour at in a divided piece and endlesse volume" (I, 15). These familiar ideas are conveyed in so characteristically subjective a tone that the underlying concepts receive little stress as compared to the sense of personal discovery.

In Section 16, Browne recapitulates the tenor of discussion initiated after the rhapsody in 9 ("Thus there are two bookes from whence I collect my Divinity; besides that written one of God, another of his servant Nature"), summarizing, in effect, by identifying the eternity and wisdom of God respectively with the revelation of Scripture and revelation through the creatures. The ultimate oneness of these is indicated in his handling of the natural religion of heathens and, harking back to the issue raised in 1, the discrimination of his interest in natural studies, his urging of Christians "to suck Divinity from the flowers of nature," from an atheistic naturalism. The section concludes with an attempt to dismiss as a pseudo-issue the Stoic opposition of nature and art: "Now nature is not at variance with art, nor art with nature; they being both the servants of his providence: Art is the perfection of Nature: Were the world now as it was the sixt day, there were yet a Chaos: Nature hath made one world, and Art another. In briefe, all things are artificiall, for Nature is the Art of God." At the level of art as human invention, however, where the issue is that of nature vs. custom, Browne, as we shall see, takes a very different position.

Section 17 represents a new departure: the apparent exceptions to the rule of God's wisdom which men call fortune. From this point on, the most heterogeneous topics of philosophic, scientific, and religious inquiry and speculation are brought within the field of Browne's attention. The impossibility of outlining the *Religio* is too well known to require emphasis here; critics have despaired of locating any principle of structure or even of tracing the kind of articulated arrangement one might expect in a discursive treatise. Instead, they have sought unifying principles in the personality of the author, in the general cast of his mind, and, more recently, as in Professor Huntley's study, in patterns of allusive metaphors. My own attempt to demonstrate a discursive order in the early sections of the *Religio* cannot reverse this judgment about the work as a whole, nor was it intended to. I mean rather to show that Browne reveals an underlying habit of thought, not directly, but, as we have seen, implicitly through the juxtaposition of certain issues as he introduces them and through the stance he adopts toward them. The surface of the work, however, remains disorganized. Thus a discussion which proceeds sequentially from section to section can do little more than list the various topics and paraphrase the author's opinions.

For this reason, the analysis of the *Religio* that follows in Chapters V and VI pretty much ignores Browne's arrangement. My interest lies in exhibiting an intellectual structure which renders the particulars of Browne's essay more intelligible by relating them to one another in the light of the Platonic epistemology defined in the introductory chapters of this study. My approach assumes, then, that, as with a play or a novel, the formal nature of the *Religio* is more significant than its material nature. But the fact remains that we are not dealing with a fictive work whose elements need correspond to each other only self-consistently within a given framework of artifice and convention. The materials of a discursive work like the *Religio* bear explicit reference to the actual world of thought in which its author lived. This means that its structural principle is of a different kind and operates in a different way from that of a novel or a play. While it does comprehend and illuminate the material of which the *Religio* is composed, this structure of thought has an a priori existence extrinsic to the *Religio* and is therefore also dependent upon intellectual history for elucidation, as are, of course, the individual topics themselves.

It must be stressed, too, that the Platonic epistemology to which Browne subscribed, with its hierarchical valuation of custom, nature, and Idea encompassing all experience and knowledge, required no overt presentation. There was no need to state these implicit assumptions; nor could such assumptions be the intended theme of the *Religio*. To reconstruct the philosophical orientation of an author and then to offer that orientation per se as the purpose, meaning, or effect of the author's work is to indulge a very naïve historicism. Those elemental attitudes which the scholar labors to recover were, we must not forget, taken for granted by the author and by his audience. They are accordingly of obvious importance to readers who wish to avoid gross misjudgments stemming from ignorance of a writer's intellectual and aesthetic presuppositions. But it is difficult to see how a writer could have as the primary focus of a work the presentation of what he and his readers already take for granted.[18]

Without understanding the implicit attitudes of a writer we cannot grasp those unstated norms which enable us to respond properly to the living issues which *are* his theme. These attitudes, however, cannot unfold to us the purpose or the unifying principle of an individual work (if this were so, all of an author's works as well as the writings of his like-minded contemporaries would be of identical import). What they allow us to see are the possibilities of signification for the issues and arguments which, though they take their final meaning only in relation to the entire work, have to be in-

[18] Unless, of course, one is dealing with a work intended as a compendium of commonplaces, but the response to the *Religio* should rule out our reading its significance as such.

terpreted accurately as particulars in order for them to produce in combination the total effect which in turn gives them individual meaning. The context in which a writer thinks about what he writes is neither the meaning itself of his work nor the determinator of that work's meaning in a simple cause-effect relation. It is rather the arena of his meaningfulness.

Browne did not write the *Religio* to argue for his Platonic epistemology or, consciously or unconsciously, to exhibit how that epistemology provided the solution to the issues he chose to treat. The Platonic definition of the relative authority of custom, nature, and Idea was Browne's implicit norm for classifying and judging the particulars which constitute his essay. As this norm is applied repeatedly through the *Religio*, a pattern is established, a pattern which I call, analogically, an "action." This pattern or action cannot be discerned at the level of surface organization, though it is briefly glimpsed in the disposition of certain topics at the outset. The intellectual action into which Browne plunges us at the opening of his work provides the *Religio* with such unity as it possesses. It is not, of course, the unity imparted by plot, or sequacious development of feeling, or reiterative theme, symbol, or image to a dramatic, narrative, or lyric work. The "action" is the reconciliation of apparently incompatible religious and intellectual postures by a highly personal application of the traditional Christian and Platonic valuation of their relative levels of truth.

The next two chapters will therefore analyze the two major actions of the *Religio* within the context of Browne's assumptions about Idea, nature, and custom. Before turning to this examination, however, I should like to consider two features of the religious and intellectual temper of the *Religio* which have always attracted a great deal of attention and have been subject, I think, to distortions interfering with a clear view of the work.

3

The exact coloration of Browne's religious feeling and doctrinal positions is highly elusive. It is safe enough to talk about his deeply religious temper; there is no risk of error in tracing his approach to all issues back to this, since for conservative thought, especially with a strong admixture of Platonism, everything was still subsumed under religion. But as soon as one focuses on the specifics of Christian faith questions arise. One is the relatively perfunctory role the Son plays in Browne's thought. This is apparent to any reader, whether or not with a special axe to grind, and must also be acknowledged by those who stress (accurately, I think) Browne's Augustinianism as opposed to the more purely rational, almost Deistic, religion of near contemporaries like the Cambridge Platonists.

While Browne's best-known work may be called a meditation as well as an essay, no one would suggest that the tradition of formal meditation which, thanks to Professor Martz, has deepened our understanding of Donne and Herbert is relevant to the *Religio*. This might be explained by the fact that Browne's sensibility was alien to Anglo-Catholicism, but that cannot account for the secondary role Christ plays in the thought of a religious writer of the seventeenth century. There is no trace of the slightest Socinianism in Browne; speaking of the hope of salvation, he clearly affirms that all salvation is through Christ. But this idea inspires neither awe nor joy in the young physician. What occurs to him is the fate of virtuous heathens. "It is hard to place those soules in Hell whose worthy lives doe teach us vertue on earth" (I, 54).

Browne prefers to comprehend God's wisdom through "those impressions hee hath left on his creatures" rather than through "Contemplations Metaphysicall" (I, 13). His religious experience tends to focus upon the creatures rather than upon the mysteries of divinity, which draw him into religious *speculation*, or than upon the things of the Cross, which hardly appear at all. This would seem to relate him to Vaughan and Traherne in the tradition of meditation associated with Bonaventura. Nonetheless, the most famous passage in the *Religio* springs from questions raised by Christian mystery. The celebrated *o altitudo* is not, I think, as many have taken it, the key to what is most central in Browne's religious sensibility. It is, however, his most important treatment of a question no man could evade, whatever the direction of his religious interests. For this reason it is crucial to see precisely what this passage does and does not reveal about Browne.

> As for those wingy mysteries in Divinity and ayery subtilties in Religion, which have unhindg'd the braines of better heads, they never stretched the *Pia Mater* of mine; me thinkes there be not impossibilities enough in Religion for an active faith; the deepest mysteries ours containes, have not only been illustrated, but maintained by syllogisme, and the rule of reason: I love to lose my selfe in a mystery, to pursue my reason to an *o altitudo*. 'Tis my solitary recreation to pose my apprehension with those involved aenigma's and riddles of the Trinity, with Incarnation and Resurrection. I can answer all the objections of Satan, and my rebellious reason, with that odde resolution I learned of *Tertullian*, *Certum est quia impossibile est.* I desire to exercise my faith in the difficultest points, for to credit ordinary and visible objects is not faith, but perswasion. (I, 9).

I would suggest that what is described here is primarily an intellectual experience, not a devotional one. Someone engaged in meditation, whether according to Ignatian or Salesian method, or seeking, less formally, interior illumination as conceived by Augustine, is hardly concerned with subduing "rebellious reason" or resolving the riddles and apparent impossibilities of dogma into the paradoxes of faith. Such questions do not arise to him. He directs his effort toward being filled with love for God and toward building a holy life through the operation of sensation, emotion, intellect, and will upon these mysteries. Browne, on the other hand, is describing the intellectual and emotional process whereby he has come to hold and frequently revitalize his settled belief in the Christian faith. This passage is free from the kind of intense emotion that marks the attachment of the meditative devotee to his object. Its tone, despite the elevation of the subject, remains mellow, even comfortably relaxed. In sum, Browne is not talking about the deepest experience of worship, nor certainly, as some suggest, of mystical union,[19] but of his speculative consideration of divinity.

Some remarks of Jeremy Taylor are here especially relevant to Browne. Taylor defines meditation as "an attention and application of spirit to divine things; a searching out all instruments to a holy life, a devout consideration of them, and a production of those affections which are in direct order to the love of God and a pious conversation."[20] This is a milder, though no less steadfast, spirit of devotion than that proposed by Loyola in his *Spiritual Exercises* or by St. Francis of Sales in *An Introduction to a Devout Life.* It is the kind of meditative practice that a man like Sir Thomas Browne – so close to Taylor in personal temper and religious position – might be expected to observe. For this reason, some further remarks of Taylor are of peculiar value in accurately judging the kind of religious experience represented by the *o altitudo* passage. "For if we think of hell, and consider the infinity of its duration, and that its flames last as long as God lasts, and thence conjecture, upon the rules of proportion, why a finite creature may have an infinite, unnatural duration; or think by what ways a material fire can torment an immaterial substance; or why the devils, who are intelligent and wise creatures, should be so foolish as to hate God, from whom they know every rivulet of amability derives; *this is to study, not to meditate.*"[21] A good many of the issues Browne raises and which draw the man of sci-

[19] Robert Sencourt in *Outflying Philosophy* (London, 1923), sees Browne as a true mystic. He attempts, equally unsuccessfully, to make a similar case for Donne and Henry Vaughan. Dean Finch raises the question: "Was Browne a mystic?" but leaves the answer indefinite: "Browne had moments of vision, when his reason bowed to the lure of faith and he groped toward things unseen" (*Sir Thomas Browne,* p. 272). W. P. Dunn declares: "But of course Browne is not a mystic. He is always too much interested in finding out why grass is green and blood is red" (*Sir Thomas Brown,* p. 172).

[20] *Works,* ed. Heber and Eden, II, 130.

[21] *Ibid.,* II, 131. My italics.

ence and the philosophic amateur into curious speculation would afford Taylor grounds for banishing the *Religio* from the realm of meditation to that of study. Of course, elsewhere in the *Religio*, especially toward the close of the first part and throughout the second, Browne's reflections are often as "humble, fruitful, and practically mysterious" as Taylor would wish. Considerations such as will "rectify an untoward inclination, or purchase a virtue" [22] appear again and again in Browne who was not least of all a Christian moralist.

Our measurement of the *o altitudo* passage against Taylor's standards and definitions of religious experience may be profitably concluded with the distinction Taylor draws between meditation and contemplation:

> For beyond this I have described, there is a degree of meditation so exalted, that it changes the very name, and is called contemplation; and it is the unitive way of religion, that is, it consists in unions and adherences to God; it is a prayer of quietness and silence, and a meditation extraordinary, a discourse without variety, a vision and intuition of divine excellencies, an immediate entry into an orb of light, and a resolution of all our faculties into sweetness, affections, and starings upon the divine beauty; and is carried on to ecstasies, raptures, suspensions, elevations, abstractions, and apprehensions beatifical.[23]

Only rhetorically can Browne's religious experience be claimed to be anything like Taylor's picture of contemplation.

How, then, should the *o altitudo* be viewed? Browne pursues his reason to its limit and then beyond into the realm of matters above reason and finally of matters above and against reason where Tertullian's resolution ceases to be an odd paradox and becomes an obvious verity. One is reminded not a little of the leap to faith which for Pascal must

[22] *Ibid.*
[23] *Ibid.*, II, 139.

crown the deliberate mounting of the steps to reason. And, of course, Browne is admitting to fideism here, but treatment of it will be deferred until a later chapter. What is clear is that Browne is giving us a picture of his habit of mind, not of devotional practice. He cites Tertullian as extricating him from the intellectual problems posed by the mysteries. Another great Churchman and Neoplatonist, Richard of St. Victor, scholar and mystic, can also shed light on Browne. Richard distinguished six genera of contemplation, of which "two exist in imagination, two in reason, two in intelligence." The highest of these, existing in intelligence, are the fifth, "above, but not beyond reason," and the sixth, which "exists above reason and appears to be beyond reason." [24] Richard's amplified definition of the sixth type is strikingly pertinent to the *o altitudo* passage:

> The sixth type of contemplation has been called that which deals with those things which are above reason and which seem to be beyond, or even against, reason. In this, as it were, the supreme and most worthy form of all contemplations, the mind truly rejoices and exults, at that time when from the reflection of the divine light, it recognizes and regards those things against which every human reason protests. Such are almost all the things we are commanded to believe concerning the Trinity of the persons. When the human reason thinks about these things, it seems nothing other than contradiction.[25]

[24] *De gratia contemplationis* 1. 6 (Migne, *Patrologia Latina,* CXCVI [Paris, 1855], col. 70). "Quintum est supra, sed non praeter rationem. Sextum supra rationem, et videtur esse praeter rationem."

[25] *Ibid.*, col. 72. "Sextum contemplationis genus dictum est, quod in his versatur quae sunt supra rationem, et videntur esse praetur, seu etiam contra rationem. In hac utique suprema omniumque dignissima contemplationum specula tunc animus veraciter exsultat atque tripudiat, quando illa ex divini luminis irradiatione cognoscit atque considerat quibus omnis humana ratio reclamat. Talia sunt pene omnia quae de personarum Trinitate credere jubemur. De quibus cum humana ratio consulitur, nihil aliud quam contraire videtur."

Richard of St. Victor was a mystic. Sir Thomas Browne was a man who liked to entertain mystical thoughts, but whose nature was not of the kind to attain, or even really to strive for, actual mystical experience. He had an unbounded capacity for feeling sweetness and wonder, but none of the strenuous impulses of the true mystic who follows the unitive way. The divine mysteries that Browne seizes when he pursues his reason to an *o altitudo* do not come to him as transforming illumination achieved in the state of mystic union. They are rather his personal comprehension and conviction – reached through individual speculation – of God's revelation of himself as available to all through the doctrines and creeds of the Church. A deeply reverent spirit is not to be confused with the extraordinary effort and capacities of the mystic.

If Browne is subject to distortion by the unhistorically minded,[26] it is partly because of the very feature of his religious life I have endeavored to point out: the relative unimportance of the *personal* sense of devotion to Christ and to the mysteries of the Passion. While this in no way weakens his orthodoxy as a believer, it does mean that his religious experience has a profoundly different substance and color from that represented by the divine poetry of Donne or Herbert. Moreover, these men derived much of their best poetry from the experience of spiritual combat, from their personal struggle over rebellion and obedience, exile or union, in relation to God and to God in Christ. Such struggle was evidently not an aspect of Browne's religious life. Certainly it does not account for the vitality of *Religio Medici* or for its greatness. Browne's religious genius was not nourished on the ground of Gethsemane or Calvary by the workings of an agitated heart, nor in a spiritual desert by a man

[26] Perhaps the most extreme position is the one taken by Mr. D. K. Ziegler: that Browne did not believe in the existence of religious truth and employed religious thought as mere gymnastics for his metaphoric imagination; and, equally untenable, that his toleration was the result of his relativism and failure to lend genuine credence to the mysteries of faith. *In Divided and Distinguished Worlds* (Cambridge, Mass., 1943), pp. 88–89.

thirsting for revivifying water. While he shared with Herbert a deep pleasure in the order and beauty of the English Church, this was not the source, as it was not for Herbert either, of his greatest expression. It is in the garden of created nature that Browne cultivated, with serene assurance, his best plants of divinity.

4

If the *Religio* is very different in substance and spirit from the devotional poetry of Donne or Herbert, it also discloses attitudes that place it at a significant remove from the best and most characteristic poetry of Henry Vaughan or the *Centuries of Meditation* of Traherne, writers whose use of the Platonic and Christian tradition of meditation on God's works has inevitably resulted in frequent association with Browne. A common interest in Hermeticism, occult science, and the concept of nature as symbol has readily linked Vaughan and Browne as parallel seventeenth-century figures. Vaughan's best-known poem opens with a superbly imagined embodiment of the Hermetic symbol for God's eternity – a symbol that Browne favored above any metaphysical definition.

> I saw Eternity the other night
> Like a great *Ring* of pure and endless light,
>   All calm, as it was bright,
> And round beneath it, Time in hours, days, years
>   Driv'n by the spheres
> Like a vast shadow mov'd, In which the world
>   And all her train were hurl'd . . .[27]

Vaughan contrasts Eternity's perfection of form, repose and luminosity to the fragmented agitation and the murkiness of Time – a contrast that appears in Browne, Marvell, Traherne, and in writers of Platonic disposition of all centuries.

For Browne, however, the pilgrimage of the soul toward interior illumination or mystical ecstasy is not what is primarily sought in the study of the creatures. He regards the

[27] "The World," *The Works of Henry Vaughan*, ed. L. C. Martin, 2d ed. (Oxford, 1957), p. 466.

two Books of God, the Book of Scripture and the book of the creatures, as emblems to be read symbolically or allegorically and laments that so many Christians "disdain to suck Divinity from the flowers of nature" (I, 16). But Browne's stress falls more on intellectual delight of a speculative character rather than on the meditative or devotional illumination of spirit that Vaughan and Traherne seek. The book of the creatures provides Browne with his favorite way of contemplating the wisdom of God. This contemplation, he tells us, "recreates" his understanding, while the consideration of God's eternity, through the definitions of philosophy, or, more congenially, through the assaults of metaphor, confounds his understanding. Though Browne shares many fundamental premises about God's works and wisdom with fellow seventeenth-century Platonists, his differences from them are significant.

A good way of getting at Browne's Platonic view of nature, modified by his inclination toward Baconian empiricism, is to compare the first of the poems interspersed in the *Religio* with some stanzas from Marvell's "The Garden." No one has ever claimed any poetic distinction for the verse passages scattered through the *Religio*, but their very mediocrity and approximation of the poetry of statement make them useful as direct presentations of Browne's ideas. The poem is introduced at the close of the section in which Browne speaks of God's wisdom, which man should study and endeavor to understand as the debt for the reason God has bestowed upon him. "The wisedome of God receives small honour from those vulgar heads, that rudely stare about, and with a grosse rusticity admire his workes; those highly magnifie him whose judicious enquiry into his acts, and deliberate research of his creatures, returne the duty of a devout and learned admiration" (I, 13). The key phrases are "deliberate research" and "learned admiration." Man is duty-bound to gain knowledge of God's works as "the homage wee pay for not being beasts." For the moment, the emphasis is not on perceiving the divine and "invisible fabrick" through the visible word of created nature. "Therefore," Browne enjoins,

Search while thou wilt, and let thy reason goe
To ransome truth even to the Abysse below.
Rally the scattered causes, and that line
Which nature twists be able to untwine.
It is thy Makers will, for unto none
But unto reason can he ere be knowne.
The Devills doe know thee, but those damned meteours
Build not thy glory, but confound thy creatures.
Teach my endeavours so thy workes to read,
That learning them, in thee I may proceed.
Give thou my reason that instructive flight,
Whose weary wings may on thy hands still light.
Teach me to soare aloft, yet ever so,
When neare the Sunne to stoope againe below.
Thus shall my humble feathers safely hover,
And though neere earth, more then the heavens discover. (I, 13)

Only man is equipped to discern the principles that govern the universe, and to this task he should devote the best powers of his freely inquiring mind. In invoking support for his endeavors to learn God's works so that through them he may proceed to God, Browne is fully within the Christian and Platonic tradition of meditation on the creatures. But beginning with "Teach me to soare aloft" he introduces an attitude that marks off the area where he ceases to resemble Marvell. This couplet, with its indirect allusion to Icarus, cues the reader to expect the usual Renaissance admonition against the overreaching intellect. The words "my humble feathers safely hover" would seem to confirm that such a warning against intellectual presumption is planned. However, the next line, "And though neere earth, more then the heavens discover," throws the stress in another direction. Browne says, in effect, that the fruits of learning to be reaped on earth are more valuable than what can be gathered in heavenward flight, that scanning the immediate and concrete may yield man richer discoveries than an assault upon the distant and invisible beyond. This strain of mundane absorption is never fully silenced by Christian and Platonic wonder; nor, on the other hand, does it inhibit his characteristic striving toward the single truth that binds the universe to God. This idea of staying close to earth recurs in Browne years later in the *Christian Morals.* "Let thy Studies be free as thy Thoughts and Contemplations, but fly not only upon the wings of Imagination; Joyn Sense unto Reason, and Experiment unto Speculation, and so give life unto Embryon Truths, and Verities yet in their Chaos."[28]

To see the significance of this more fully, let us contrast the conclusion of Browne's poem with the great climactic stanzas of Marvell's "The Garden."

VI.

Mean while the Mind, from pleasure less,
Withdraws into its happiness:
The Mind, that Ocean where each kind
Does streight its own resemblance find;
Yet it creates, transcending these,
Far other Worlds, and other Seas;
Annihilating all that's made
To a green Thought in a green Shade.

VII.

Here at the Fountains sliding foot,
Or at some Fruit-trees mossy root,
Casting the Bodies Vest aside,
My Soul into the boughs does glide:
There like a Bird it sits, and sings,
Then whets, and combs its silver Wings;
And, till prepar'd for longer flight,
Waves in its Plumes the various Light.[29]

The context of contemplation in "The Garden" is the Stoic and Horatian retirement from the struggles of public life – from the efforts "To win the Palm, the Oke, or Bayes" – and

[28] *Works*, I, 261–62.

[29] *The Poems and Letters of Andrew Marvell*, ed. H. M. Margoliouth, 2d ed., 2 vols. (Oxford, 1952), I, 49. Spenser's Neoplatonic treatment of the contemplative steps to mystical vision in "An Hymne of Heavenly Beautie," especially lines 22–28, offers an interesting comparison to Marvell and still another contrast to Browne.

the rejection of sexual passion. However, the sensuous delights of the garden – only a "pleasure less" than the mind's meditation on its own symbolic alphabet "where each kind/Does streight its own resemblance find" – preclude an ascetic denial of the material world, for either ethical or epistemological reasons. In the repose and beauty of the garden, the soul can be restored to the condition it enjoyed in Eden, thus enabling it to fly up to the transcendent pattern that irradiates the beauty of the garden.

Life in the world of nature is seen, then, not as an imprisonment of the soul but as a preparation, through proper meditation on the creatures, for an eternal contemplation of the Creator. The actual Yorkshire garden in which the poem is set becomes a stepping-stone toward the garden of Heaven to which the soul will take its "longer flight." Thus when the soul casts the "Bodies Vest aside," it is not gathered up into the realm of *nous*; *ekstasis* carries it rather into the boughs of a tree where it engages, in the fullest and strictest sense of the word, in meditation on the creatures. In the spiritual preparation of meditation, the soul is resolved in perfect composure: "it sits, and sings,/Then whets, and combs its silver Wings;/And, till prepar'd for longer flight," the Plotinian ecstasy which transports the soul to its final resting place in the One, allows "the various Light" of created nature to envelop and illuminate it.

Browne and Marvell are very close in their metaphysical assumptions about nature and their assurance of its cognitive value. But in their ethical stress on what man should derive from the creatures they diverge. The very images employed by each indicate a fundamental split. Marvell envisions the tranquil movements of the birdlike soul in meditative communion. Browne uses the figure of the industrious bee:

And then at last, when homeward I shall drive
Rich with the spoyles of nature to my hive,
There will I sit, like that industrious flye,
Buzzing thy prayses, which shall never die
Till death abrupts them, and succeeding glory
Bid me goe on in a more lasting story. (I, 13)

The bee lacks silver wings to absorb and refract the light of nature, and it offers no graceful and melodious response to the rainbow colors of the creatures. Having gathered "the spoyles of nature," having done its empirical "deliberate research," "that industrious flye" returns home to buzz the praises of God. The metaphor is perhaps unfortunate, certainly unlovely; yet it makes Browne's point unmistakably clear. The praises that the bee-like scientist buzzes to God, his "devout and learned admiration," consist in the principles and universal laws he has discovered in nature. While Marvell seeks a temporary suspension of soul from body until the soul is ready for its final transcendence, Browne seeks understanding of the creatures through methodical investigation and therefore insists upon returning to the world. Marvell is the meditative poet in "The Garden," representing the use of the creatures as a Plotinian experiential ladder to God. Browne is the Platonic scientist, fulfilling his duty of worship by discovering through natural reason the laws governing the creatures. While the ultimate justification for this activity is knowledge of the Creator, and the "more lasting story" may be compared to the "longer flight," Browne's stress does not fall here on this end; rather upon the rational activity itself, upon the value of knowing nature for its own sake. Though religion provides both the framework and the rationale for his scientific endeavors, Browne, it goes without saying, does not keep his eye fixed solely upon it. This would have ruled out the kind of practical investigation which was his everyday study and which accounts for the bulk of his writings.

What is interesting about this necessary practical focus and curiosity of the scientist is their presence where Browne is thinking about the quest for knowledge in the broadest and loftiest terms. In other words, Browne's empirical scientific studies and his traditional Platonic and Christian outlook exert a mutual influence upon each other. Not only did the religious emphasis of meditation on the creatures guide and shape Browne's actual study of nature, his presuppositions in those studies, and his conclusions, but likewise his role as practical student modified the temper of the Christian Platonist, giving it a dimension it did not ordinarily possess.[30]

On this side, then, Browne reaches out toward the ideals of Bacon and the empirical impulse of the age. Despite his nominalism, Bacon, it should be remembered, was interested in the universal principles of nature, since these "forms" could explain most inclusively and generally the laws of operation in matter. I offer this comparison of Browne to Marvell and Bacon not to point out what we all know: that Browne was a man of science as well as a man of faith in whom the empirical motive mingles, as it did elsewhere in the seventeenth century, with Platonism. Rather, because striking similarities in intellectual interests, metaphysical view, and even vocabulary and imagery have led to a too facile yoking of Browne with writers like Marvell and Vaughan. Their similarities, in the total picture, are more important than their differences; just as, in the last analysis, Browne's differences from Bacon are more important than his similarities. Yet the balance is delicate and unless one carefully marks off the areas where Browne fully resembles figures to whom he is closely allied from those where he diverges and leans toward men of quite different mind, one cannot hope to reach an accurate view of him. Browne cannot be understood either by assigning him wholesale to any one current of the seventeenth century

[30] Some remarks of Marie-Sofie Røstvig, who has studied the various attitudes toward nature in seventeenth-century poetry, may appropriately be noted here: "There is one interesting question which arises once the theory of the benefits accruing from a contemplation of nature has been accepted: can the book of the creatures be read only by the trained philosopher-scientist, or is it possible also for the ignorant person to approach the wonders of the world and obtain some understanding of them intuitively?

"Opinion on this point was divided, both among the poets and the philosophers, and it is even possible to find both views held by the same person. While Henry Vaughan (and Thomas Traherne) associated contemplative nature appreciation with inborn intuitive powers, Abraham Cowley and John Dryden associated it with a knowledge of letters and philosophy. Joseph Glanvill and Henry More took pains to stress the intellectual qualifications required, while Sir Thomas Browne vacillated between the two views." *The Happy Man* (Oslo, 1954), pp. 38–39.

through explaining away bothersome contradictions or by unravelling single threads of his tangled intellectual fabric onto their proper skeins. One method violently distorts him; the other obliterates him entirely. The only profitable definition Browne lends himself to is definition in the literal sense of the word – tracing his limits and boundaries so as to draw his own outline as sharply as possible. In this way we can hope to see the individual character of his thought which, encompassing much that is apparently contradictory, frustrates any attempt at clinically pure schematization.

The problem is increased by Browne's capacity for imaginative projection into many, and often conflicting, attitudes. To cite a crucial example, one may wonder which represents his true feeling about the quest of knowledge: the eloquent call to "deliberate research" that will issue in "a devout and learned admiration," or the resigned, other-worldly note struck in Part II of the *Religio* as Browne thinks: "it is a vanity to waste our dayes in the blind pursuit of knowledge; it is but attending a little longer, and wee shall enjoy that by instinct and infusion which we endeavour at here by labour and inquisition: it is better to sit downe in a modest ignorance, & rest contented with the naturall blessing of our owne reasons, then buy the uncertaine knowledge of this life, with sweat and vexation, which death gives every foole gratis, and is an accessary of our glorification" (II, 8).

Which, we may ask, is the real voice of Sir Thomas Browne? That of the energetic and disciplined Baconian investigator, or that of the modest and devout Christian who rejects formal study? To argue for one or the other as his true position is futile. We have seen running through the Platonic tradition an implicit double view of the soul's status and activity: the religio-mystical longing of the exile for reunion with the Absolute and, opposed to this, a rational activity, a shaping force that gives significance to the world of sensibles. This double view operates at many levels. In epistemology, Browne alternates between certain equivalents of the two sides of this basic Platonic dilemma. On one is the impulse compounded of scientific Christian Platonism and the empiricism, more or less critical, of the new science; on the other is the Augustinian version of Plotinian illumination through contemplation, the gift of complete knowledge through grace which was once the natural possession of man.

Within a Neoplatonic framework this opposition is resolved as a hierarchical union wherein the soul's dual condition becomes a special glory. Its exile from the One is made up for by its transmission of form to what lies below and by the creation of beauty. Transferred and adapted to a specifically Christian context in which time and history, irrelevant to the pagan Platonists, assume crucial importance, the dilemma of ethical choice between the active and contemplative life is raised to a plane where virtue and beauty, noble ideals and noble action are consolidated. From this Platonic world view derive both the matter and the method of a poem like *The Faerie Queene*. The upward movement of Spenser's human heroes, striving for the soul's perfection through achievement of the universal ideals of virtue for which they are named, has as its necessary counterpart the downward movement through which these ideals can be embodied in the world of time and action, thus directing the providential scheme of Christian and national history. As Spenser's allegory looks both up to philosophical absolutes and down to their actualization in the process of history, so Browne's strategy of truth operates in two directions: the revelations of positive religion and those of the creatures; the confounding of his mind by the paradoxical mysteries of faith and the recreation of his mind by the mysterious order of nature.

This double view underlies the countless oppositions running through the *Religio*, functioning not as mutually exclusive choices but as interdependent necessities. The world is a place to be studied, but also a hospital to die in. God reveals himself through nature, "that streight and regular line, that setled and constant course," but also through fortune, the term men unthinkingly apply to his providence, "that serpentine and crooked line," which does not "lie expans'd unto the eyes of all" (I, 16, 17). Moreover, Browne's Platonic orientation provides not only an explanation for the shifting intellectual positions in the *Religio*; it accounts for much of the richness of the work. It is a commonplace that Renaissance Platonism, when subject to critical scrutiny, collapses as philosophy in the strict sense, while offering to the arts a uniquely usable vision of life. Such a view can be supported whether we apply the standards of Sir Philip Sidney on the peculiar nature and function of poetry or the definition of a modern poet like Yeats who felt that the poet dramatizes an attitude or mood, "dwell[s] in the presence of certain ideas." [31] Belief to enrich experience along with moral commitment to make it "meaningful," but without absolutes to shackle its existential freedom, is the paradoxical demand of twentieth-century sensibility, a demand mirrored in much of the great fiction and poetry of our time with its assumption that only those values personally and hence fragmentarily apprehended can be honestly and significantly embodied in art. The Renaissance assumption of absolutes and of the unity of experience finds its characteristically richest paradoxical expression in a potently imagined, but deeply uncritical, Platonic synthesis of humanistic reason and Christian faith, in the happy illusion of the convergence of all truth.

We can look too, then, to Browne's Platonism to ask how he may in a real sense be considered a poet. The term is frequently applied to him as a label of praise, though the Renaissance concept of poetry as a fiction, as something feigned or made up, clearly does not apply. Stylistic merits alone, such as his prose rhythm, seem an inadequate measure; visual imagination is strikingly absent. The religious view of nature and his profound spirit of devotion create an elevation, a sense of the sublime, which for Browne's age was closely allied to poetry, but which we cannot identify with it per se. Without attempting anything so futile as a definition of poetry we can say that one of its attributes or effects that we especially acknowledge today is notably present in the *Religio*: the confrontation of thought and feeling in such a way as to produce a discourse that can sustain and dramatize

[31] Quoted from Richard Ellmann, *The Identity of Yeats* (New York, 1954), p. 43.

the contraries of the whole spectrum of human experience – what the New Critics in our own time have chosen to call, in their special sense, "ambiguity," "tension," "paradox." Like other artists of his time, Browne was fortunate in that at the heart of the intellectual and religious orientation to which he was instinctively drawn lay an articulated system of contraries.

The speculative mind eager for knowledge and the devout spirit moved by faith are both present in the *Religio*; yet they do not meet in implacable combat (that would be impossible in Browne's frame of reference in which all truth is finally one); nor do they achieve perfect fusion (the assault of genuinely new currents of thought as well as the inherent inconsistencies of Platonism itself would prevent this). Rather these two tempers play against one another in a fugue of countersuggestions and irresolutions. Or as Ficino defined the co-existence of the impulses of knowledge and belief: "we see that by a natural instinct every soul strives in a continuous effort both to know all truths by the intellect and to enjoy all good things by the will." [32]

[32] *Epistolae* 2. 1 (trans. Josephine L. Burroughs as "Five Questions Concerning the Mind," in *The Renaissance Philosophy of Man*, ed. Ernst Cassirer, Paul O. Kristeller, and J. H. Randall, Jr. [Chicago, 1948], p. 201).

CHAPTER V

RELIGIO MEDICI: THE LIMITS AND VALUE OF CUSTOM

My conclusion is this, That it is the part of a wise rationall man, as to consider diligently how farre forth *custome* both in matter of Religion and in other things is considerable, lest hee trouble himselfe and others without cause: So to consider as diligently wherein it is altogether against reason, lest conforming to the vulgar in those things, hee himself become one of them; that is, a man that is led by *custome* and not by reason.

MERIC CASAUBON, *A Treatise of Use and Custome* (1638), p. 186.

Mutual agreement and indearments was the badge of Primitive Believers, but we may be known by the contrary *criterion.* The Union of a Sect within it self, is a pitiful charity: it's no concord of *Christians,* but a conspiracy against Christ; and they that love one another, for their *opinionative concurrences,* love for their *own sakes,* not their *Lords*: not because they love his *image,* but because they bear one *anothers.*

JOSEPH GLANVILL, *The Vanity of Dogmatizing* (1661), p. 230.

HAVING considered certain broad aspects of *Religio Medici,* we shall now turn to a detailed examination of the first of the two arguments which constitute its action. Within the context of Browne's Platonic thought, sectarian differences are intimately bound up with the authority of human opinion and traditions; i.e. custom. The close relevance of custom to the controversies raging among Puritans, Anglo-Catholics, and Latitudinarians was recognized by all factions, though each drew sharply variant conclusions. In the first passage quoted above, Casaubon concludes that the intellectual limits of custom are defined by reason, while its practical force, as either coercion to conformity or as a pointless and divisive refusal to conform, must never violate charity. Browne's response to sectarian strife over customs is also the application of charity.

When Browne was composing the *Religio* in the mid-1630's the religious situation in England was seething; by the time of its publication the Civil War had erupted. Behind the troubling questions reflected in his meditative essay lay a history of many decades. But there is little exposition of these matters in the *Religio*, since the issues, their history, and their partisan answers were all too familiar. Besides, Browne was not writing as a churchman nor as a controversialist seeking to win an audience to his views. He makes no attempt to give a coherently articulated statement of his position, but reflects and comments from a highly personal vantagepoint. We must therefore define his position in terms of certain fuller and more systematically presented arguments. Then it will be possible to see its significance in the larger structure of thought of *Religio Medici*.

1

The real conflict between Anglicans and Puritans was not doctrinal, but disciplinary, hinging especially on church government. This was, in general, as true for Browne's time when Anglicans had adopted Arminianism as for the age of Elizabeth when the Anglican and Puritan parties of the Church alike inclined to Calvinism.[1] When a Puritan pro-

[1] Douglas Bush has pointed out, on the authority of Thomas Fuller, that "Dalmatian Archbishop of Spalatro, who was in England during 1616–22, was the first to use 'Puritan' in a doctrinal sense, as opposed to Arminian" (*English Literature in the Earlier Seventeenth Century*, p. 337).

ponent for complete and immediate reformation hurled the epithet "Arminian" at a supporter of Laud, a High Churchman, he was not arguing theology primarily; the doctrinal differences on free will, soteriology, and so forth, though very real, were taken for granted by their inclusion within a broader frame. What was really at stake was the government of the church (was it to be Episcopal or Presbyterian?) and such related questions as the role of preaching, ritualism, and the form of the Prayer Book. Intellectually, the acute problem was *where to seek authority for determining truth* in religious discipline and dogma. It is no coincidence that Donne's powerfully searching examination of the vexed religious situation in "Satire III" is also one of the most passionate responses to the problem of truth in the literature of seventeenth-century England.

The Puritan and Anglican parties grounded their positions on church government in two opposed views of the Bible. The Anglicans held that no final model for church government was set forth in Scripture, a position that had been argued at length by Hooker's superior, John Whitgift, who, as Vice-Chancellor of Cambridge in the early 1570's, had engaged in controversy with Thomas Cartwright, a fellow of Trinity College and a Puritan. "The Word of God," Cartwright declared, "containeth the direction of all things pertaining to the church, yea, of whatsoever things can fall into any part of man's life." [2] Whitgift countered by denying that the Bible "doth set down any one certain form and kind of government of the church, to be perpetual for all times, persons, and places, without alteration." [3]

Anglicans like Whitgift and Hooker tended to reduce the absolute truth of Christian theology – the divinely decreed law – to the facts of the Apostles' Creed, the two sacraments of Baptism and the Eucharist, and the supernatural virtues of faith, hope, and charity. They did not place everything in Scripture on a level of equal authority, but distinguished

[2] Donald J. McGinn, *The Admonition Controversy* (New Brunswick, N.J., 1949), p. 378.

[3] *Ibid.*, p. 56.

those things essential to salvation from "indifferencies" which need not be adhered to. Their stance was drawn delicately between Rome and Geneva and, appropriately for those who held the reins of power, was more notable for reasonableness than for strict logic. While believing that everything necessary for salvation was to be found in Scripture (refusing to recognize as essential the "superfluous" doctrines and observances of the Roman Church), they did not believe everything in Scripture was necessary for salvation or that everything not in Scripture, so long as it does not touch essentials, must be rejected (denying the Puritan position on these two points). The separation of fundamental articles of faith from non-fundamentals was the characteristic strategy of Anglicans for meeting the Puritan insistence upon strict and full observance of every word in the Bible and upon prohibition of everything else. This task required a broader philosophic underpinning than Whitgift had provided, and Hooker's *Laws of Ecclesiastical Polity* was designed to extend the argument by showing the efficacy of natural reason in all but the divinely ordained fundamentals.

Anglicans regarded ecclesiastical government, form of worship, and ceremony as indifferent to salvation and reserved to the Church (in effect, to the civil government whose instrument the Church was) the authority to prescribe as it saw fit in these areas. According to Whitgift, no claim to revealed truth is necessary to justify the Church's practice in these matters. "That no ceremony, order, discipline, or kind of government may be in the church except the same be expressed in the Word of God is a great absurdity and breedeth many inconveniencies."[4] The Church is therefore free to establish the form of government and worship it deems proper and expedient in particular times and places.[5]

[4] *Ibid.*, p. 378.

[5] The position of the English Church on the question "Of Ceremonies, why some be abolished and some retayned," had been set forth in the *First Book of Common Prayer* (1549), which argues, on one hand, against the superfluities of Rome and, on the other, against the abolition of Ceremonies desired by the complete Reformers.

Hooker defended "The Sumptuousness of Churches" against the

Though Hooker's broader discussion reduced the liability of this Erastian position to the charge of relying merely on human and arbitrary custom, the Puritans remained unsatisfied. Unflinchingly absolutist in mentality, they contended that final truth exists in all matters touching religion, that this truth is to be found in Scripture, and that it should be rigidly enforced.

Certain glaring inconsistencies are apparent on both sides. To their adversaries, it seemed that the Anglicans, while denying the existence of a divinely prescribed form of ecclesiastical government, would yet command the obedience of all Englishmen to the observance of what they themselves acknowledged, at bottom, to be only custom. Hooker's attempt to equate rational natural law with divine law through a refutation of the Calvinist split between nature and grace was an intellectual triumph, but it failed to convince the Puritans. Nor did the fact that nothing in the Bible directly opposed an Episcopal form of government carry any weight with them; they insisted not only on the need to conform to the pattern they believed set forth in Scripture but also to forbid everything not expressly enjoined therein.

For Hooker to assert that positive laws cannot bind universally, to assign church government to the realm of positive law, and yet to bind men to Episcopacy, must have seemed to the Puritans not only the indulgence of a false assumption but the drawing of a contradictory conclusion. Yet the existence of the state and the continuity of an ordered national church depended upon just such a split between theory and actual ecclesiastical rule. Hooker had defended Episcopacy by demonstrating that natural law and reason were for most matters as true revelations of the divine will as Scripture. However, Anglicans in general, while welcoming this philosophic support for their position, felt their Church justified by tradition, by expediency, and by its orderliness of

Puritans, who pointed to the simplicity of the buildings of the early Church, by distinguishing the state of "the Church in the times of universal persecution" from "the other when God hath enriched it with plenty." *Ecclesiastical Polity* 5. 15. 3 ([London, 1907], II, 48–49).

government and worship – in short, by the sanction of revered custom.

As for the Puritans, despite their emphasis on the individual Christian conscience shaped through reading of the Bible, the last thing they sought was liberty either for individuals or sects. Universal truth must be universally observed; and since they found in the complete and infallible code of Scripture the injunction for a Presbyterian form of government, nothing else would do either for themselves or for others. Thus, both parties endorsed the employment of force to maintain a particular form of church discipline. The Anglicans made a broad allowance for individual feeling and conviction and supported the observance of much that was edifying, while admitting it to be nonessential. But both parties demanded a single visible Church, the Anglicans on grounds of reason and expediency, the Puritans on grounds of divine truth. The time had not yet come for the acceptance of pluralism and hence of religious toleration in the modern sense.

2

Between the seemingly irreconcilable positions of Anglican and Puritan there developed a mediative attitude toward custom in religion and toward sectarian differences in general. The Latitudinarians were notable for their temperateness of opinion and restraint of expression in an age when belief too readily distorted itself into fanaticism. Their call for a rational and peaceful solution to the bitter religious strife went unheeded; moderates like Falkland, Hales, and Chillingworth were impotent to prevent the upheaval of the Civil War. But though they failed to exert immediate influence, their ideas were of more enduring importance than the ideas of the extreme left or right, which by the end of the seventeenth century came to appear unimaginably outworn.[6]

Sir Thomas Browne stood, or rather moved, in the 1630's

[6] The fullest and still the best discussion of this group of thinkers is John Tulloch, *Rational Theology and Christian Philosophy in England in the Seventeenth Century*, rev. ed., 2 vols. (London, 1874), Vol. I, *Liberal Churchmen*. These same figures are approached from a differ-

on this middle ground, considerably to the left of the High Church party and quite far to the right of the Puritans. Writing at that moment, he inevitably invites comparison with these loyal supporters of the national Church who undertook three thankless tasks: defending the English Church against both the claims of Rome and the clamor of the Presbyterians while also seeking a liberal definition of the Anglican communion and practice that was deeply suspect to the Laudian establishment. Though our interest is not the historical question as such, but custom as an intellectual and ethical component of the structure of thought of *Religio Medici*, the relevance of custom cannot be understood apart from certain specific controversial issues. Moreover, while Browne has frequently been grouped with Falkland and his fellows, accurate definition of his attitude, as distinct from general labelling, requires that we discriminate among shades of liberal opinion. For our purposes, the differences, though subtle, are more important than the larger similarities.

The idea of religious freedom developed in close relation to certain liberal answers to the question of custom in religion. What was custom? What was divine command? What were the bases for distinguishing one from the other? To what extent might the civil authority legitimately reach in regulating religious matters admitted to be custom and not divine truth? The Latitudinarians steered a course between and above the Laudian Anglo-Catholics and the Puritans. While their conception of the Christian communion was not unlike Hooker's, they were closer to the spirit of a more primitive Protestantism, which nevertheless placed them at even a further remove from seventeenth-century Puritanism than from the Anglo-Catholic party. They regarded all who subscribed to the few simple beliefs necessary to salvation as members of the Christian communion. Anything in excess

ent interest by Wilbur K. Jordan, *The Development of Religious Toleration in England*, 4 vols. (Cambridge, Mass., 1932–40), Vol. II, *1603–40* (1936). While my own account focuses upon the special problem of custom, I am greatly indebted to these two vast works of scholarship for their general perspective.

of this, whether concerning doctrine, the administration of the Church, or the external forms of worship, was nonessential and therefore beyond the legitimate reach of coercion. Irrespective of excrescences and corruptions in doctrine and form of worship, any church that preached the fundamentals necessary to salvation was a true church whose "errors" should be regarded with charity. Though different from Browne in religious temper, Chillingworth, like Browne, granted that the Roman Church (to which he converted and from which he soon broke) was a true church.[7]

The Latitudinarians insisted that salvation is an individual duty in which private conscience illuminated by the Bible bears final responsibility, a responsibility that cannot be shifted to any external authority which claims to possess a sole or infallible way. The bulk of their controversial writings were directed against Rome, it should be remembered. Falkland and his fellows valued inwardness in religion at the expense of a visible church of whatever doctrinal or outer form. Milton was to carry this position much further, finding refuge finally in a personal church such as this position tends to build—a church in which the individual is priest and congregation within his own conscience.

There is an obvious relation between such attitudes and Christian Platonism, characteristically more concerned as it is to achieve a universal religion than to build the single "true" visible church. Differences in external signs or in the particular formulas used to express dogma do not represent threats to the communion of believers. Indeed, such diversity reinforces the unity of faith by gathering the strength of truth from many sources. On the other hand, a faith depending upon precise agreement on all points of dogma and practice, however minor, must be weak since it is built upon an accord of prejudices. In the passage from *The Vanity of Dogmatizing* that serves as an epigraph for this chapter, Joseph Glanvill states this liberal attitude in the face of sectarian narrowness with great force and acuity. This same position can be traced with remarkable essential consistency through

[7] Jordan, II, 380.

Florentine humanists like Pico,[8] the Tudor humanists, Falkland and his fellow moderates, and the Cambridge Platonists. A motto Ficino used as a chapter heading in *De Christiana religione* epitomizes the liberal Platonic position most concisely: "Omnis religio boni habet nonnihil, modo ad Deum ipsum creatorem omnium dirigatur, Christiana syncera est." [9]

The individual emphasis so basic to the Latitudinarian idea of toleration was therefore hardly new. It represented a reaffirmation of the trust in the individual conscience from which Protestantism had drawn its profoundest impulses. In the seventeenth century this value was greatly in need of restoration, since the two warring parties had discarded it under the pressure to gain a hardened efficiency in combat. At the heart of Protestantism had lain a spirit of free inquiry and trust in the individual perception of truth that had preceded the actual split with Rome. With the Reformation, this animating spirit of the Platonic humanists of the Tudor period was focused on the Bible. Saving truth was to be discovered by the individual using the Bible to guide his reason and conscience. Reliance on the promptings of private feeling allowed for a greater freedom than could be easily compassed in a single institutional frame, and it was perhaps inevitable that this original view should have been narrowed.

The beliefs essential to salvation, the Latitudinarians held, were clearly and unmistakably revealed in the Bible; God had not clouded the momentous essentials of faith. Though they were not in perfect agreement as to what these necessary beliefs were, none of them would have claimed more things essential than Hooker had; Chillingworth evidently held that observance of Christ's simple injunction to believe in Him and to love one's neighbor as oneself was sufficient. Beyond these fundamentals the individual should enjoy complete freedom within the Church to speculate about those

[8] See Cassirer, "Pico," *Journal of the History of Ideas*, 3: 335.

[9] *Opera omnia*, ed. M. Sancipriano and P. O. Kristeller, photographic reproduction of Basel ed., 2 vols., 1576 (Turin, 1959), I, 4 (chap. 4). The chapter heading reads: "Every religion has something good in it; so long as it is directed to God the Creator of all things, it is a true Christian religion."

other doctrines and beliefs which require no determination. By holding firm to the fundamentals and searching without bias for truth, men cannot be in danger of damnation, nor the Church of deformation. To speak of "heretics" in a Church defined in these terms is a solecism, since all who assent to the essentials and who worship God are members.

Moreover, the Latitudinarians saw that unnecessary fear of error leads to an insistence upon conformity of creed that destroys the spiritual life of religion. Distaste for compulsion is natural to rationalists and skeptics, since compulsion can be justified only by the possession of final truth. It would be inaccurate, though, to confuse Falkland and the circle of moderates who gathered about him at Great Tew with secular rationalists who are concerned only with keeping the mind free of the shackles of authority. They were equally concerned with the damage that inflexible external authority could do to religion itself, whose greatest strength is individual and internal. Chillingworth summed up the consequences of dogmatism wedded to force: "for human violence may make men counterfeit, but cannot make them believe, and is therefore fit for nothing, but to breed form without, and atheism within."[10] Browne sounded this note with still greater resonance when he inveighed against persecution as self-defeating: "The Jew is obstinate in all fortunes; the persecutions of fifteene hundred yeares have but confirmed them in their errour: they have already endured whatsoever may be inflicted, and have suffered, in a bad cause, even to the condemnation of their enemies. Persecution is a bad and indirect way to plant Religion; It hath beene the unhappy method of angry devotions, not onely to confirme honest Religion, but wicked Heresies, and extravagant opinions" (I, 25).

In Chillingworth, whose *Religion of Protestants* (1637) offers the fullest statement of the Latitudinarian position, two lines of attack on dogmatism and bigotry are discernible. These lines meet at a point where the comprehensive Chris-

[10] *The Works of William Chillingworth*, 3 vols. (London, 1820), II, 271.

tian Church stands. This church is very loosely framed externally and takes as many precise shapes as there are individual Christians; its coherence rests on the essentials to which all the members subscribe. This lack of conformity does not threaten to result in irreligion or anarchy, since free and compatible men, each holding his belief through inner conviction, make a stronger Christian body than individuals bound together by repressive tyranny.

Chillingworth aimed first at dissolving the barriers that separate sects from one another by stressing the saving truth that all possess while dispelling the notion of exclusive and infallible saving power for any one sect. The illiberal mind demands conformity to its own narrow version of truth and thus endlessly multiplies sects that become increasingly harsh and further isolated from the majority of other Christians. He wished to avert the discord of numerous schisms as much as the tyranny of an ascendant sect—whether minority or majority—over individual Englishmen. Nothing pained him so much as the kind of fanaticism that was not content to formulate a doctrine without attempting to enforce the precise assent of others. What could be more arrogant and uncharitable than to damn men by narrow laws of one's own making that were never ordained by God? This sentiment appears in Browne, who shared Chillingworth's dismay at those who claimed exclusive possession of the path to salvation and would consign to damnation any who wandered from their narrowly defined way: "nor must a few differences more remarkable in the eyes of man than perhaps in the judgement of God, excommunicate from heaven one another, much lesse those Christians who are in a manner all Martyrs, maintaining their faith in the noble way of persecution, and serving God in the fire, whereas we honour him but in the Sunshine" (I, 56).

The wish of Chillingworth to keep the Church simple and free of extra-fundamental accretions did not derive from any zeal for primitive purity. Rather, he realized that inessential doctrines and practices become confused with fundamentals (as witnessed by the history of the Roman Church) and that this leads to the two scourges of tyrannous enforcement of nonessentials and the multiplication of sects and schisms. His stress on the private exercise of reason and on a broad and simple Church was nevertheless interpreted by some as Socinianism and worse. There is the famous and ugly story related by the Presbyterian Francis Cheynell who persecuted Chillingworth on his death bed, unwilling to accept his refusal to consign Turks, Papists, and Socinians either to Heaven or to Hell; and at Chillingworth's funeral Cheynell inveighed against *The Religion of Protestants* after casting a copy of the book into the author's grave.[11]

In the seventeenth century, skepticism like Chillingworth's was always liable to interpretation as a wicked disloyalty to truth. A man who claimed to hold final truth in all matters of religion and then attempted to win others to his position, damning those who would not be won, was an understandable and manageable adversary. The polemical artillery of the day was expressly designed for firing at such fixed targets. But Chillingworth and his fellows, who saw bits of truth scattered everywhere, refused to proclaim any final answers, indeed denied that any could exist beyond the fundamentals, and therefore offered a most disturbing challenge to men of doctrinaire opinion. While Roman Catholics, High Churchmen, and Presbyterians were insisting on the separateness of their particular truth, the Latitudinarians were pondering the ambiguities of truth and error, and, most important, wished to create an atmosphere in which the individual quest of religious truth would be possible.

3

Browne's casually expressed opinions on custom take on a larger perspective against the more formal tracts and treatises of the Latitudinarians in the 1630's. Likewise, a particular slant of his attitude, crucial for the complex relation of custom to truth within his Platonic epistemology (not only in the *Religio* but also, as we will see, in *Urn Burial*), takes

[11] *Chillingworthi Novissima; or the Sicknesse, Heresy, Death, and Buriall of William Chillingworth* (London, 1644).

on greater precision through reference to the ideas of a somewhat later writer: Jeremy Taylor. Within the wide spectrum of liberal opinion there were naturally variations of emphasis, some of which could amount to important differences. A High Churchman and a chaplain to Laud, Taylor nevertheless achieved as liberal a stance on religious freedom as Chillingworth and lived long enough to be even more deeply pained at the ravages of bigotry. His continued emphasis upon private reason and the Bible in *The Liberty of Prophesying* (1647) places him very close to the position of the Latitudinarians. Tulloch stressed the resemblance between this work and *The Religion of Protestants* and argued that Chillingworth's and Taylor's assumptions and conclusions are substantially identical.[12]

Our own interest in Taylor must focus more narrowly upon how his attitude toward ceremony and custom, developed in his massive exercise of casuistry, *Ductor dubitantium* (1660), illuminates Browne's position toward custom in *Religio Medici.* Dedicated to the newly restored monarch Charles II, this longest of Taylor's works represents his maturest thought, ripened under pressure of the years of national upheaval, as applied to cases of conscience.[13] The disenchantment borne of conflict and tyranny did not shake Taylor's liberalism. He still held, as he had in *The Liberty of Prophesying,* that acceptance of the Apostles' Creed and a virtuous life were the only requirements of salvation. Nor did his profound attachment to extra-Biblical traditions and non-fundamental practices betray him into demanding the exact compliance of others. His insistent awareness of the limits of custom is the cornerstone of his liberalism.

> Truth and divine commandments need no prescription, but have an intrinsic warrant and a perpetual abode, but that which is warranted by custom hath but an accidental obligation, and is of human

[12] *Rational Theology,* I, 404–406.

[13] The place of *Ductor dubitantium* in the larger patterns of seventeenth-century thought has been treated by Herschel Baker, *The Wars of Truth* (Cambridge, Mass., 1952), pp. 233–38.

> authority. The laws of Christ are or ought to be the parents of custom; but custom cannot introduce a divine law or obligation: our customs ought to be according to Christ's commandment; but from our customs we cannot conclude or infer that this is the will or commandment of Christ.
>
> . . . .
>
> Custom can thus in cases of destitution of other topics declare the meaning of a law; but custom of itself cannot be the interpreter of the will of Christ, or a sufficient warrant of a law, or immediately bind the conscience as if it were a signification of the divine pleasure: much less ought it to be opposed to any words of scripture or right reason, and proper arguments derived from thence.
>
> . . . .
>
> When custom is consonant to some other instrument of probation, when it is apparently pious and reasonable, and of the analogy of faith, it is an excellent corroborative and defensative of truth, and warrant to conscience; but when it stands alone, or hath an ill aspect upon other more reasonable and effective ways of persuasion, it is very suspicious and very dangerous, and is commonly a very ill sign of an ill cause, or of corrupted manners.[14]

Where Taylor does defend the observance of custom, his defense is entirely undogmatic and derives from the conciliatory and order-loving impulses of the liberal Anglican temper at its best.

> In such cases where there is no law, the manners of Christians introduce a law so far, that we cannot recede from it without probable cause; or if we do, we cannot do it without scandal and reproach. And indeed it is an act of love to conform to the customs of Christians with whom we do converse, who either will think you blame their custom, or despise their persons, if you comply not.

[14] *Works*, ed. Heber and Eden (London, 1847–54), IX, 692, 693, 694.

> It is a catholic custom, that they who receive the holy communion, should receive it fasting. This is not a duty commanded by God: but unless it be necessary to eat, he that despises this custom, gives nothing but the testimony of an evil mind.
>
> It is a custom in the church of England to uncover the head or to bow the knee when the name of Jesus is named: the custom is not only innocent but pious, and agreeable to the duty of every Christian, and therefore abstracting from the injunction, the custom itself is sufficient to exact conformity of all modest persons. But if a son of the church of England shall come into other protestant churches who use it not, he is to comply with them in the omisson, unless himself be persuaded that it is a divine commandment; and yet even then also the specification and the circumstances of time and place may be undetermined, and leave him in a capacity to comply for a time, and in a limited place.[15]

Taylor is scrupulous to place the authority of private conscience above any custom, whether prescribed by one's own church or by another. Earlier in his career, he had, like the Latitudinarians, noted that the responsibility for salvation devolves finally upon the individual. "Some men are so fond as to think heaven is entailed upon a sect or an opinion, and then nothing is wanting to them, when they once have entered their name into that persuasion."[16] At the same time, the passages quoted above reveal aspects of Taylor's thought that differentiate him from a Latitudinarian like Chillingworth or Hales.

First, there is in Taylor the assumption that customs, though frequently sources of contention, do have a legitimate place; visible acts and ceremonies are useful supports of worship and are ineluctable unless rigidly suppressed. It is unfortunate that inflexible minds cause needless disputes

[15] *Ibid.*, X, 358, 360 f.
[16] *Ibid.*, I, 126.

over such customs, since they are nonessentials. Looking back at the terrible years of the 1640's and 1650's, Taylor remarks not without bitterness: "And we see it by a sad experience, that those who are enemies and stubborn to the innocent customs of a church, intend nothing but to get the government into their own hands." [17] Second, he goes beyond the flexibility of toleration to participation in customs that diverge from those of his own Church. Where customs offer no injury to conscience, refusal to unbend is inexcusable: "For a custom obliges by being amongst them with whom we do converse, and to whom in charity and prudence we are to comply." [18] And even when a divine commandment is involved, conscience is not broken by a compliance "for a time, and in a limited place." "Though every subject is tied to the custom of his own church, yet he is not to give offence when he converses with another church that hath a differing custom." [19]

Taylor's concept of charity thus extends as far as that of the Latitudinarians and has the depth of another dimension as well. For he seeks to minimize sectarian conflict not through a leveling down or stripping away of religious customs but by widening the range of customs which the individual Christian may accept. In striving for a deeper toleration of varying forms and ceremonies, he is concerned with preserving them as things of unique value and not merely with depriving them of their divisive power.

Falkland and Chillingworth deny the justice of forcing men to observe non-fundamental doctrines and abhor the disunity that conflicting customs breed among Christians. Their characteristic solution is to simplify the Church to the point where all Protestants could join its communion without injury of conscience to any. This solution is eminently rational. Yet for an Anglican like Taylor, liberal though he was, such a solution would have been unsatisfactory, because, by undermining the Church's appeal to memory, sense,

[17] *Ibid.*, X, 368.
[18] *Ibid.*, X, 361.
[19] *Ibid.*, X, 360.

and emotion, it would tend to strip religion of much of its sustaining power. Taylor is in perfect concord with the desire of these moderates to put an end to conflicts, persecutions, and schisms stemming from disagreement about nonfundamentals. But while he will make his reason bow to no authority but divine command, his religious life would starve if only the rational part of it were fed.

The Latitudinarians saw that bigotry breeds hypocrisy and crushes the true spirit of religion. We are inclined to sympathize with their feeling that religion is largely a private matter that may enrich the mind and spirit of the individual, but becomes a menace when it unfurls creeds and dogmas like so many flags that must be publicly saluted. Yet for all their clarity and humaneness of vision, their solution to the problem of custom inevitably took much of the vital force out of religion along with the destructive sting.

They are linked to a liberal Puritan like Milton by a common distrust of external forms and by a lack of felt need for them. To many this may attest more surely to the genuineness and depth of their spiritual life. On the other hand, it is safe to guess that more men, and not necessarily less gifted ones, require some sense of connection between their physical and spiritual existence. For Taylor the beauty of ritual and the suggestiveness of liturgical symbolism provide a relationship at once splendid and intimate between the individual Christian and the realm of spirit with which he seeks communion. Or, as Hooker defended the celebration of religious festivals: "They are the splendour and outward dignity of our religion, forcible witnesses of ancient truth, provocations to the exercise of all piety, shadows of our endless felicity in heaven."[20] In one sense as liberal as Chillingworth, Taylor wished the Church to be a community of believers, but he was also a traditionalist, rather than a rationalist, and valued the Church as an institution in which the worship of God was practiced with the order and the beauty of ancient rites.

[20] *Ecclesiastical Polity* 5. 71. 11 ([London, 1907], II, 372–73).

4

The bitter religious contention of the 1630's was inescapable even for a young physician who was just getting under way in his profession, and whose real interests lay in quite different areas. Browne's natural feelings ring with unmistakable clarity. "I could never divide my selfe from any man upon the difference of an opinion, or be angry with his judgment for not agreeing with mee in that, from which perhaps within a few days I should dissent my selfe: I have no Genius to disputes in Religion . . ." (I, 6). The attitudes toward religious conflict in *Religio Medici* are an accurate reflection of Browne's personality. They took definite shape, however, in reaction to the dogmatic assertiveness of the times and cannot be understood on the basis of temperament alone. What Browne says in the *Religio* bears reference to the specific issues that men at the left and right were arguing so heatedly. Though he had no direct association with members of the Latitudinarian group or with liberal churchmen of Jeremy Taylor's stature, his assumptions and outlook indicate how closely attuned he was to their ideas.

While the second and much shorter of the two parts of *Religio Medici* bears the heading "Charity," the relevance of this highest of the theological virtues is not confined to the final fifteen sections. We have seen that Browne introduces charity into Section 1 and then applies it to differences among contemporary schools of philosophy. The charitable voice of toleration raised by Falkland, Chillingworth, and Taylor in the hope of harmonizing divergent opinions is everywhere in the *Religio.*

> I cannot fall out or contemne a man for an errour, or conceive why a difference in opinion should divide our affection: for controversies, disputes, and argumentations, both in Philosophy and in Divinity, if they meete with discreet and peaceable natures, doe not infringe the Lawes of Charity; in all disputes, so much as there is of passion, so much there is of nothing to the purpose; for then reason like a

> bad hound spends upon a false sent, and forsakes the question first started. (II, 3)

Conscious application of charity to the conflicts raised by religious customs had a long tradition to which men in the seventeenth century could look back. Augustine was sensitive to the two chief errors that lie at opposite poles of the crux of custom—a bigoted provinciality that rejects all unfamiliar customs as unnatural and a moral anarchism that concludes there is no right or wrong. That sudden emancipation from the first of these errors could drive an individual into the second troubled Augustine. Against the persecution and moral anarchy that attend these erroneous attitudes, he offered the antidote of Christian charity.

> When men, ignorant of any other manner of living, happen to read about these deeds, unless they are deterred by an authority, they consider them sins. They cannot understand that their own entire mode of living, in connection with marriage, banqueting, dress, and the other necessities and refinements of human life, seems sinful to people of other nations and other times. Aroused by this diversity of innumerable customs, some souls, drowsy so to speak, who were neither settled in the sound sleep of folly nor able to waken fully to light of wisdom, have thought that justice did not exist of itself, but that each nation regarded as right that which was its own custom. Since this or that custom is different for every nation, while justice must remain immutable, it becomes evident that there is no justice anywhere. They have not understood (not to multiply instances) that the maxim, "Do not do to another what you do not wish to have done to you" cannot be varied in any way by any national diversity of customs. When this rule is applied to the love of God, all vices die; when it is applied to the love of our neighbor, all crimes vanish. No one wants to despoil his own house. Therefore, he should not dishonor the house of God, namely, himself. Further, no one is willing to be injured by

> another; then, neither should he himself harm anyone.[21]

The remedy for differences of custom that Augustine prescribed was pleasant indeed for Sir Thomas Browne. Conscious effort only bolstered what in Browne was a natural inclination to charity.

> Now for that other Vertue of Charity, without which Faith is a meer notion, and of no existence, I have ever endeavoured to nourish the mercifull disposition, and humane inclination [which] I borrowed from my Parents, and [to] regulate it to the written and prescribed Lawes of Charity; and if I hold the true Anatomy of my selfe, I am delineated & naturally framed to such a piece of vertue: for I am of a constitution so generall, that it consorts and sympathizeth with all things; I have no antipathy, or rather Idio-syncrasie, in dyet, humour, ayre, any thing; I wonder not at the *French*, for their dishes of frogges, snailes, and toadstooles, nor at the Jewes for Locusts and Grasse-hoppers, but being amongst them, make them my common viands; and I finde they agree with my stomach as well as theirs; I could digest a Sallad gathered in a Church-yard, as well as in a Garden. I cannot start at the presence of a Serpent, Scorpion, Lizard, or Salamander; at the sight of a Toad, or Viper, I feel in me no desire to take up a stone to destroy them. I finde not in my selfe those common antipathies that I can discover in others: Those nationall repugnances doe not touch me, nor doe I behold with prejudice the *French*, *Italian*, *Spaniard*, or *Dutch*; but where I finde their actions in ballance with my Countreymens, I honour, love, and embrace them in the same degree; I was borne in the eighth Climate, but seeme to bee framed, and constellated unto all; I am no Plant that will not prosper out of a Garden. All places, all ayres, make unto me one Countrey;

[21] *Christian Instruction* 3. 14 (trans. J. J. Gavigan, O.S.A., *Writings of Saint Augustine*, 17 vols. [New York, 1947–59], IV, 134–35).

> I am in *England* every where, and under any meridian. (II, 1)

The terms of Browne's exaltation of charity above faith, the gap between "existence" and "notion" or realization and impulse, are not merely a personal interpretation, but precisely orthodox. Aquinas had said that the endowment of the soul that corresponds to faith is "vision," while that which corresponds to charity is "fruition."[22]

In his disavowal of provinciality Browne indulges the kind of healthy, if elementary, skepticism that has always challenged the narrow claims of custom most effectively. While Browne's *philosophic* skepticism is very different from Montaigne's and derives from an exactly opposed assumption about nature, this passage reveals a close resemblance between the skeptical tempers of the two writers. In his essay "Of Vanity," Montaigne expresses similar views.

> I have my bodies complexion as free, and my taste as common, as any man in the world. The diversity of fashions betweene one and other Nations, concerneth me nothing, but by the varieties-pleasure. *Each custome hath his reason.* Bee the trenchers or dishes of wood, of pewter or of earth: bee my meate boyled, rosted or baked; butter or oyle, and that of Olives or of Wall-nuts: hot or colde; I make no difference; all is one to me: And as one, that is growing old, I accuse the generous facultie; and had need that delicatenesse and choise, should stay the indiscretion of my appetite, and sometime ease and solace my stomacke. When I have beene out of *France*, and that to do me curtesie, some have asked me, Whether I would be served after the French maner, I have jested at them, and have ever thrust-in amongst the thickest tables and fullest of strangers. I am ashamed to see our men besotted with this foolish humor, to fret and chafe, when they see any fashions contrary to theirs. They thinke themselves out of their element, when they are out of

[22] *Summa theologica* 1. 12. 7 (Dominican translation, I, 136).

> their Village: Where ever they come they keepe their owne country fashions, and hate, yea and abhorre all strange manners . . .[23]

To withhold condemnation when faced with unfamiliar customs is to exercise reason. The attitudes here expressed by Browne and Montaigne go beyond such toleration to the sweeter virtue that allows the individual to enjoy other customs as if they were his own. The ability to respond in this way depends also, perhaps, on a certain power of imagination and on spontaneity. A charitable participation in the material customs of others is encountered frequently enough not to seem remarkable. What makes Sir Thomas Browne unusual in his age is that he maintains this same depth of charity in religion.

In the *Religio*, Browne's toleration, his desire to include others in his charity and to be included in theirs, while seemingly universal, is specifically directed primarily at the Roman Catholics. This concern to minimize conflict between the English and Roman Churches, together with an attachment to traditional forms of worship, has led some to regard Browne as a Laudian Anglican.[24] Though recent scholarship has modified the old view of Laud as an inflexible tyrant, his place in the Anglican *via media* remains far to the right of Browne. While Browne stresses the Apostolic succession and treasures the special continuity of his Church, restored to its native beauty after "the fatall corruption of times," he makes no such claims for its divine origins as Laud.[25] And most important, while the doctrine, government, and ritual of the Church of England accord with his own inclinations, Browne insists upon the rights of reason and conscience

[23] *Essayes*, III, 232–33.

[24] See, for example, Ruth Wallerstein, *Studies in Seventeenth-Century Poetic*, p. 245 f.

[25] Nor, of course, does Hooker. The claim of divine authority for Episcopacy was first asserted by Richard Bancroft (1544–1610) in a sermon delivered at St. Paul's Cross, 9 February 1588–89. It was not until Bancroft became Archbishop of Canterbury (1604) that this position began to be stressed officially.

privately exercised in such a way as to emphasize the claims of the inner church. "I condemne not all things in the Councell of *Trent*, nor approve all in the Synod of *Dort*. In briefe, where the Scripture is silent, the Church is my Text; where that speakes, 'tis but my Comment; where there is a joynt silence of both, I borrow not the rules of my Religion from *Rome* or *Geneva*, but the dictates of my owne reason" (I, 5).

At the same time, he confesses a fondness for ceremony: ". . . at my devotion I love to use the civility of my knee, my hat, and hands, with all those outward and sensible motions, which may express or promote my invisible devotion" (I, 3). So sensitive, it would seem, is Browne to the external instruments of devotion that he draws no firm restrictions against Roman practices. "I could never heare the *Ave Maria* Bell without an elevation, or thinke it a sufficient warrant, because they erred in one circumstance, for me to erre in all: that is in silence and dumb contempt. Whilst therefore they directed their devotions to her, I offered mine to God, and rectified the errour of their prayers by rightly ordering mine owne" (I, 3). He may be recalling an experience shared with fellow English students on the Continent, as he continues: "At a solemne Procession I have wept abundantly, while my consorts, blinde with opposition and prejudice, have fallen into an eccesse of scorne and laughter" (I, 3).

Such practices, though not approved by his own Church, are innocent and need not be scorned or shunned. They are externals, neither necessary to salvation nor capable, through corrupt observance, of depriving the individual of salvation. It is the quality of the inner devotion that is crucial; if a man's faith is rightly ordered the external forms are indifferent. The aesthetic appeal of customs and ceremonies, however mistaken, may induce a religious fervor perfectly consistent with one's own beliefs: "There are questionless both in Greek, Roman, and African Churches, solemnities, and ceremonies, whereof the wiser zeales doe make a Christian use . . ." (I, 3). Browne's attitude is very like what we have seen in Jeremy Taylor: both men require the formal beauty of ceremony in their worship, but because they do not confuse this ceremony with the essentials of salvation are able to participate outwardly in the ceremony of other sects without sacrificing their own beliefs. One could hardly find a better example of the proverbial flexibility of the Anglican mentality.

Intellectually, Taylor and Browne recognize the minimal importance of external forms to man's salvation. Both abhor any coercion or separation that results from enforcing uniformity or insisting upon an exclusive purity in these matters of custom. Browne, for example, regards the passive suffering of the religious martyr as greater valor than the soldier's heroism on the battlefield (I, 25). Nevertheless, "as all that die in warre are not termed Souldiers, so neither can I properly terme all those that suffer in matters of Religion Martyrs" (I, 26). Martyrdom "on such a trifle" as "the cause of *Antipodes*" inspires pity both for Bishop Virgilius who suffered for so small a point and for "those of ignorance and folly that condemned him" (I, 26). Browne wonders if perhaps Socrates, "that wise Heathen, that suffered on a fundamentall point of Religion, the Unity of God" is not a more perfect martyr than many whose names are inscribed in the Christian Martyrologies. He takes a rational position on the conflict between custom and conscience: "I would not perish upon a Ceremony, Politick point or indifferency: nor is my beleefe of that untractable temper, as not to bow at their obstacles, or connive at matters wherein there are not manifest impieties" (I, 26).

It is difficult to see how these statements can be reconciled with Laud's inflexible views on external uniformity. True, like Laud, Browne loved ceremony, but he valued it for its aesthetic and emotional power to induce a devotional mood. He undoubtedly approved Laud's program for beautifying the Church, but would not have condemned any man who objected to these innovations whether, totally, on Puritan principles or, singly, over some particular point. Browne had no doctrinaire position on the visible church, nor any unalterable notion of how its liturgy and ceremony should be ordered. While he leaned naturally toward Anglican practices, he was never so rigid that some difference in ritual could drive him out of his own Church or drive him in hatred against another.

If Browne took deep offense at anyone, it was at those who would restrict salvation to themselves and to those who assented precisely to their notion of saving truth. Beneath the intellectual arrogance and spiritual smugness of such bigots lurks a callous disregard of the Christian message. Though "the bridge is narrow, the passage straite unto life; yet those who doe confine the Church of God, either to particular Nations, Churches, or Families, have made it far narrower than our Saviour ever meant it" (I, 55). This intolerance evokes a mordant response from Chillingworth; Browne comments on this folly with quiet irony: "Thus whilst the mercies of God doe promise us heaven, our conceits and opinions exclude us from that place. There must be therefore more than one Saint *Peter*; particular Churches and Sects usurpe the gates of heaven, and turne the key against each other; and thus we goe to heaven against each others wills, conceits and opinions, and, with as much uncharity as ignorance, doe erre I feare in points, not onely of our own, but one anothers salvation" (I, 56). Browne's skepticism in matters of religious controversy results in an undogmatic temper and a pervading sympathy.

But even these gentle, and seemingly harmless, opinions could render a man suspect. With characteristic breadth of mind, Alexander Ross warned the young physician that "doubting is not the fruit of humilitie, but of infidelitie," and, chiding him more sharply, "you encline too much to the doubtings of the Church of *Rome*."[26] Where thought fails, the tongue leaps to the rescue. A master of the indiscriminate charge, Ross repeatedly hurls at Browne the most popular red herring of the day — heresy. In the seventeenth century, however, heresy could be a vital concern of some of the best minds as well as a crude weapon of demagogues.

Looking back upon his own beliefs, Browne confesses that he was not immune to "Heresies, Schismes, or Errors." His

[26] *Medicus medicatus*, p. 66.

"greener studies have beene polluted with two or three" (I, 6), including "that of the *Arabians*, that the soules of men perished with their bodies, but should yet bee raised againe at the last day, . . . that of *Origen*, that God would not persist in his vengeance for ever, but after a definite time of his wrath hee would release the damned soules from torture . . . ," and, thirdly, "prayer for the dead" to which he "was inclined from some charitable inducements . . ." (I, 7). He assures the reader that he is now free of these mistaken ideas. But more interesting than the errors themselves is his attitude toward the holding of incorrect beliefs:

> These opinions I never maintained with pertinacity, or endeavoured to enveagle any mans beliefe unto mine, nor so much as ever revealed or disputed them with my dearest friends; by which meanes I neither propagated them in others, nor confirmed them in my selfe, but suffering them to flame upon their owne substance, without addition of new fuell, they went out insensibly of themselves; therefore these opinions, though condemned by lawfull Councels, were not Heresies in me, but bare Errors, and single Lapses of my understanding, without a joynt depravity of my will: Those have not only depraved understandings but diseased affections, which cannot enjoy a singularity without a Heresie, or be the author of an opinion, without they be of a Sect also . . . (I, 7)

Browne vents his distaste for those who aggravate the errors of their understanding by infecting others and evinces a particular aversion to those who, for the sake of some small difference, will separate themselves from the communion of other Christians and further multiply sects and schisms. His attitude toward heresy and schism is like that of John Hales, who argued similar views in an important pamphlet published in the same year as the *Religio*. Indeed, Hales's *Tract Concerning Schisme and Schismaticks* (1642), probably written about 1636, perhaps at the request of Chillingworth,[27] provides an excellent gloss on the passage just quoted from Browne. "Schisme," Hales defines, "is nothing else but an unnecessary separation of Christians from that part of the visible Church, of which they were once members."[28] A division is inexcusable when it does not proceed from the fact that "nothing will serve to save us from guilt of Conscience, but open separation."[29] Passion, distemper, and avarice, which are the most frequent causes of separation, are insufficient. The division of community may be excused and men absolved from the guilt of schism *only* by "true and unpretended conscience."[30]

Discussion of schisms "arising upon occasion of opinion" leads Hales into the problem of heresy. Arianism, Nestorianism, and others "are but names of *Schisme*; howsoever in the common language of the Fathers, they were called *Heresies*, for *Heresie* is an act of the will, not of the reason, and is indeed a lye and not a mistake."[31] For both Hales and Browne, then, only those who invent and deliberately teach errors commit heresy, not those who "fall upon it by error or mistake." This very generous definition of heresy at once encourages charitable assumptions about the motives of those who hold "unorthodox" beliefs and discourages the hasty employment of punishment and suppression. Together with the characteristic attitude of these liberals toward customs and nonessentials, this view of heresy could have made possible as profound a spirit and as full a practice of religious toleration as England had ever known.

The familiar identification of Browne with the Latitudinarians in the historical development of the liberal position toward religious conflict, and hence toward toleration, is obviously correct. However, by focusing upon the peculiar ambiguity of his attitude toward custom and the role of that ambiguity in the total intellectual structure of *Religio*

[27] Tulloch, I, 201–202.
[28] P. 2.
[29] *Ibid.*
[30] *Ibid.*, p. 4.
[31] *Ibid.*, p. 9.

Medici, we soon discover why Browne's liberal Platonic Christianity is less purely rational than that of many of his like-minded contemporaries. His unwillingness, like Taylor's, to see custom merely as what he knew it *theoretically* to be—the troublesome bottom plane of the hierarchy of truth—is a measure of his imaginative attachment, at once pious and poetic, to human traditions of worship.

To see where Browne parts from the more purely rational temper of the Latitudinarians on religious custom, we may consider the following remarks of John Hales, written, we should recall, almost in the same year that Browne composed the *Religio*, and also first published in 1642:

> . . . why may I not go, if occasion require, to an *Arian Church*, so there be no *Arianisme* exprest in their Liturgy; and were Liturgies and publick Forms of Service so framed, as that they admitted not of particular and private fancies, but contained only such things, as in which all Christians do agree; *Schismes* on opinion were utterly vanished; for consider of all the Liturgies that are and ever have been, and remove from them whatsoever is scandalous to any party, and leave nothing but what all agree on, and the evil shall be, that the publick Service and Honour of God shall no ways suffer. Whereas to load our publick Forms, with the private fancies upon which we differ, is the most soveraign way to perpetuate *Schisme* unto the worlds end; Prayer, Confession, Thanksgiving, Reading of Scriptures, Administration of Sacraments in the plainest and the simplest manner, were matter enough to furnish out a sufficient Liturgy, though nothing either of private opinion, or of Church Pomp, of Garments, or prescribed Gestures, of Imagery, of Musick, or matter concerning the Dead, of many superfluities which creep into the Church, under the name of Order and Decency, did interpose itself.[32]

[32] *Ibid.*, p. 10.

It is not surprising that Hales's *Tract* was received without favor by Laud, for these comments seem to have been aimed directly at Laud's whole policy on Church service. The opening of this passage might have been written by Taylor or Browne and indeed parallels what Browne says of the Roman Catholics: "there is between us one common name and appellation, one faith, and necessary body of principles common to us both; and therefore I am not scrupulous to converse or live with them, to enter their Churches in defect of ours, and either pray with them, or for them" (I, 3). That a charitable fraternization need not involve betrayal of conscience was a position held in common by moderates.

However, to the problems raised by the elaborate and varying ceremony of the Church, Hales, like Chillingworth, applies what might be called a negative eclecticism. This tends to invert the traditional strengths of Anglicanism — its flexibility and richness — and leaves in their place an apparently more consistent Church, but one stripped of much of its power to compel the religious imagination. The things that the Latitudinarians were eager to sacrifice as inimicable to a broad and inclusive Church — pomp, vestments, "prescribed Gestures," imagery, and music — were as important to Browne as they were to Laud, though for rather different reasons. While a Church framed about essentials was an irenic ideal urged by all Anglican moderates, for Browne such a bare frame alone was insufficient. The "Broad Church" that Hales and Chillingworth hoped could include all Protestants by giving offense to none, though plausible in view of the exigencies of the moment, was apt to deteriorate into a feeble institution incapable of nourishing a profound religious spirit either among men like themselves or among men of less strictly rational temper.

Because the position of Hales and Chillingworth is primarily rational, it lends itself to relatively easy definition. The outlook of Sir Thomas Browne, however, on matters of religious belief, practice, and toleration is more difficult to define. He is very close to the liberal Anglicanism of Jeremy Taylor — a position that is nebulous enough even in the lucid and orderly prose of that great preacher and artist. But Browne himself was not trained for the Church; and he addresses himself only sporadically to these issues, leaving us relatively little in mass and less in system pertaining to them. They definitely constitute the secondary "action" of the *Religio*, but could hardly be avoided by a man setting out to examine his religious position.

Browne's liberating rationality, his skepticism about custom, and his striving for individual experience of mind and emotion within the ordered and beautiful framework of formal ritual are hardly consistent either logically, as among themselves, or in practical relation to the demands of the time. He typifies the liberal Anglican who did not so much profess a fully defined position as he cultivated a religious mood founded on a relatively simple creed, supported by personal emotion and enriched by formal ceremony. For Browne, the divine injunction of *caritas* was the essential principle for a right view of custom. But charity, he felt, had to work two ways: for toleration of differences by reigning authority so that coercion would not multiply dissenting sects and damage unity of faith, but also for acceptance of the reasonableness and value of tradition and ceremony. Understandably, he was more distressed by the Puritans: "'Tis the generall complaint of these times . . . that charity growes cold; which I perceive most verified in those which most doe manifest the fires and flames of zeale . . ." (II, 4). Nonetheless, his stance is opposed to the absolutism of Laudians and Presbyterians alike.

Browne required liberty of mind for the proper functioning of inquiry according to the norms of his Platonic epistemology, while his dedication to the traditional view of natural law required order. In the seventeenth century, in both politics and religion, men confronted a choice between these two seemingly incompatible goods: liberty and order. Factions on the left and right pursued their separate concepts of a just religious order with a single-mindedness that could end only in the tragedy of violence and tyranny. The Latitudinarians assumed that by freeing religion from the authority of custom, the rent in the Church would be repaired and individual devotion fostered. As for moderate but traditional Anglicans, the very indefiniteness of their *via media* required a spacious liberty in which to operate. But if this liberty was not to weaken absorption in the divine and to diffuse devotional attention, it required forms and ceremonies in which thought and emotion, the rational and the affective apprehension of faith, could find a concrete focus. Jeremy Taylor provides the age's fullest and most eloquent statement of such dedication to religious liberty within the traditional order of the national Church. And the *Religio Medici* provides the most intimate and attractive picture of a man enjoying this version of the Anglican way.

CHAPTER VI

RELIGIO MEDICI: ENDEAVORS OF SCIENCE AND RELIGION

THOUGH the issue of religious liberty figured momentously in the 1630's and 1640's, it plays in the *Religio Medici* a distinctly secondary role to certain broader and more philosophic questions. Not only does Browne devote less space to this issue, but it draws a less urgent response from him. If we recall his Platonic disposition, then his instinctively liberal attitude toward religious differences and the ease with which he combines his own traditional Anglicanism with views like those of the rational Latitudinarians are not difficult to understand. Exclusion and coercion — the unfortunate consequences of conflicting religious opinions — are readily obviated for Browne by the virtue of charity. In any case, they pose no significant questions about the problem of knowledge. The insistence of human custom upon conformity can be dismissed, at least in theory, as prejudice convinced of its identity with truth.

The clash of faith and philosophy is less amenable to solution. For Browne could not relinquish the cognitive value of either, or abandon his certainty of their ultimate harmony. When he turned to the two planes of experience higher than human custom, he encountered the kind of problems with which he best liked to grapple and which evoked his most characteristically complex responses. However obscure at times the texture and purpose of his works, it becomes evident to any reader that Browne's absorbing interest was the problem of knowledge, which is both a motivating impulse and integrating theme of his writings.

The primary intellectual concern in *Religio Medici* may

no longer seem as urgent, or even as interesting, as it did in the seventeenth century or, in different terms, during the Victorian Age. The conflict between science and religion and the pressing need to resolve that conflict derive from expectations our own century has pretty widely abandoned. First among these is the idea that religion is one of man's sources of knowledge about the actual nature of things. The value religion retains in our own world is not usually for any verifiable system of knowledge it can afford but as a mode of personal experience. The epistemological issues of the seventeenth century have a special importance exactly because our assumptions rest upon redefinitions of the cognitive value of religion initiated during that period. While it cannot be claimed that Browne himself contributed anything to that redefinition, his was an unusually receptive mind, readily stirred to speculation in many fields and always eager to trace the difficulties arising from contradictory evidence and opposed ways of knowing.

The most essential point about Browne's epistemology is that the problem of knowledge is for him, as a Christian Platonist, not merely an intellectual problem and therefore one that cannot be approached through the process of intellection alone. His outlook is conditioned by the assumption of the relatedness and superiority of revelation and intuition to reason. This means more than belief in the adequacy of Scripture as an explanation of the world. It means that the truths Scripture propounds to faith are ultimately rational and that the workings of nature, analyzable by reason, can be traced up to the divine.

The opposing claims of faith and philosophy were not of course new to the seventeenth century. We saw in Chapter II of this study that this was a recurrent issue in the history of Western thought. Philo Judaeus had attempted to wed the Old Testament to Greek philosophy and yet to avoid conflict between religious beliefs accepted on faith and directed at building a holy life and philosophic explanations attained through the exercise of logic and aimed at purely intellectual ends. The construction of a philosophic theology by the Church Fathers who were trained in Greek thought transformed Christianity from an ethic grounded in a simple commitment of faith into a system for explaining the structure and meaning of the universe. The fusion of Greek ideas about the *logos* or objective reason – at once metaphysical entity, cognitive end, ethical guide, and mystical experience — with the Christian concept of the triune God produced a religion of unique intellectual endeavor in which faith could extend into matters of physical fact and natural reason could attempt to anatomize God.

The relation between natural knowledge and faith thus became a perennial issue in Christianity. The growth and disruption of various systems for reconciling faith and philosophy and the accompanying shifts in emphasis and definition have proved a challenge to artists as well as to scientists, philosophers, and men of religion. In Browne's age this continual process of readjustment reached a crisis that the perspective of three centuries permits us to label a revolution. In this revolution Browne was not a leader of either the "modernist" or "traditionalist" camp, if indeed we can be sure that he clearly belonged to either, or even if such definite lines of demarcation can be validly drawn in the age. But perhaps more than any other writer in seventeenth-century England, he reflects the impact of this revolution with all its ramifications for the science and religion, the art and sensibility which define the culture of the age.[1]

I

The very title *Religio Medici* indicates an awareness of the challenge that faith and philosophy offer each other.[2] The

[1] A comprehensive and richly documented account of the major issues is Paul H. Kocher, *Science and Religion in Elizabethan England* (San Marino, Cal., 1953), which is relevant for Browne even though it does not go beyond 1610. Richard S. Westfall, *Science and Religion in Seventeenth-Century England* (New Haven, 1958), provides a rather external account, from the standpoint of the important scientists, and is not very useful for students of literature.

[2] The title Browne gave to his essay was itself widely imitated. Geoffrey Keynes lists eighty-five works whose titles indicate their indebtedness to *Religio Medici*. *A Bibliography of Sir Thomas Browne* (Cambridge, 1924), pp. 186–208.

fact that Browne is a physician and a man of science leaves him, he recognizes, peculiarly vulnerable to the charge of atheism, of being a man of no faith.[3] Those who followed a "naturall course" of studies had been open to this charge in the past, but such an accusation was invested with added likelihood at a time when the recurring clash of faith and philosophy was intensified by certain fresh currents of thought. Browne, as suggested earlier, is seeking from the first words of his meditation to show the harmonious coexistence of religion and science in a life dedicated to the pursuit of both. In the course of this demonstration, however, he discloses some fascinating tensions between the two.

Simultaneous resistance to a purely material interpretation of nature and support of empirical study represent a situation not untypical in the seventeenth century. Examination of this position within its Platonic context has shown that it was not as hopelessly at odds with itself as might appear. Gordon Chalmers, in an important article on Browne's scientific method, emphasizes that Browne regarded the object of research to be, not Truth, but probable and plural truths or hypotheses.[4] This attitude is closer to that of modern science than the more assertive position of many of Browne's greater scientific contemporaries; it is also perfectly consistent with his Platonism. Discursive reason, operating on sense data, provides at best probabilities which are always subject to correction in the light of enlarged knowledge. Only in the area of first causes and divine mysteries does Browne rest in the absolutes of faith. His inclination toward traditional rational theology did, however, influence his thinking as a man of science. Egon Merton points out, for example, that Browne consistently adheres to vitalistic rather than mechanical biological theory, and that his "teleology is in no way modified by his manipulation of the atomic theory."[5] And it is impossible to deny that his attempt

[3] See Paul H. Kocher, "The Physician as Atheist," *Science and Religion*, pp. 239–57.

[4] "Sir Thomas Browne, True Scientist," *Osiris*, 2 (1936): 73.

[5] *Science and Imagination in Sir Thomas Browne* (New York, 1949), p. 82.

as a scientist to render a visible picture of reality was sometimes at war with his desire as a man of faith to enjoy through intuition and imagination the invisible world that lay behind the picture.

Though the *Religio* was written too early for Browne to have the challenge of Hobbesian materialism specifically in mind, he proclaims his belief in the seniority of spirit over matter and in a vital governing force in nature as unmistakably as do the Cambridge Platonists. Despite his quite serious empiricism, the neglect of first causes is unthinkable. "There is but one first cause, and foure second causes of all things; some are without efficient, as God; others without matter, as Angels; some without forme, as the first matter; but every Essence, created or uncreated, hath its finall cause, and some positive end both of its Essence and operation; This is the cause I grope after in the workes of nature, on this hangs the providence of God . . ." (I, 41). Since the first cause is prior to all others, a science which ignores it cannot reach ultimate knowledge. Moreover, the first cause cannot be derived from the others but must be grasped as a whole. Therefore, while one should observe the particular workings of nature, one should proceed as well from the whole to the parts. Behind this reciprocal approach lies the Plotinian doctrine of an animating spirit and regulating force that descends from the One through *nous* into the world soul of nature.

And, though Browne speaks of the ordained laws of God which man seeks to learn through reason, nature is not conceived solely as a deliberate instrument, or as the art, of God. Within his Platonic framework, he conceives of nature not only as a creation sustained and governed by its Creator, but also as an emanation from His plenitude, bearing the spirit of its source in its particulars but not diminishing that source. The two views mingled in Christian theology and in Browne's own thought:

> Now, besides these particular and divided Spirits, there may be (for ought I know) an universall and common Spirit to the whole world. It

> was the opinion of *Plato*, and it is yet of the *Hermeticall* Philosophers; if there be a common nature that unites and tyes the scattered and divided individuals into one species, why may there not bee one that unites them all? However, I am sure there is a common Spirit that playes within us, yet makes no part of us; and that is the Spirit of God, the fire and scintillation of that noble and mighty Essence, which is the life and radicall heat of spirits, and those essences that know not the vertue of the Sunne; a fire quite contrary to the fire of Hell: This is that gentle heate that brooded on the waters, and in six dayes hatched the world; this is that irradiation that dispells the mists of Hell, the clouds of horrour, feare, sorrow, [and] despaire; and preserves the region of the mind in serenity: whosoever feels not the warme gale and gentle ventilation of this Spirit, (though I feele his pulse) I dare not say he lives; for truely without this, to mee there is no heat under the Tropick; nor any light, though I dwelt in the body of the Sunne. (I, 32)

According to Plotinian doctrine, this emanation of divine love as shaping spirit into the great world of nature and into the little world of man means that God or the One can be known only through a return of that love. If nature provides a ladder to God, as traditional rational thought held, that ladder cannot be scaled by reason alone. Though God remains transcendent, his spirit infuses the world; he does not regulate it from afar through a merely external law. Reason, working either inductively on the data of sense or deductively from principles of teleology, seeks to formulate laws which *describe* nature. But the full and immediate grasp of truth which is alone real knowledge of God is attainable through the turning of the divine spirit implanted in men back to its original source.

The pluralistic epistemology Browne derives from this complex of beliefs inevitably raises difficulties when he turns from the general outline of the realms of matter and spirit to their specific manifestations. In working out patent discrepancies between observable fact and assumptions about a teleologically ordered universe he frequently indulges the kind of speculation, at once casuistical and fanciful, that has helped to earn his reputation for "quaintness." Whatever difficulty he faces, Browne steadfastly refuses to admit a divorce between matter and spirit. Nature is run according to established laws, but ultimate control lies elsewhere. "Nor do I so forget God, as to adore the name of Nature; which I define not with the Schooles, the principle of motion and rest, but, that streight and regular line, that setled and constant course the wisedome of God hath ordained the actions of his creatures, according to their severall kinds" (I, 16). He is careful always to avoid the identification of God with nature, or natural law, or an abstract notion of reason. Though God prefers to follow the "forelaid principles" of his art rather than order the world through his simple word, these principles are only his instruments and do not limit his power. Sometimes, "to acquaint the world with his prerogative," God acts directly and not through nature, "lest the arrogancy of our reason should question his power . . ." (I, 16). This is why miracles are still possible and why fortune is a misnomer; "for there is no liberty for causes to operate in a loose and stragling way, nor any effect whatsoever, but hath its warrant from some universall or superiour cause" (I, 18).

In an age when nature and the problem of understanding it were being gradually detached from the realm of spirit and from moral and theological presuppositions, it became increasingly difficult to maintain the traditional view that nature, while rationally coherent, was not mechanically uniform and determined. With politic, if not wholly convincing, piety, Bacon secured the truth of religion in a fortress accessible only to revelation. Neither reason nor the light of nature could provide the key to unlock the mysteries of faith; for they could be properly and profitably applied only to the physical world. The place of reason in religion had previously been discredited by Calvin who revived and adapted the darker side of Pauline and Augustinian thought. Calvin, like

Bacon, rejected the optimistic epistemology of the Schoolmen and, alienating nature from grace, denied to man in his natural condition any knowledge of the divine.

Their motives of course were quite different. Bacon wished to emancipate reason from the prescriptive rationality of scholastic theology and focus it on the physical world as a secular instrument of observation and analysis. So long as the study of nature proceeded from the assumptions of teleology and was aimed at demonstrating qualitative correspondences between matter and spirit, between "real" things and abstract universals, it could never yield "true and solid and living axioms, on which depend the affairs and fortunes of men. . . ."[6] Calvin, on the other hand, sought to prevent the contamination of faith by discursive reason and to demolish any claim of access to grace by those not among the elect. Bacon, in effect, sought to isolate religion in a remote castle where, if it was safe from attack, it was also barred from activity in the wide world outside. Calvin, having banished Theology's traditional handmaiden Reason to the natural world, invested Faith with the absolute power of an arbitrary and inscrutable Queen, courted by all and granting her favor to few. These apparently similar conferments of privileged status upon religious faith by exempting it from the standards of reason were actually diametric opposites—Bacon tending to reduce faith to irrelevance, while Calvin raised it to the awesome position of man's central and all-absorbing concern.

Bacon's skepticism and fideism, unlike Browne's, were not fundamental impulses of his mind but chiefly tactical devices for liberating natural studies from theological prescription. He was quick to upbraid any doubt of the efficacy of human reason to pierce the secrets of nature.[7] The problem was one of correct method, not of man's capacity or the orderliness of nature. He believed that forms or general principles did underlie particulars and that they were the ultimate objects of natural knowledge. That is why sensation, which could be

[6] *Novum organum* 1. 104 (*Bacon*, ed. R. F. Jones, p. 317).
[7] *Novum organum* 1. 68.

misleading, required systematic control and why experimental data had to be submitted to inductive analysis in order to yield basic truths. What had to be avoided was the application of a priori assumptions derived from scholastic logic, mere categories irrelevant to reality which the human mind imposed on nature. "For the world is not to be narrowed till it will go into the understanding (which has been done hitherto), but the understanding to be expanded and opened till it can take in the image of the world, as it is in fact."[8]

The value of reason was retained by Bacon only after it had been redefined through a stripping away of assumed notions of universal order that could be applied to individual things without scrutiny of the things themselves. He narrowed the area of its deployment and restricted the direction of its march so as to reject a conclusion like that of Ficino, who without hesitation could answer the question of "whether or not the intellect can attain a clear understanding of everything which is included under being" with a ringing "Certainly it can."[9]

But however Bacon reconstructed reason and modified its role in knowledge, it remained for him the only instrument sturdy enough, when properly repaired, to do real scientific work. This was not the outcome of the attack on rationalism by certain absolute skeptics who denied to man intellection of both God and nature. Such a position, allied to the stance of ultra-piety, is well exemplified in Henry Cornelius Agrippa's *De incertitudine et vanitate scientarium et artium* (1531). Agrippa rested on an extreme fideism that prided itself in dispelling (for the greater glory of God and the confusion of human presumption) the Scholastic illusion of man's rational powers. But in fact he only discharged an impenetrable smoke screen of obscurantism, further thick-

[8] *Bacon*, ed. R. F. Jones, p. 354. The cognitive absolutism which Bacon assumes in the phrase "as it is in fact" is, one should note, as outdated in its way as are the differently Platonic assumptions of Browne.

[9] "Five Questions Concerning the Mind," trans. J. L. Burroughs, *Renaissance Philosophy of Man*, ed. Ernst Cassirer *et al*, p. 199.

ened by his fantastic notions about magic, between man and truth.

Montaigne was a more intellectually respectable proponent of fideism. His famous comparison of man and the animals, with its sardonic attack on the uniqueness of man's intellectual prowess, was at bottom a denial of man's capability to abstract essential forms from sensibles and therefore of his power to proceed from a knowledge of things to knowledge of God. Though not immediately recognized as such, this represented something even more serious than Bacon's fracturing of the premise that rational endeavor speeds man along the road of truth to the goal of piety. Montaigne ruled truth in any sphere out of man's natural grasp and therefore enjoined him to rely entirely and unquestioningly on the revealed word of God.

Yet, curiously enough, he does not completely reject intellectual endeavor, but only the claims of those who insisted they hold truth. Aware of the frailty of the senses as well as of the rational faculty, the Skeptic, whom Montaigne applauds as the wisest philosopher, assumes an attitude of uncertainty toward human knowledge. He neither rejects all ideas as false nor embraces any one with dogmatic certitude. Instead, he engages in a continual search for truth by holding conflicting ideas in balanced and suspended judgment. If Montaigne's attack on reason reduces man to an abject creature before God, it also endows him with an attractive humility before his fellows. His fideism is accompanied by a spirit of toleration quite foreign to the mentality of Agrippa. An anti-intellectualism deeply concerned with the right ordering of the life of the mind, stressing the vanity of dogmatism as much as the vanity of learning, cannot be dismissed as mere obscurantism. The bleak picture limned in the *Apology* of man's epistemological status is lightened everywhere by a generous ethic. This shading has inevitably given rise to doubts as to the significance of Montaigne's attack on reason and has invested that attack with perennial interest.

This combination of fideism and liberal toleration within a fundamentally conservative temper makes Montaigne an illuminating point of departure for defining Browne's own version of skepticism. Both men held skeptical attitudes toward custom and prescriptive rationality and stressed in varying degrees the limits of reason. It may also be said of both that their skepticism was more a tendency of mind than a systematic method. Montaigne's attitude was the expression of a mind more responsive to diversity than to uniformity, that envisioned nature — including his own nature — as variegated and changeable. This sensitivity to the separateness of things made him distrustful of the comprehensive systems which traditional rationalism had built on the assumption that the principle of individuation was not ultimately real but merely created in time.

Browne, on the other hand, though conscious of his personal vagaries of thought, felt a deep assurance about the unity of things and was inclined to seek out likenesses and the principles that bind things together. His Platonic premise that particulars are part of the One and exemplify the One — which is only concealed but not destroyed in individuality — disposed him to seek correspondences. He was inclined in his natural studies to reject or at least to doubt pronouncements about particulars inferred from an assumed rationality without the benefit of direct observation. Empiricism here protected his scientific endeavors from the dangers inherent in his Platonism, dangers against which Bacon issued a famous warning: "The human understanding is of its own nature prone to suppose the existence of more order and regularity in the world than it finds. And though there be many things in nature which are singular and unmatched, yet it devises for them parallels and conjugates and relatives which do not exist." [10] But that matter and spirit did correspond to one another he never doubted.

A man who worked from Platonic presuppositions was bound, however, to run into trouble when he employed his reason empirically. Browne directed his skepticism at targets precisely opposite from those of Montaigne: at the apparent

[10] *Novum organum* 1. 45 (*Bacon*, ed. R. F. Jones, p. 280).

singularities and deviations from rationally induced patterns instead of at the assumed unity of things. His skepticism, therefore, was at times inevitably directed at his own empiricism. When the data of sense pointed to a conclusion supporting a nominalist or materialist interpretation of the world, the Christian Platonist stepped in to assert the regulation of nature by moral principle.

Browne's confidence in the harmony of phenomena with religious truth is the source of many of the most glowing passages in the *Religio.* When he confronts, for example, the question of how the resurrection of the dead can occur in view of the ordinarily accepted operations of nature, he simply invokes, as it were, the highest plane of the hierarchy of truth and asserts that "to beleeve onely possibilities, is not faith, but meere Philosophy" (I, 48). The *how* of the resurrection is irrelevant to his assurance "that our estranged and divided ashes shall unite againe; that our separated dust after so many pilgrimages and transformations into the parts of mineralls, Plants, Animals, Elements, shall at the voyce of God returne into their primitive shapes, and joyne againe to make up their primary and predestinated formes." And toward the end of this section he demonstrates the reality of such apparently impossible resurrections by drawing upon scientific observation of his own:

> A plant or vegetable consumed to ashes, to a contemplative and schoole Philosopher seemes utterly destroyed, and the forme to have taken his leave for ever: But to a sensible Artist the formes are not perished, but withdrawne into their incombustible part, where they lie secure from the action of that devouring element. This is made good by experience, which can from the ashes of a plant revive the plant, and from its cinders recall it into its stalk and leaves againe. What the Art of man can doe in these inferiour pieces, what blasphemy is it to affirme the finger of God cannot doe in these more perfect and sensible structures? This is that mysticall Philosophy, from whence no true Scholler be-

> comes an Atheist, but from the visible effects of nature, growes up a reall Divine, and beholds not in a dreame, as *Ezekiel,* but in an ocular and visible object the types of his resurrection. (I, 48)

Such expressions beautifully embody the characteristic ease with which Browne, falling back upon fideism and Platonism, can bring his scientific and religious endeavors to perfect agreement. For our purposes, however, it is more important to recognize and appraise the points of friction between his empiricism and his Christian orthodoxy, since they generate the primary action of thought in *Religio Medici* and are thus the components of the reconciliation which is so visible at the surface of the work. To gain a fuller perspective on Browne's assumptions in this crucial area, especially his skepticism toward apparent singularities and purposeless elements in nature, our best recourse is Browne's second published work—that voluminous encyclopedia of knowledge, *Vulgar Errors.*

2

In the seventeenth century, science was a popular amateur pursuit as well as the absorbing occupation of some of the age's greatest minds. The dilettanti or virtuosi (as they were dubbed after the Restoration when numerous enough to attract the ridicule of Shadwell and Butler) practiced science with varying degrees of competence and sincere, as opposed to fashionable, interest. They all tended, however, to share a bias which sets them off from the true scientists of the age. Their predilections both as collectors and experimenters were definitely in the direction of the "extraordinary" or "wonderful."

To the nineteenth century, *Vulgar Errors* revealed its author as just such an enthusiastic and indiscriminate collector of curiosities. In this most pragmatic of his major works Browne displayed a wide command of out-of-the-way facts in human and natural history and a capacity for subduing his credence to the most outrageous wonders. Modern scholarship has done much to lay to rest this erroneous view of

Browne as a mere chaser of oddities.[11] But if this misconception dies hard, perhaps it is because Browne was in fact a great collector — of information, books, coins, bones, shells, and whatnot. Yet, an examination of his motives for amassing these bits of the unusual in the pages of *Vulgar Errors* and for cramming his cabinets with them will show why this earlier view was mistaken.

On superficial consideration it might seem that Browne, the professional man of medicine, shared the quest for rarities with a figure like Sir John Evelyn, the most celebrated virtuoso of the century and a correspondent of Browne. At a time when great discoveries were being made in mathematics and physics, Browne, with his collector's instinct and fascination with biological oddities, may seem more proper to the company of Evelyn than of Boyle. But despite his fondness for materials that typically attracted the dabbler and his love of the curious and puzzling, Browne's basic approach was that of the serious scientist. For like Bacon and Boyle, he sought the underlying and universal principles in nature rather than astonishing prodigies. The prodigies had to be attended to, but their interest always extended beyond themselves. They offered the challenge, perhaps even harbored the secret, to the universal principles which regulate nature. Browne's concern to understand the principles concealed beneath particulars and his use of an experimental method for observing the particulars mark him as a modernist. He differs from Bacon, though, in his assumption that the principles natural study aims at are an intelligence which guides nature and not merely the laws of formed matter in motion. It is this metaphysical bias, in the last analysis, that imparts to *Vulgar Errors* its distinctly old-fashioned flavor.

The book was nonetheless a living and growing witness to Browne's dedication to the endeavors of science. It first appeared in 1646 and went through six editions by 1672, with most of these containing new or revised information that

[11] The question of Browne as "virtuoso" or "true scientist" is discussed by Egon S. Merton, *Science and Imagination*, pp. 3–10. Mr. Merton's book on Browne is especially valuable for *Vulgar Errors*.

shows Browne keeping abreast of the latest developments. The full title—*Pseudodoxia Epidemica: or Enquiries into Very many received Tenents, And commonly presumed Truths*—would suggest that its scope was determined by the need for a calendar of popular errors that Bacon had voiced early in the century in *The Advancement of Learning* (1605). This calendar was to be an enumeration of popular errors "chiefly in natural history, such as pass in speech and conceit, and are nevertheless apparently detected and convicted of untruth: that man's knowledge be not weakened nor embased by such dress and vanity."[12] Browne's massive work is, however, more than a raking away of pseudoscientific debris, more even than an encyclopedia of knowledge in the tradition of Pliny's *Natural History* or La Primaudaye's *French Academie*. For it is concerned throughout with an inquiry into the method for attaining truth.

The first book of the *Pseudodoxia* is devoted to an exposition and analysis of the causes of error. Browne enumerates the following enemies of truth: the general infirmity of human nature attested, for example, by the delusion of reason by passion in the Fall; "those democratical enemies of truth," the untutored masses, "the most deceptable part of mankind"; credulity and supinity; adherence to antiquity and authority; and, finally, the endeavors of Satan, that "great promoter of false opinions." The resemblance between all these obstacles to truth (except the last) and Bacon's idols of the mind has been regularly noted, and it has been generally assumed that Browne must have had Bacon in mind as he wrote. This assumption has been cogently denied by Egon Merton, who concludes of Browne's account: "Like Bacon's, it is an independent, if less brilliant, critique by a modern scientist of the causes of ancient error."[13]

Browne is less systematic in presenting the method of truth than in listing its snares. Not until the third book does

[12] Francis Bacon, *Works*, ed. J. Spedding and R. L. Ellis, 7 vols. (London, 1857–59), VI, 233.

[13] *Science and Imagination*, p. 23.

he mention "the three Determinators of Truth, Authority, Sense, and Reason," employed by the scientist. Like the three Platonic realms of experience, these "determinators" are listed in ascending order of epistemological value, but correspond only very roughly to custom, nature, and Idea. Authority, inextricably identified with antiquity for a Renaissance writer, is, like custom, a source and crystallization of opinion. Browne regards adherence to antiquity as the "mortallest enemy unto knowledge" and points out that many of the wise sayings of the ancients are mere commonplaces deserving no special reverence. As further proof of the weakness of authority, he offers the fact that the ancients themselves often disagreed with one another, a point very like the one usually stressed by critics of custom as a guide to knowledge. Finally, the statements of authority must always be put to the test of reason and experiment.[14]

The kind of authority Browne is concerned with in *Vulgar Errors* is not that of revelation, but simply the accumulated knowledge of the past. Authority is not so much opposed to sense as it is a heterogeneous record of the observation and opinion of learned men in previous centuries. That record must be taken into account, and, like a good scholar, Browne always brings together "what has been done" on a problem, weighing the observations and conclusions of various authorities against one another before offering his own data and thought on the subject. But he especially approves Harvey's discovery "in that excellent discourse *of Generation*; So strongly erected upon the two great pillars of truth, experience and solid reason."[15] The greatest victories of truth are won, it would seem, quite independently of the support of authority.

Like Bacon, Browne recognizes that sense, while the basis of natural knowledge, is a very fallible instrument. Thus the observable fact that the ostrich takes iron into its mouth and swallows it does not prove that the bird actually digests iron. A more critical kind of observation, such as an examination of

[14] Bk. I, chaps. 6 and 7.

[15] Bk. III, chap. 28. (*Works*, II, 265).

what happens to the iron in the ostrich's stomach, would be needed to demonstrate the truth of this popularly held notion. When Browne speaks of "Sense" in *Vulgar Errors* he is not referring to discursive reason but to the raw data of sensation upon which discursive reason works.

The third of the "determinators," reason, includes a number of concepts and methods but in no way overlaps the Platonic realm of intelligible Ideas. First, reason winnows out observed data that are true from those that are deceptive; it distinguishes experiment from simple sensation. An example of an error of sense is the notion that the bear "brings forth her young informous and unshapen" and that her constant licking of them serves to make up for what nature has left undone. Actually, "the Cub comes forth involved in the Chorion, a thick and tough Membrane obscuring the formation, and which the Dam doth after bite and tear asunder; the beholder at first sight conceives it a rude and informous lump of flesh, and imputes the ensuing shape unto the Mouthing of the Dam; which addeth nothing thereunto, but only draws the curtain, and takes away the vail which concealed the Piece before."[16] Reason also serves as a corrective for logical and verbal errors. Throughout *Vulgar Errors* Browne inveighs against literalness in the interpretation of figures of speech as a major source of error. The false notion that the pigeon or dove has no gall springs from a literal acceptance of the metaphoric statement that these are mild and gentle creatures.[17]

But when Browne speaks of some notion as contrary or repulsive to reason he is not referring to a logical fallacy such as false analogy or *post hoc, ergo propter hoc*. By reason, Browne most often means certain broad ideas either induced from a sufficient number of specific instances or accepted a priori as a general principle of purpose and efficiency in nature. He employs inductive and deductive method side by side to refute popular errors. In Books II, III, and IV of the *Pseudodoxia*, most of the errors Browne exposes involve some

[16] Bk. III, chap. 6. (*Works*, II, 172–73).

[17] Bk. III, chap. 3.

supposed singularity in nature. While the endless variety of natural phenomena is fascinating, Browne goes beyond the dilettante collector's relishing of variety for its own sake to meet the challenge posed to the order of nature. Anything which contradicts without meaningful purpose some common attribute of creatures is repulsive to reason. Since all animals are constructed to multiply their kind, and the young of every kind are protected and nourished by their dam, it is inconceivable that among the vipers alone "the young ones eat through the womb and belly of the female."[18] This extraordinary birth through matricide contravenes the design of nature that is everywhere evident and therefore must be rejected as false. Such alleged singularities are always examined from a highly skeptical position so that reason alone, without the evidence of dissection, assures Browne that pigeons must have a gall. And the "informous" birth of the bear is "injurious unto Reason, and much impugneth the course and providence of Nature, to conceive a birth should be ordained before there is a formation."[19]

Browne furthermore subscribes to a principle of efficiency according to which no part or attribute of a creature exists without a function. The dictum of Aristotle – nature does nothing in vain – to which he assents so warmly in the *Religio,* is invoked again and again in *Vulgar Errors.* It is contrary to the reason of nature for the lamprey to have nine eyes since not all of them could be necessary for vision.[20] Browne consistently opposes any implication that the general laws of nature are suspended for some creatures or that anything in nature is superfluous.

It is typical of Browne that his aversion to any suggestion of chaos in nature, his scorn of the vulgar, who are prone "to translate a remarkable quality into a propriety," does not extend to matters of human custom. He is neither surprised to find men living in ways utterly different from his own nor inclined to condemn them for doing so. A survey of the

[18] Bk. III, chap. 16. (*Works,* II, 207).
[19] *Works,* II, 172.
[20] Bk. III, chap. 19.

course of diet in different nations shows that flesh considered a delicacy by one people is deemed unfit for human consumption by another. Browne catalogues the endless variety of dietary practice, at once delighting in its curiosities and puncturing man's assurance about the rightness of what, in fact, is peculiar to one time or place: "while we single out several dishes and reject others, the selection seems but arbitrary, or upon opinion; for many are commended and cryed up in one age, which are decryed and nauseated in another."[21] Here one is reminded of Montaigne and of Browne's own avowal in the *Religio* of universally flexible taste.

The method employed in *Vulgar Errors* flows quite naturally from the interests and cast of mind exhibited in the *Religio*: from the empirical impulse which allies him to Bacon and which is modified by an even sharper awareness of the deceptiveness of bare experience; from the non-utilitarian search for truth of a man of science who is no secularist, but who places "felicity in things removed from sense, and the intellectual enjoyment of God";[22] from the Platonic disposition that sees everything stemming from the One as rationally ordered and morally purposeful, while things of human contrivance are diverse, chaotic, arbitrary. *Vulgar Errors* differs significantly from the *Religio*, however, because of the absence of the whole dimension of *o altitudo*. Since this scientific work is chiefly a consideration of God's wisdom, Browne's understanding is not confounded as in his religious meditation where consideration of God's eternity rouses his poetic imagination and puts his reason to St. Paul's Sanctuary (*Religio*, I, 11).

As a scientist, Browne has Bacon's distrust of abstract speculation and Descartes' distrust of experience; yet he uses both and checks one against the other. If he stresses the importance of experiment over authority he is nonetheless addicted to learned citation. His recognition of the importance of hypotheses may, as Chalmers suggests, make him

[21] Bk. III, chap. 25. (*Works*, II, 248).
[22] *Works*, II, 28.

in one sense a truer scientist than either Bacon or Descartes.[23] But his scientific method was eclectic and his vision of nature comprehensive at a time when the advancement of knowledge depended upon the rigorous pursuit of more narrowly defined methods and the breaking down of complex wholes into simple constituent parts. As Leroy, the French biographer of Browne, noted: "Le monde des analogies, non de la dialectique, est le sien."[24]

Up-to-date in his information, Browne was more receptive to the ideas of the New Science than Bacon and was a patient, even laborious, experimenter and observer. His failure to achieve great things as a scientist is best explained by the same obvious lack that applies to the majority of dedicated men of science in any age: he simply was not endowed with talent of the order that produces great discoveries or new systems of thought. Furthermore, his Platonic disposition was at odds with the needs of science. The Timaean vision of the world is ultimately moral and poetic, while the seventeenth century's great contribution was a redefinition of the quantitative and materialist view. Of all the Greek philosophers who considered the physical world, it was Democritus whom Bacon thought most "worthy to be rescued."[25] Though Browne championed modern scientific method as consistently as anyone in an age strangely compounded of the old and the new, his outlook remained teleological and Platonic. It is perhaps instructive to note Paul Shorey's insistence that "the *Timaeus* rightly understood and interpreted is more in harmony with the spirit of modern science than Aristotle or almost any other philosophy of the past."[26] "Modern" is the most relative of terms, since modernity is regularly antiquated and the old-fashioned can be renovated to modernity. Though Browne's interest in first causes was rapidly becom-

[23] "Sir Thomas Browne, True Scientist," pp. 54, 62.

[24] *Le Chevalier Thomas Browne (1605–1682), médecin, styliste, & métaphysicien* (Paris, 1931), p. 123.

[25] Fulton H. Anderson, *Francis Bacon* (Los Angeles, 1962), p. 328.

[26] *Platonism Ancient and Modern* (Berkeley, 1938), p. 109. Of course, from Shorey's standpoint, Browne and his contemporaries did not rightly understand and interpret the *Timaeus*.

ing obsolete in terms of the critical direction of seventeenth-century science, in our own century science has shown a renewed interest in what to Bacon might look suspiciously like metaphysics. The spirit of Bacon, though it marches along the main road of modern thought with Hobbes, Locke, the Enlightenment, and the logical analysts, has itself been twice antiquated – once by Kant and, in altogether different terms, by the undermining of the quantum theory. In the intellectual history of the West it is possible perhaps to interpret the advancement of knowledge as a strategic alternation of renewed forms of nominalism and realism. And it is not surprising that just when the realist outlook was ceasing to be useful for science, its rich suitability for poetry should be reaffirmed in so much of the greatest writing of the period.

3

While *Vulgar Errors* represents Browne's systematic and substantial assault on the scientific and learned questions of the day, it is in the casually organized *Religio Medici* that the author's strategy of truth becomes most fully visible. For in the *Religio* Browne considers the entire range of epistemological assumptions and problems in the context of what may be called their ultimate terms: the relation of empirical scientific endeavors to Christian Platonism. The method of *Vulgar Errors* is, as I have suggested, implicit in the *Religio*. Yet what emerges from the *Religio* is not a program of knowledge capable of definition from the standpoint of the discipline of the history of ideas. To trace the pattern of what for lack of a looser term I have been calling Browne's epistemology is not the same thing as exhibiting a philosophically valid or even a coherent system of thought.

Nor is Browne's pluralism in epistemology a conscious philosophic position. He neither sought nor achieved the kind of fixed and deliberate composite of thought of the formal eclectic. He moved instead among a group of unintegrated positions, now subscribing to one method, now apparently renouncing it in favor of another, then returning to the view originally expressed from an unexpected direction. "The book is apparently a succession of moods which run the gamut of orthodox submission, persistent skepticism, mystical flights, scientific and philosophical argument, idle curiosity, and Stoic world-weariness" – such is W. P. Dunn's description of the impact of the *Religio* on the reader.[27]

The instability suggested by various modes of knowledge and erratically shifting moods is augmented by a disparity between certain firmly, and seemingly consistently, held convictions and the encyclopedic range of subjects which could rouse his interest and compel his mind. Consider one of the more striking contradictions between a consistently stated bias and an habitual focus of his attention. Browne regularly derides antiquity, disclaiming interest in it or reverence for it since eternity is a more worthy object of contemplation. In the *Religio* he explains that "one reason I tender so little devotion unto reliques is, I think, the slender and doubtfull respect I have alwayes held unto Antiquities: for that indeed which I admire is farre before antiquity, that is Eternity, and that is God himselfe . . ." (I, 28). He believes there are too many books in the world and therefore cannot "deplore the combustion of the Library of *Alexandria*"; indeed, he would like to see a "generall Synod . . . for the benefit of learning, to reduce it as it lay at first in a few and solid Authors; and to condemne to the fire those swarms and millions of *Rhapsodies*, begotten onely to distract and abuse the weaker judgements of Scholars, and to maintaine the Trade and Mystery of Typographers" (I, 24). We have touched upon the view of antiquity expressed in *Vulgar Errors* and have seen that its authority is only very grudgingly and conditionally admitted among the determinators of truth. In *Christian Morals*, he congratulates his own age for throwing off the bondage of authority and for engaging in a free search for truth: "There is nothing more acceptable unto the Ingenious World, than this noble Eluctation of Truth; wherein, against the tenacity of Prejudice and Prescription, this Century now prevaileth."[28] Yet there is no need to document Browne's immer-

[27] *Sir Thomas Browne*, p. 43.
[28] *Works*, I, 262.

sion in the past and his delight in antiquity. Though he consistently assigns it a negative value, he is also fascinated by it to a degree that not even the learned temper of Renaissance humanism, which he would appear to be disclaiming, can account for. And his own library – formidable in size and in range – poses the most impressive denial of his assertion that the world were better off had more ancient books been lost.

Perhaps Browne himself provides the clearest explanation for his incurable eclecticism and constant shifting of intellectual stance. "I have runne through all sorts, yet finde no rest in any; though our first studies & *junior* endeavors may stile us Peripateticks, Stoicks, or Academicks, yet I perceive the wisest heads prove, at last, almost all Scepticks, and stand like *Janus* in the field of knowledge. I have therefore one common and authentick Philosophy I learned in the Schooles, whereby I discourse and satisfie the reason of other men; another more reserved and drawne from experience whereby I content mine owne" (*Religio*, II, 8). To some, this will suggest intellectual frivolity, to others the seriousness of a man for whom the life of the mind is an inextricable part of the life of the man and not simply a set of disciplines to master. Nor should we overlook the similarity of this attitude to the position which Montaigne develops in his great essay "On Experience." Browne's striving for a personal experience of truth as well as a publicly valid system of thought marks him a man of letters rather than a philosopher. His natural studies, aimed at a clarification of the physical world, formed part of this larger personal experience. The spirit of science and the spirit of poetry concur and finally merge in the concrete order of discourse he preferred to dialectic.

He is very aware of having two kinds of discourse or modes of definition at his command and sometimes cues the reader that he is going to shift from one to the other:

> . . . indeed he only is, all other things have beene or shall be, but in eternitie there is no distinction of Tenses; and therefore that terrible terme, *Predestination*, which hath troubled so many weake heads

> to conceive, and the wisest to explaine, is in respect to God no prescious determination of our estates to come, but a definitive placet of his will already fulfilled, and at the instant that he first decreed it; for to his eternitie which is indivisible, and altogether, the last Trumpe is already sounded, the reprobates in the flame, and the blessed in *Abrahams* bosome. Saint *Peter* spoke modestly, when hee said, a thousand yeares to God are but as one day; for to speake like a Philosopher, those continued instants of time which flow into a thousand yeares, make not to him one moment; what to us is to come, to his Eternitie is present, his whole duration being but one permanent point without succession, parts, flux, or division. (I, 11)

Though the movement here is untypical of Browne — from the metaphoric and Biblical to the abstract and philosophic — there is no diminishing of expressive power. He invests the abstract statement with a casual majesty attesting to the impact of the naked idea on his mind. Elsewhere, one feels that Browne works at a definite disadvantage with abstract discourse. For example, this bit of scholastic jargon, though nimbly handled, is triumphant only in obfuscation:

> . . . a production of something out of nothing; and what is that? Whatsoever is opposite to something or more exactly, that which is truely contrary unto God: for he onely is, all others have an existence with dependency and are something but by a distinction; and herein is Divinity conformant unto Philosophy, and generation not onely founded on contrarieties, but also creation; God being all things is contrary unto nothing out of which were made all things, and so nothing becomes something, and *Omneity* informed *Nullity* into an essence. (I, 35)

Philosophical abstraction is the part of Browne's intellectual activity that relates him to the community of professional thinking men. His characteristic approach, however, the one that unquestionably satisfies him more deeply, is concrete:

> [God] . . . holds no Councell, but that mysticall one of the Trinity, wherein, though there be three persons, there is but one minde that decrees, without contradiction; nor needs he any, his actions are not begot with deliberation, his wisedome naturally knowes what's best; his intellect stands ready fraught with the superlative and purest Idea's of goodnesse; consultation and election, which are two motions in us, are not one in him; his actions springing from his power, at the first touch of his will. These are Contemplations Metaphysicall; my humble speculations have another Method, and are content to trace and discover those impressions hee hath left on his creatures, and the obvious effects of nature . . . (I, 13)

What is most interesting is that poetry and science are intimately connected in the symbolic comprehension of God and the world. Browne regards the materials both of abstract thought and of natural studies as symbols to be interpreted as well as physical facts or distinct ideas to be analyzed. He definitely prefers to dwell on the suggestiveness of nature rather than reduce it to a flat and confined mechanism. "The severe Schooles shall never laugh me out of the Philosophy of *Hermes*, that this visible world is but a picture of the invisible, wherein as in a pourtract, things are not truely, but in equivocall shapes, and as they counterfeit some more reall substance in that invisible fabrick" (I, 12). Analogous to the oblique cognitions extractable from a symbolic nature are the insights provided by the symbolic definitions not only of Scripture but of somewhat dubious mystical works. "I am now content to understand a mystery without a rigid definition in an easie and Platonick description. That allegorical description of *Hermes* [*Deus est Sphaera cuius centrum ubique, circumferentia nullibi*] pleaseth me beyond all the Metaphysicall definitions of Divines . . ." (I, 10).

To speak of what one prefers or finds more pleasing in the method of truth struck Sir Kenelm Digby, as it still may many others, as intolerable egotism. But the feeling that truth has value as delight need not be identified with an attitude of idle amusement. The contemplative and aesthetic appeal of truth was at times present even to Bacon who ordinarily conceived the value of knowledge in utilitarian terms. A kind of heaven is established on earth, he felt, when a man's mind "turn[s] upon the poles of truth."

Browne's cavalier juggling of different epistemologies and his fluctuating personal attitudes have seldom presented obstacles to appreciation for his audience. The major stumbling block for modern readers — the issue to which all discussion of his epistemology must at last turn — is his fideism. Moderns are likely to be repelled by the attitude of fideism unless, as with Montaigne, they can feel that it was only an escape hatch for a man somewhat inclined to libertine atheism who also liked to play it safe. But in Browne's fideism there is neither evasiveness nor desperation. Where it is not joyous, it is perfectly deliberate and serene:

> . . . where I cannot satisfie my reason, I love to humour my fancy; I had as leive you tell me that *anima est angelus hominis, est Corpus Dei*, as *Entelechia*; *Lux est umbra Dei*, as *actus perspicui*: where there is an obscurity too deepe for our reason, 'tis good to sit downe with a description, periphrasis, or adumbration; for by acquainting our reason how unable it is to display the visible and obvious effects of nature, it becomes more humble and submissive unto the subtilties of faith: and thus I teach my haggard and unreclaimed reason to stoope unto the lure of faith. . . . and this I think is no vulgar part of faith to believe a thing not only above, but contrary to reason, and against the argument of our proper senses. (I, 10)

Translation of matters above reason into metaphor provides training for accepting matters contrary to reason. More important, this passage reveals a very characteristic side of Sir Thomas Browne, yet one which must qualify our usual conception of him as a Christian humanist. While traditional epistemology distinguished the proper ways of knowing the natural and the spiritual, it was loath to admit a gap between them that could be bridged only by a blind leap of faith. Hooker, after all, had insisted that only through reason could man know that Scripture was indeed the Word of God.[29] Browne draws the limits of reason more sharply, indicating his place in the revival of an antirational and Augustinian pietism that is a significant feature of religious thought in the earlier seventeenth century. This, I think, may explain why Ficino, Pico, and even Hooker are likely to seem a good deal closer to later liberal theology and religious sensibility than Browne, not to mention the more obvious difference in the case of Donne. While Anglican thinkers of the period, and Milton too, stoutly maintained the Platonic continuity between sensibles and intelligibles, nature and grace, reason and revelation, there was still an underlying awareness that this continuity was not an identity or an equality. It is when this final distinction, often so vague, receives occasional necessary stress and the modern reader confronts an uncompromising Augustinian orthodoxy that discomfort sets in and intellectual sympathy is likely to be cut off, as in this passage of Browne and, to cite a greater and more oblique example, Christ's rejection of classical culture in *Paradise Regained.*

Browne is among the last of the Christian Platonists in whom this distinction still clearly matters, if only sporadically. His fideism is obviously related to this attitude which marks off the area where the general label of Christian Platonist cannot be usefully applied unless defined more precisely. We can refine the definition by contrasting this aspect of Browne's thought with certain basic assumptions of an allied figure and near contemporary like the Cambridge Platonist Benjamin Whichcote (1609–83), whose intellectual relation to Brown has been regularly noted.

Both men defended a vital and spiritual interpretation of nature and shared the liberal attitude toward religious differences exemplified in men like Taylor and Chillingworth. Whichcote's posthumously published *Moral and Religious*

[29] *Ecclesiastical Polity* 3. 8. 12.

Aphorisms are studded with irenic and charitable statements about religious controversy that are reminiscent of Browne:

> 53. He that never *changed* any of his opinions, never *corrected* any of his Mistakes: and He, who was never *wise* enough, to find any mistakes in Himself; will not be *charitable* enough, to excuse what he reckons mistakes in Others.
>
> 73. We may maintain *Unity* of Verity, in point of Faith; and Unity of Charity, in point of Communion; notwithstanding all *Differences* in point of Apprehension.
>
> 130. Our Fallibility and the Shortness of our Knowledge should make us peaceable and gentle: because I *may* be Mistaken, I *must* not be dogmatical and confident, peremptory and imperious. I *will* not break the certain Laws of Charity, for a doubtful Doctrine or of uncertain Truth.[30]

The Cambridge circle of Puritan Platonists stressed the results that religion should produce in a man's conduct and inner life, what Whichcote called the "habit of sanctification." John Smith echoes this recurring idea of the century: "There is an inward beauty, life and loveliness in Divine Truth, which cannot be known but onely then when it is digested into life and practice."[31] A list of the bonds of kinship between these men and an Anglican like Browne could be indefinitely extended. To those already mentioned or implied one might add a preference for the life of contemplation to that of action, and for understanding the physical world rather than controlling it. Nevertheless, one cannot follow the ties of mind and temper between Browne and the Cambridge group very far without encountering some stubborn knots whose unravelling discloses a definite split in the implications of their thought.

The major differences may be traced to Browne's vein of Augustinian orthodoxy, which, though certainly not the con-

[30] Ed. W. R. Inge (London, 1930), pp. 8, 10, 17.

[31] E. T. Campagnac (ed.), *The Cambridge Platonists* (Oxford, 1901), pp. 3–4.

trolling impulse of his mind, is a consideration we cannot neglect without blurring our picture of him. It is not Augustine's position on free will that is specifically relevant. Browne is typically Anglican in eschewing the radical depravity of the natural condition professed by strict Calvinists. "Insolent zeales that doe decry good workes and rely onely upon faith, take not away merits: for depending upon the efficacy of their faith, they enforce the condition of God, and in a more sophisticall way doe seeme to challenge Heaven" (I, 60). Though he derides the extreme position of Calvinists, he adheres quite literally to the doctrine of the Fall and to the need for supernatural grace: "by the letter, and written Law of God, we are without exception in the state of death; but there is a prerogative of God, and an arbitrary pleasure above the letter of his owne Law, by which alone wee can pretend unto salvation . . ." (I, 57).

The orthodox Christian side of Browne inevitably modifies, even contradicts, certain aspects of the Platonism he shared with the Cambridge men. For while God as Creator is like the Platonic One in eternally sustaining and governing His creation, God as Reedeemer does not fit so readily into a Platonic structure of thought. Though Browne may express the spiritual link between God and man Platonically, as in the beautiful passage (I, 32), p. 172 above, he still subscribes quite literally to the need for redemption through the special act of grace. Devout though they were, this was not the case with the Cambridge Platonists. The emanation of a creative love from the One into the *logos* of the soul implied to them a natural spiritual force in man which is constantly at work carrying him to the divine. This concept of an eternally operative force tends to minimize the doctrinal importance of the Incarnation and Crucifixion as well as to render grace superfluous.[32] This tendency may be taken as having originated with Ficino's efforts to establish a harmonious relation, if not an actual identity, between basic Christian

[32] This represents something quite different from the relatively minor role we have seen that the mysteries of faith play in the *devotional* experience of Browne.

doctrines and Platonic concepts. Of course, from the Gospel of St. John onward, Platonic thought had provided the intellectual structure for Christian faith, and the language, imagery, and spiritual idealism of Platonism and Christianity became increasingly interwoven. So long as this synthesis depended upon symbolic concepts, mythologizing, and comparable imaginative embodiments of the relation between the human and the divine, matter and spirit, the very fundamental differences between the two did not tear that synthesis asunder or submerge what was essentially Christian.[33]

However, the intellectual pressures of the mid-seventeenth century, as Basil Willey stressed in his classic study of the thought of the age, compelled a *philosophic* statement of Christian Platonism if rational religion was to be preserved from Hobbes's reduction of nature and mind to matter in motion and from Cartesian metaphysics which Henry More finally rejected when he saw that spirit could have no place in a world regulated by mathematical laws of magnitude. The rational religion of Hooker had recognized that it was attempting to explain to reason in the terms of reason things contrary to reason, or at least ungraspable by it. To the Cambridge Platonists, on the other hand, whatever was contrary to reason was contrary to religion; they would have demurred at taking refuge with Browne in "Saint *Pauls* Sanctuary." Not only explanations about religion but also the substance of religious dogma itself had to be "intelligible, rational, accountable."[34] Since the Cambridge men firmly subscribed to the essentials of Christian dogma, but could not, as Ernst Cassirer points out, allow *credo quia impossibile* as a genuine religious attitude,[35] they set about to rein-

[33] Such syncretic efforts did not always win acceptance even from men who may be considered Christian Platonists. In his edition of Colet's marginalia on Ficino's *Epistolae*, Sears Jayne emphasizes the anti-intellectual and Augustinian tendencies in Colet which precluded his assent to many of Ficino's leading ideas. *John Colet and Marsilio Ficino*, pp. 56–76.

[34] Whichcote, *Aphorisms*, p. 27, No. 220.

[35] *The Platonic Renaissance in England*, trans. James P. Pettegrove (Austin, 1953), p. 39.

terpret the mysteries of faith in the conceptual terms of rational idealism. What had formerly been expressed in the language of paradox had now, it was felt, to be rendered in clear and distinct ideas.

In so doing, it was inevitable that abstract concepts of universal spiritual truths should emerge as prior and therefore superior to the particular historical events upon which Christianity rests, so that the mysteries of faith cease to be the innermost core of truth and, reversing in effect the Augustinian formula, are themselves referred to a more general, more rational, and thus higher authority. Ficino had similarly undercut Augustinian orthodoxy by subordinating the exclusive importance of events in time which miraculously shaped the eternal fate of the world to a Platonic stress upon the naturalness and usualness of spiritual and divine influx into matter and into man. Our concern, however, is not with the well-known consequences of this rational emphasis of the Cambridge Platonists for the history of liberal theology, but with the significance of the dimension of traditional orthodoxy in the religious discourse of Sir Thomas Browne. The rational and universalized attitude toward religious truth professed by Whichcote and his fellows appears, of course, in Browne too, as it does in varying degrees in all Christian Platonists; and there is no reason to believe that Browne or even these more formal thinkers were conscious that such ideas were opposed to orthodox Christian Doctrine.[36] What is important for our consideration of Browne is that his approach to the mysteries of faith through paradox or in an *o altitudo* was still a viable channel of religious expression. As such it accounts for the felt difference in tone and imaginative quality between *Religio Medici* and the whole drift of thought presented in a writer like Whichcote.

Browne's exercise of the habit of paradox to grasp the mys-

[36] Anthony Tuckney's attempts to convince Whichcote that his opinions bordered on Socinianism and Arminianism brought forth an eloquent reaffirmation of his rational principles.

teries of faith and also to enhance the sense of wonder surrounding them naturally enough pervaded and shaped his sensibility in other areas of religious thought. We have amply noted his basic preference, both in explicit statements and characteristic practice, to comprehend religious truth metaphorically. This concrete and symbolic mode accompanies and reinforces a sense of wonder and of the miraculousness of all things. There is a poignant recognition of the mysteriousness, the otherness, of spirit and of the obscurity in which it remains shrouded.

> Thus are we men, and we know not how; there is something in us, that can be without us, and will be after us, though it is strange that it hath no history, what it was before us, nor can tell how it entred in us. (I, 36)
>
> . . . there is therfore some other hand that twines the thread of life than that of nature; wee are not onely ignorant in Antipathies and occult qualities, our ends are as obscure as our beginnings, the line of our dayes is drawne by night, and the various effects therein by a pencill that is invisible; wherein though wee confesse our ignorance, I am sure wee doe not erre, if wee say, it is the hand of God. (I, 43)

The dark intuitions through which Browne approaches first causes and the realm of spirit are foreign to the temper of the Cambridge Platonists. They see the spiritual simply as a higher form of the rational that is linked to it in a straight line illuminated at every point. Whichcote gives memorable statement to this attitude:

> The *Spirit of God* in *us,* is a Living *Law,* Informing the Soul; not Constrained by a Law, without, that enlivens not; but we act in the Power of an *inward Principle* of Life, which enables, inclines, facilitates, determines. Our *Nature* is reconciled to the law of Heaven, the Rule of Everlasting Righteousness, Goodness, and Truth.[37]

[37] *Aphorisms,* p. 72, No. 625.

The profound difference between Browne and Whichcote is determined more by tone and attitude than by any definition of religious doctrine. It is impossible not to admire the warm strength and the clarity of Whichcote's thought. One can hardly fail to see in his language and sensibility an anticipation of the assured ethical tone of eighteenth-century deism and benevolism. Though more attractive in many ways than the religion of Browne's age, this rationalism represents the end of a tradition in which truth was carried to the believer with radiant associations that, joined with gifts such as Browne's, could be productive of literature of the highest value.

4

By stressing one or another of its elements we have seen how a case can be made for *Religio Medici* as a religious exercise, an essay about faith and philosophy, an inner biography, or an apologia for Anglicanism in general or for the Anglicanism of one man in particular. It definitely lacks the drama of Augustine's *Confessions*, the drama that issues from religious conversion. Nor does it partake of the spiritual melodrama of Donne's divine poems and prose meditations — the passionate urgency of dwelling perpetually at the frontier of life and death, sin and regeneration, as though every moment were his last. But nowhere else can we find a presentation of a mind so securely anchored in the Anglican *via media* that is equally compelling. Never has complacency been so dazzling and the transport that accompanies the contemplation of mysteries so serene.

For all his orthodoxy and indulgence of commonplaces, Browne had a kind of original religious genius. He was unsurpassed at revitalizing traditional beliefs that had long sustained men precisely because his witty paradoxes and skeptical reflections could shake men loose from routine ways of thinking and feeling about what they believed. He was neither a mystic nor a theologian and least of all a prophet with a new vision. A poet who drenched whatever he touched in the freshness of his individuality, Browne yet depended upon traditional Christian and Platonic attitudes and employed the oblique resources of art to afford renewed strength for long-possessed truths.

The strategy of truth in *Religio Medici* proceeds from an implicit set of norms for judging two of the great intellectual controversies of the day. The Platonic paradigm of knowledge and the Christian virtues of faith and charity test and are tested by specific conflicts between science and religion and between human custom and divine command. The hierarchical integrity of custom, nature and Idea and the right practice of faith and charity emerge as intimately interdependent epistemological and ethical standards. Browne applies these norms in so personal a manner, with such sensitivity to inherent ambiguities, that the result is not a discourse shaped simply by an a priori system of thought and therefore inviting reduction to an intellectual formula. The *Religio* achieves instead the status of what may profitably be called a mimetic essay. For as in a work of fictive literature, its effect and meaning are unique to it and inseparable from the concrete power of its material particulars. The effect we must finally seek to experience is not then the system of thought Browne assumes and employs in the *Religio* but the action of thought he creates.

CHAPTER VII

URN BURIAL: THE ETHICS OF MORTALITY

BEFORE we could analyze *Religio Medici* certain questions about genre and intention had to be raised and at least provisionally answered. *Urn Burial* and *The Garden of Cyrus* pose such questions in an even more acute form. The relationship of the *Religio* to the personal essay, autobiography, and various forms of religious writing allowed us to employ, as an initial step, methods appropriate to those types. No such literary starting points are available for the companion pieces, even though they are Browne's most purely literary efforts. Response to them is certainly more for themselves as distinct from anything they are about than is the case with the *Religio*, which Browne's speculations about philosophic, religious, and scientific issues invest with the interest of a document in intellectual history. Yet the companion pieces are learned treatises; each is definitely about something extrinsic to itself or to the personality of the author; the perspective of the *Religio*, on the other hand, is, as we saw, always the first person, however wide-ranging its subject matter.

Analysis and interpretation of *Urn Burial* and *The Garden of Cyrus* have proceeded from considerations such as their simultaneous publication in the volume of 1658, their dedicatory epistles, and the division of each into five chapters — these being taken as clues to Browne's formal literary intention. The question much recent criticism has started from is the reason for the simultaneous publication and the significance of the order of the two prose works. It is now customary to assume that a profitable approach to the companion pieces must provide single access to both. Accordingly, explanations like that of Sir Edmund Gosse have been dismissed, that *The Garden of Cyrus* was added to *Urn Burial* because the one work was too short to be published by itself.[1]

Two recent studies exemplify the tendency to read these treatises as companion pieces in a strict sense by tracing their parallels and contrasts in materials, themes, and symbols. The older view of two fortuitously joined works has been replaced by an assumption of complementary relation which calls to mind *L'Allegro* and *Il Penseroso* and would seem to require analysis such as has long been afforded to Milton's companion poems. Indeed, Margaret A. Heideman implies a thematic relationship similar to the one existing between *L'Allegro* and *Il Penseroso*, what may be called a co-ectype of the same pattern.[2] Miss Heideman finds that *Urn Burial*'s "dominant and unifying symbol . . . is that mystery of similitude which Browne finds in the burial urn and the human womb."[3] In *The Garden of Cyrus* there is the reiteration "in a variety of aspects under one dominant conception" of the image of light, and the entire work "is as inspired with quiet joy as the *Hydriotaphia* with penetrating sadness."[4]

Frank L. Huntley provides the most cogent reading of the companion pieces as the two parts of an encompassing vision.[5] A summary cannot do justice to the reasoning and elaboration of his thesis, but no serious student can now read these "twin essays" without Huntley's study in mind. Showing how the number five operates geometrically, structurally, and symbolically, he goes on to examine the relation of subject matter, design, and epistemology in the two prose pieces. Pro-

[1] *Sir Thomas Browne* (London, 1905), p. 121.

[2] "*Hydriotaphia* and *The Garden of Cyrus*: A Paradox and a Cosmic Vision," *University of Toronto Quarterly*, 19 (1950): 235–46.

[3] *Ibid.*, pp. 235–36.

[4] *Ibid.*, pp. 245 and 241.

[5] Huntley's study originally appeared as "Sir Thomas Browne: The Relationship of *Urn Burial* and *The Garden of Cyrus*," *Studies in Philology*, 53 (1956): 204–19; this article was revised in his book on Browne (Ann Arbor, 1962), chap. 13.

fessor Huntley points out — not with absolute originality, but certainly with a very original force of definition — that *Urn Burial* is concerned with death, the body, passions, accident, and substance, while *The Garden of Cyrus* is concerned with life, the soul, reason, design, and form. The chaotically irregular materials of one are fraught with the uncertainties of human ignorance, while the Platonic-mathematical uniformity of the quincunx witnesses the certainty of divine order.

It is now an accepted premise that each of the companion pieces gains in fullness and precision of interpretation when placed beside the other. But the relationship, I would insist, is not equal. For there are issues and resolutions in *Urn Burial* more profound than any schematic paralleling with its sequel can reveal. To establish the true stature of *Urn Burial* it is necessary to examine it primarily as in independent creation rather than as a mutually important foil for *The Garden of Cyrus*.[6] I plan, therefore, to treat each work individually. A significant relationship between the two can nonetheless be exhibited — one in essential agreement with Professor Huntley's conclusions — though arrived at through a different route, and providing, along with an individual view, the perspective of the larger context of Browne's thought.

1

The disparity between the prosaic archaeological occasion of *Urn Burial* — the unearthing of forty or fifty sepulchral urns — and the extraordinary imaginative height to which this work rises has always seemed a little preternatural. To the nineteenth century, the fifth chapter showed how Browne, fired with the nobility to which his subject was

[6] J. M. Cline offered the first significant demonstration of the unity of *Urn Burial*: "*Hydriotaphia*," *University of California Publications in English*, 8 (1940): 73–100. George Williamson's analysis, aimed at defining the "rational structure of its eloquence," unfortunately appeared after my own study was substantially completed and has not been taken into real account: "The Purple of *Urn Burial*," *Modern Philology*, 62 (1964): 110–17.

allied, could abandon his modest scholarly purpose and a pedestrian scholarly style to seize upon the poetic possibilities of mortality, transforming what had started out as an antiquary's report into a work of undeniable, if baffling, greatness. This view of Browne as artist in spite of himself has been exorcised by modern criticism. The evidence that he intended *Urn Burial* to be a literary composition and made conscious use of the resources of art now appears overwhelming. This in no way diminishes the wonder at Browne's power to show mundane things in a magical light; indeed, the wonder increases as the deliberateness of his design unfolds.

Browne was not "carried away" from an original antiquarian purpose, but exploited the discovery of the burial urns "In a Field of old *Walsingham*, not many moneths past" to fulfill an intention that was literary from the outset. The dedicatory epistle addressed to Thomas Le Gros, a Norfolk neighbor of Browne's, may be adduced first to support this contention. Both its style and substance indicate that the larger (what we might call the "liberal" as opposed to the "specialist") aspects of "the fate of [men's] bones" provided the motive and the emphasis for his treatment. "We were hinted by the occasion, not catched the opportunity to write of old things, or intrude upon the Antiquary" (*Works*, I, 132). He disavows any predisposition to "discourses of Antiquities"; the discovery of the urns forced the occasion upon him. That Browne almost certainly wrote the dedication after the treatise itself was completed scarcely matters. His interest in the urns and his treatment were clearly not in the line of routine scholarly investigation; this is implicit in the cadenced periods and elevated tone (anticipatory of the final chapter) of the prefatory dedication.

> 'Tis opportune to look back upon old times, and contemplate our Forefathers. Great examples grow thin, and to be fetched from the passed world. Simplicity flies away, and iniquity comes at long strides upon us. We have enough to do to make up our selves from present and passed times, and the whole stage of things scarce serveth for our instruction. A

> compleat peece of vertue must be made up from the *Centos* of all ages, as all the beauties of *Greece* could make but one handsome *Venus*. (*Works*, I, 132)

The sense of a great heritage that outweighs any present or future possibilities and is in danger of being swept away; the transitoriness of human glory, decaying to nothingness unless transferred to the plane of memory and imagination which alone partakes of permanence—these haunting themes of the concluding chapter are emphatically foreshadowed in this dedication, and, it is reasonable to assume, Browne wished to establish their tone as the proper perspective for reading *Urn Burial*.

Browne's organization provides further evidence that the urns and specifically archaeological questions they might raise did not provide the real focus of his interest. Instead of beginning with the circumstances of the discovery or other first-hand data, he devotes the first chapter to an historical survey of burial customs. But it is a survey with a difference. It is not the mass of encyclopedic information and heterogeneous curiosities we might expect from the author of *Vulgar Errors*. Nor, significantly, is it composed in the low style suited to factual material, but in the middle, meditative style of individual intellectual exploration. The first chapter has, moreover, a firm thematic shape that anticipates the two final chapters.

The expectations of ordinary discursive strategy may well lead us to read Chapter I simply as background which introduces and places in larger context the particular discovery to be detailed in Chapters II and III. However, Browne structures this historical account of burial customs so as to direct our attention to certain other questions. The opening paragraphs picture the secrets of nature and history that lie buried within the earth. "Time hath endlesse rarities, and shows of all varieties; which reveals old things in heaven, makes new discoveries in earth, and even earth it self a discovery" (I, 135). Things as yet unknown, "the treasures of time," like these long-buried bones, are "still in the Urne unto us." The urn becomes symbolic of all that man does not know, of all that he may discover ("That great Antiquity *America* lay buried for thousands of years . . ."), and of much more that he will never know, the inevitable incompleteness of human knowledge.

In the fourth paragraph Browne turns to the announced subject of his discourse by making a broad generalization about burial customs.

> Many have taken voluminous pains to determine the state of the soul upon disunion; but men have been most phantasticall in the singular contrivances of their corporall dissolution; whilest the sobrest Nations have rested in two wayes, of simple inhumation and burning. (I, 136)

The major interest in death is the destiny of the soul, but the chief practical activity has necessarily been the disposal of the body. The subsequent paragraphs of Chapter I develop as a comparative examination of inhumation and burning, with Browne ransacking history and literature for examples obvious or recherché of these alternative methods.

He begins in the manner of a formal disputation with a comparison of the relative antiquity of the two. "Carnall interment or burying, was of the elder date," its origins associated with the Hebrew Biblical world; "the practice of Burning was also of great Antiquity," as shown in Homer and other sources of our knowledge of the pagan world. The introductory maneuver is the traditional oratorical one of comparing two opponents in relation to certain *topoi.* When Milton, as a Cambridge student, argued "Whether Day or Night is the More Excellent," he arranged this academic exercise about a comparison of the antiquity, origins, and associations of each—all topics that a textbook of rhetoric like Aphthonius' would prescribe. But, of course, Browne, while borrowing from this habit of discourse, does not really follow it, since he is not trying to persuade his audience of the greater praiseworthiness of burning or burying. His aim, rather, is to discern and evaluate the bases on which different civilizations or sects have opted for one practice or the other. What is significant about these practices are the assumptions upon which they are built and, indeed, that they stem from attitudes having a broader base. Browne seeks to define the rationales underlying the welter of differing customs. "Now as all customes were founded upon some bottome of Reason, so there wanted not grounds for this; according to severall apprehensions of the most rationall dissolution" (I, 137). The variations in burial customs are to be understood, then, as the product of varying conceptions of material nature, of the make-up of the human body, of fire and water, and of the way these interact.

> . . . Some being of the opinion of *Thales*, that water was the originall of all things, thought it most equall to submit unto the principle of putrefaction, and conclude in a moist relentment. Others conceived it most natural to end in fire, as due unto the master principle in the composition, according to the doctrine of *Heraclitus*. And therefore heaped up large piles, more actively to waft them toward that Element, whereby they also declined a visible degeneration into worms, and left a lasting parcell of their composition. (I, 137)

The natural philosophy and views on the continued existence of the soul have determined for each civilization the outcome planned and hoped for in the dissolution and preservation of human remains. And while "Some apprehended a purifying virtue in fire," others found the rationale for burning not in the attempt to withstand the effects of nature or to cooperate with them, but in the practical expedient of foiling predatory human action. "Others pretending no natural grounds, politickly declined the malice of enemies upon their buried bodies. Which consideration led *Sylla* unto this practise; who having thus served the body of *Marius*, could not but fear a retaliation upon his own . . ." (I, 137). The Chaldeans, "the great Idolaters of fire," avoided cremation because of religious considerations: they "abhorred the burning of their carcasses, as a pollution of that Deity." On the other hand, "The Ægyptians were afraid of fire, not as a Deity, but a devouring Element, mercilesly consuming their bodies, and leaving too little of them; and therefore by precious Embalments, depositure in dry earths, or handsome inclosure in glasses, contrived the notablest wayes of integrall conservation" (I, 138). Browne does not claim any special scientific authority for the opposition of Christians to burning, but simply gives the rationale for their practice, as he does for others, in terms of their religious beliefs and tradition.

> Christians abhorred this way of obsequies, and though they stickt not to give their bodies to be burnt in their lives, detested that mode after death; affecting rather a depositure than absumption, and properly submitting unto the sentence of God, to return not unto ashes but unto dust againe, conformable unto the practice of the Patriarchs, the interrment of our Saviour, of *Peter*, *Paul*, and the ancient Martyrs. (I, 138)

The rich mass of detail in Chapter I is, we can see, presented so as to explore the alternatives of burial and burning in terms of their underlying assumptions and motives. Browne, of course, settles on no answer; instead, he raises questions which must be settled at a different level altogether. The choice between interment and cremation turns upon certain larger issues—the decay or disturbance of physical remains, the life of the soul, and the preservation of men's names from oblivion—about which the chapter is organized. But the whole matter is pointedly and deliberately left in abeyance, as Browne moves into the account of the urns themselves. The final paragraph slides off the main track into a curious byway: conjecture as to whether "some examples of sepulture," which lawyers would restrict to the "Law of Nations," may legitimately be seen "in Elephants, Cranes, the Sepulchrall Cells of Pismires and practice of Bees; which civill society carrieth out their dead, and hath exequies, if not interrments" (I, 140). With a reversed Montaignesque comparison of man to the animals, Browne concludes by raising a curious epistemological question: Do man's burial practices, dictated by posited law or custom, find counterparts in the instinctive observances of animals and therefore confirmation in natural law?

Browne opens Chapter II with the announcement that "The Solemnities, Ceremonies, Rites of their Cremation or enterrment, so solemnly delivered by Authours," surveyed in the preceding chapter, "we shall not disparage our Readers to repeat." He will treat "Only the last and lasting part in their Urns," the actual materials of the discovery at Walsingham (II, 140). As he turns to this data there is an appropriate descent from the middle style of meditative exploration to the low style, with its short, unadorned sentences, pure information that is often as flat as raw notes being directly transcribed. He examines the urns and their contents, weighs the evidence as to their being Roman or British, attempts to date them by means of coins discovered nearby, speculates that Britons may have imitated the Roman custom of burning. All conjectures are kept within the bounds of his scholarly investigation; apparently tangential bits of information such as the discovery of some urns definitely not Roman in Norway and Denmark are tightly related to the problem at hand. Browne shows no inclination here for anything more than patient examination of the evidence itself and a few cautious hypotheses. There is no hint of opening up the larger aspects of the subject. Yet even this mass of data is presented with an unmistakable thematic direction. For through the entire chapter runs a strong sense of uncertainty, an almost resigned awareness of the contradictoriness of much of the evidence, and an emphasis upon the difficulty of drawing conclusions from physical and historical materials, however carefully studied. This chapter, like the first, closes with some puzzling bits of information, characteristically in the form of a problem. And Browne's final words raise a suggestive enigma: "why the *Anglesea* Urnes are placed with their mouths downward, remains yet undiscovered" (II, 147).

Chapter III, the longest of the five, continues to describe the urns and their contents, but moves freely from physical to speculative observations. The perspective shifts, now widening from "many fragments of sculs in these Urnes," suggesting perhaps "a mixture of bones," to historically recorded instances of "the Ashes of . . . nearest friends and kindred" in the same urn (III, 151); now narrowing from "the Iron Reliques . . . found all rusty and crumbling into peeces. . . . In the Monument of King Childerick" to the good state of preservation noted in "our little Iron pins which fastened the Ivory works" (III, 150). The significance of the urns is deepened by the reverberating names of the distant past, and great personages of ancient civilizations are brought into intimate relation with these very urns.

The universal truths Browne extracts from this data are expressed in the aphoristic manner of the curt Senecan style, with its tendency to reduce immediate observation and experience or accumulated learning to terse and memorable form, and also to make such inductions extend the range of moral insight to other particulars only hinted at. The following paragraph is composed almost entirely of a series of aphorisms, rhythmically harsh, syntactically disjunctive, but tightly articulated to the central idea, stated now as an essence distilled from the data under consideration, now as general truths shaped to the function of ethical suasion and reaching out indefinitely in human application.

> He that lay in a golden Urne eminently above the Earth, was not likely to finde the quiet of these bones. Many of these Urnes were broke by a vulgar discoverer in hope of inclosed treasure. The ashes of *Marcellus* were lost above ground, upon the like account. Where profit hath prompted, no age hath wanted such miners. For which the most barbarous Expilators found the most civill Rhetorick. Gold once out of the earth is no more due unto it; What was unreasonably committed to the ground is reasonably resumed from it: Let Monuments and rich Fabricks, not Riches adorn mens ashes. The com-

> merce of the living is not to be transferred unto the dead: It is no injustice to take that which none complains to lose, and no man is wronged where no man is possessor. (III, 152–53)

The peculiar success of this paragraph — its ever-widening scope of forward movement — depends upon Browne's use of the two discursive tendencies of the aphoristic style to add a larger pattern of balanced alternation to the obvious and characteristic syntactical feature of strongly marked balance and antithesis within the individual member.

Style, then, as well as statement, contributes to the larger human context of the subject; called forth in Chapter I, this context is re-established with renewed force in Chapter III. The note of uncertainty dominating Chapter II is now sounded with greater poignance. The sizes, shapes, and colors of the urns, the jewels and relics found within, the clues bones give as to the sex, race, and physiognomy of the dead, the effects of fire on different parts of the body — all have as their steady accompaniment an overwhelming uncertainty that any burial practices can achieve their desired ends. That man has employed both reason and what some would call superstition with such ingenuity and precise care in order to preserve his remains and his name — and to no purpose — destroys all assurance about any customs of burial. The most extravagant memorials have failed to preserve men's names to posterity. "The variety of Monuments hath often obscured true graves: and *Cenotaphs* confounded Sepulchres. For beside their reall Tombs, many have founded honorary and empty Sepulchres" (III, 152). The attitude of uncertainty is now invested with a sadness absent from Chapter II, where the scholarly investigator was frustrated in his search for firm conclusions. As the perspective changes to that of human involvement, the uncertainty is no longer abstract or limited to the quest for a clear view of things; it acutely touches the author, his audience, and all the living and therefore makes detachment impossible.

The history of how supposedly rational customs were defeated again and again by nature, which follows its own laws, and by chance, which follows none, points relentlessly to the same lesson. To pursue mundane remembrance and corporal preservation is to chase down a labyrinth in which wherever one turns in the maze of custom one must at last confront that twice-hideous Minotaur – Death and Oblivion. It is not necessary to consider in very great detail the material gathered into the embodiment of this argument, since there is general agreement that the information and speculation woven through the first three chapters all underscore this inescapable conclusion: the universal failure of man's efforts at self-perpetuation. While this enables Browne to insinuate a rather facile Christian irony against "*Ulysses* in *Hecuba* [who] cared not how meanly he lived, so he might finde a noble Tomb after death" (III, 147), the fate of the remains of the dead raises certain stubborn questions about the Resurrection. For, on the one hand, "that power which subdueth all things unto it self, that can resume the scattered Atomes . . . [makes] it superfluous to expect a resurrection out of Reliques." But, on the other hand, "if according to learned conjecture, the bodies of men shall rise where their greatest Reliques remain, many are not like to erre in the Topography of their Resurrection, though their bones or bodies be after translated by Angels into the field of *Ezechiels* vision, or as some will order it, into the Valley of Judgement, or *Jehosaphat*" (III, 157).

2

In the role of antiquary Browne exposes the frailty of human custom to his better self, Browne the scientific student of nature. The lengthy survey of burial customs demonstrates how they succeed only in tracing a bewildering maze of custom among the impregnable walls of nature. As Browne deepens his meditation on the paradoxes of death, the irony implicit in the earlier chapters becomes the dominant strain of Chapter IV. The irrefutable evidence that time and nature reduce all human effort to nothingness prepares for the conclusion asserted by Browne's best self in Chapter V, that only Christian faith can surmount the destruction that must finally overtake all things. Against the vanity of "hope for Immortality, or any patent from oblivion, in preservations below the Moon" (V, 168), there is the assurance that "in the Metaphysicks of true belief" lies the promise of "infallible perpetuity" (V, 171, 170).

The elements composing the theme of *Urn Burial* thus correspond to the three levels of Browne's Platonic epistemology. However, the theory of knowledge defined in this study and shown to impart thematic direction to *Religio Medici* functions quite differently in *Urn Burial*. The central issue of the earlier work is, we saw, the determination of truth: what, Browne asks, is the relative weight of the various authorities and methods – scientific, philosophic, and religious – man invokes in his quest for truth? *Urn Burial* too implies an epistemology, but the problem of knowledge focuses here upon the realm of value and is resolved in terms of it. As he points out the absurd lengths to which men have gone to preserve their remains and memory, Browne works closer and closer toward the values on which they can be clear. The meditation on death finally brings out what is significant in life.

The unfolding of these values is not limited to the anticipated declaration of Christian truth at the end, but is intrinsic to the development of the entire work. In the *Religio*, custom, nature, and Idea, functioning as epistemological norms underlying certain controversial questions, produce what we called an intellectual action. In *Urn Burial*, this same triple scheme is implicit to the historical process whereby Christian faith is discovered as the only assurance of immortality, and, therefore, as the best guide to what is valuable in mortal life. As with the *Religio*, this theme is not presented primarily through explicit argument. We can and do reduce Browne's theme to the conclusion of an argument or the solution of a problem when we summarize in one or another of the schematic approaches unavoidable for criticism. But the actual process for discovering how the futility of human effort can be transcended operates as an action within the work and is experienced as such by the reader.

The account of burial customs and the accompanying meditation on their uncertainties is an excursion into history. There is first the examination of the objects of history, the books, monuments, and relics which preserve the record of civilization. Then there is the contemplation of history as a confirmation of the revealed truth about human destiny, history as Augustine conceived of it. One study is conjecture and hope for preservation in its realm futile; only the other study produces assurance. "Study" here means not a disinterested intellectual activity but the whole direction of life as a commitment to what the contemplation of history teaches is most enduring. The value toward which Browne has been moving is also a norm upon which he operates all along. We are guided throughout toward a vantagepoint from which an increasingly insistent irony is cast upon man's attempts to deal with death from the limited perspective of natural knowledge. In the penultimate paragraph of Chapter V, the Christian norm that has functioned obliquely is stated as the true ethic of mortality.

> Pious spirits who passed their dayes in raptures of futurity, made little more of this world than the world that was before it, while they lay obscure in the Chaos of pre-ordination, and night of their fore-beings. And if any have been so happy as truly to understand Christian annihilation, extasis, exolution, liquefaction, transformation, the kisse of the Spouse, gustation of God, and ingression into the divine shadow, they have already had an handsome anticipation of heaven; the glory of the world is surely over, and the earth in ashes unto them. (V, 170)

To those rare individuals living in and for purely spiritual truth, the fact of death poses none of the problems that so disturb ordinary men. But Browne, it must be stressed, does not offer this image of mystical otherworldliness as a prescriptive guide for actual living. Despite the specifically Christian lesson toward which the meditation on death leads, he never relinquishes his very human interest in the world and in the merely human, of which burial practices themselves are one manifestation. This representation of "pious spirits" reawakens, rather, an awareness of life under its eternal aspect. Though incapable of being sustained as man's usual attitude, it provides the sense of a final perspective.

In terms of its epistemology, then, the "action" of man's long quest through history for the "patent against oblivion," culminating in the anagnorisis of Christian faith, may be defined as follows. Man frames customs according to the best lights of his reason to avoid the consequences of death for his name, deeds, glory, and mortal remnants, but finds his devices unavailing before nature. Only when he learns to place his hope for immortality in faith does he free himself from the paths of custom and soar beyond the labyrinth of human ignorance and uncertainty to a plane secure from the destructive action of nature and time. Christian faith solves one part of the problem and dismisses the other, for in its context physical remains become "indifferencies" to the glory of salvation. There is no need, therefore, to concern oneself too precisely with the disposal of the body so long as it is done with decency.

> Christians have handsomely glossed the deformity of death, by careful consideration of the body, and civil rites which take off brutall terminations. And though they conceived all reparable by a resurrection, cast not off all care of enterrment. For since the ashes of Sacrifices burnt upon the Altar of God, were carefully carried out by the Priests, and deposed in a clean field; since they acknowledged their bodies to be the lodging of Christ, and temples of the holy Ghost, they devolved not all upon the sufficiency of soul existence; and therefore with long services and full solemnities concluded their last Exequies, wherein to all distinctions the Greek devotion seems most pathetically ceremonious. (IV, 157–58)

Because what is most valuable in man can neither be saved by material preservation nor destroyed by neglect of that preservation, human endeavors at immortality are doubly futile. Browne avoids, however, the smugness of conventional piety which heaps scorn on the blindness of those not privileged to possess Christian truth. He appreciates the significance of insights like that of Socrates (traditionally afforded a special place among the ancients because of his doctrine of the immortality of the soul and his martyrdom for belief in one God) who "was content that his friends should bury his body, so they would not think they buried *Socrates*, and regarding only his immortal part, was indifferent to be burnt or buried" (IV, 158). Chapter IV draws to a close on a note of the great good fortune of Christians as opposed to the uncertainty of even the noblest pagans.

> But all or most apprehensions rested in Opinions of some future being, which ignorantly or coldly beleeved, begat those perverted conceptions, Ceremonies, Sayings, which Christians pity or laught at. Happy are they, which live not in that disadvantage of time, when men could say little for futurity, but from reason. Whereby the noblest mindes fell often upon doubtfull deaths, and melancholly Dissolutions; With these hopes *Socrates* warmed his doubtfull spirits against that cold potion, and *Cato* before he durst give the fatall stroak spent part of the night in reading the immortality of *Plato*, thereby confirming his wavering hand unto the animosity of that attempt. (IV, 163)

At the same that "Christian invention hath chiefly driven at Rites, which speak hopes of another life, and hints of a Resurrection" (IV, 158), Christians do in fact attend to the form of their burial and the preservation of their names through monuments. Likewise, the pagan's misguided quest to preserve his soul-like part through allegedly rational burial customs evidences man's continuous recognition of something uniquely valuable in himself. Browne's perspective in *Urn Burial* is manifold. He reaches the crown of his art in offering the Christian solution to the fact of death for at least two reasons other than his acknowledged potency of style: first, his presentation of the theme as an action of discovery contributes the pleasure and force of originality to what was, after all, the most familiar verity of the age; second, Browne's conception of the issue reaches beyond the ethical commonplaces and the predictable assertions of faith upon which it necessarily rests.

The entire history of burial customs may be read as a prelude in shadowy and groping types to the knowledge of wherein immortality truly consists: "if the ancient Gentiles held not the immortality of their better part, and some subsistence after death; in severall rites, customes, actions and expressions, they contradicted their own opinions . . ." (IV, 158). However fruitless the unillumined efforts of pagans to protect the treasure within man, their sense of that treasure's existence was in itself a great thing. Splendor of burial rites admittedly stands at a double remove from the real way to perpetuity through salvation, but it satisfies impulses too deep to be denied. This explains why in practice Christians "though they conceived all reparable by a resurrection, cast not off all care of enterrment"—explains it better than the reason Browne offers explicitly here, that the body is the temple of the soul. There is after all another traditional, though not quite orthodox, Christian attitude which makes the body the prison-house of the soul.

These equivocal reverberations of a mind profoundly moved by the absolutes of faith but also much given to a very humane (as distinct from fideistic) skepticism may recall, too, that in the *Religio* Browne holds human traditions to be indifferent to salvation, abhors persecution and schism resulting from them, yet shows himself keenly sensitive to and dependent upon ceremony in his own religious life. The underlying principles of opposition in *Urn Burial* and in *Religio Medici* are very similar, as are the terms of their resolution. In one work Browne shows that only Christian faith, by illuminating the true nature of the soul and its salvation, can free man from a parochial and superstitious adherence to burial customs, because it makes the body an indifferency to salvation. Carnal remains become irrelevant to immortality rightly understood, just as in the *Religio* Browne shows that rigid Laudian prescription of religious customs and zealous Presbyterian proscription of them are irrelevant to the essentials of salvation and to the fabric of a true church. Browne thus solves the problem of *Urn Burial*, as he did that of the *Religio*, in the framework of the Platonic hierarchy of custom, nature, and Idea, the epistemological scale at one with the Christian system of value it helped to formulate. In the *Religio*, where this triad of knowledge served as a norm in the exploration of various intellectual issues, no final solutions were offered. In *Urn Burial*, Browne's process of inquiry continuously intimates and finally reaches its conclusion. But this ostensibly clear-cut answer is not without its elusive shading, the product of peculiarly human tensions that resist any perfect resolution.

3

I have attempted to read *Urn Burial* as a mimetic essay and have sought its excellence in an action which illuminates the structure of values and ideas upon which it rests. In doing so I have parted from earlier criticism which tended to look almost exclusively to the final chapter, and there primarily to stylistic merit, for the distinction of the work, and also from the attention more recently paid to the work as a totality by Professor Huntley, who interprets *Urn Burial* by setting it beside *The Garden of Cyrus*. The relation between the companion pieces will, as I promised, be considered after each has been examined individually. And in the interest of an integral approach the separate status usually conferred upon Chapter V has thus far been ignored. However, no discussion hoping to account with some degree of completeness for the success of *Urn Burial* can neglect the special achievement of Chapter V. It must indeed be recognized that without the extraordinary impact of the final chapter there would be much less critical motive for locating the causes of unity in this work. At the same time, seeing *Urn Burial* as a coherent whole can enhance our appreciation of Chapter V by enabling us to read it as more than a great coda. Crowning and resolving what has already been solidly built, its effect is heightened by what it stands upon. It will doubtless continue to be read by many as a detachable part for its purple phrases and compelling rhythms, much as the *Liebestod*, say, is for many what makes Wagner's *Tristan* worth listening to. But as the transcendent effect of Isolde's love-death is fully experienced only in relation to the long anguish of Tristan and to the other scenes of the opera, so the final chapter of *Urn Burial* best conveys its effect when experienced as the climax of an integral whole.

Chapter V penetrates the profoundest reaches of time and mortality; it opens, however, by carrying the reader back to the particular remnants.

> Now since these dead bones have already outlasted the living ones of *Methuselah*, and in a yard under ground, and thin walls of clay, out-worn all the strong and specious buildings above it; and quietly rested under the drums and tramplings of three conquests; What Prince can promise such diuturnity unto his Reliques, or might not gladly say,
>
> *Sic ego componi versus in ossa velim.*
>
> Time which antiquates Antiquities, and hath an art to make dust of all things, hath yet spared these *minor* Monuments. . . . (V, 164)

The juxtaposition of "these dead bones . . . in a yard under ground, and thin walls of clay" to "all the strong and specious buildings" establishes a trenchant contrast, since these frail relics of nature have proved more enduring than many imposing and pretentious works of man. (One cannot help but recall how Donne gets at a similar point in "The Canonization": "As well a well wrought urne becomes/The greatest ashes as halfe-acre tombes," where public grandiloquence is slighted for private lyric expression.) Finally, of course, neither the "dead bones" nor the "strong buildings" really triumph, since both are pathetically weak in the face of time and mortality. This contrast serves instead to arouse emotion as well as awareness in support of the values toward which Browne is working.

The graves of obscure, private individuals may be spared, allowing them at least a nameless perpetuity, while the grandiose monuments of the illustrious have suffered complete obliteration and their remains destruction. Indeed, great tombs may defeat the very end for which they were designed. "In vain we hope to be known by open and visible conservatories, when to be unknown was the means of their continuation and obscurity their protection" (V, 164).

In Chapter V, Browne encompasses the vanity of human wishes for perpetuation in a still larger irony: the destruction of Time itself. "Pagan vain-glories which thought the world might last for ever, had encouragement for ambition, and finding no *Atropos* unto the immortality of their Names, were never dampt with the necessity of oblivion" (V, 166). The Christian's knowledge that the world will not continue forever but has its appointed surcease renders the "Vain ashes . . . Emblemes of mortall vanities" (V, 165) even more vulnerable.[7] Realization that the world has run well past the half-way mark of its career accounts for a pervasive nostalgia; more of life and time lie completed in the past than remains to the future, "one face of *Janus* holds no proportion unto the other" (V, 166). Knowledge that the universe itself is dying tells man that those in whose memory he strives to live on will themselves be reduced to ashes — to ashes, like those in the urns, which serve finally as "Antidotes against pride, vainglory, and madding vices" (V, 165). The insistent question must shift then from how best to dispose of the dead and insure their memory to how to conduct life "in this setting part of time," when " 'tis too late to be ambitious"; for "the great mutations of the world are acted" (V, 166).

To this question there can be no clear-cut answer or positive course of action, other than the stance of Christian

[7] It should here be noted, however, that Browne did not lend literal credence to the traditional calculation of 6,000 years as the "determinable" duration of the world. See *Religio Medici*, I, 45, 46; *Vulgar Errors*, Bk. 6, chap. 1 (*Works*, II, 389–410).

Stoicism. Therefore, again and again Browne sounds thematic variations on the irony of personal ambition, the nothingness of human glory.

> There is no antidote against the *Opium* of time, which temporally considereth all things; Our Fathers finde their graves in our short memories, and sadly tell us how we may be buried in our Survivors. (V, 166)
>
> Oblivion is not to be hired: The greater part must be content to be as though they had not been, to be found in the Register of God, not in the record of man. Twenty seven Names make up the first story, and the recorded names ever since contain not one living Century. The number of the dead long exceedeth all that shall live. The night of time far surpasseth the day, and who knows when was the Æquinox? Every houre addes unto that current Arithmetique, which scarce stands one moment. And since death must be the *Lucina* of life, and even Pagans could doubt whether thus to live, were to dye. Since our longest Sunne sets at right descensions, and makes but winter arches, and therefore it cannot be long before we lie down in darknesse, and have our light in ashes. Since the brother of death daily haunts us with dying *memento's*, and time that grows old it self, bids us hope no long duration: Diuturnity is a dream and folly of expectation. (V, 167–68)
>
> . . . Others rather than be lost in the uncomfortable night of nothing, were content to recede into the common being, and make one particle of the publick soul of all things, which was no more than to return into their unknown and divine Originall again. Ægyptian ingenuity was more unsatisfied, continuing their bodies in sweet consistences, to attend the return of their souls. But all was vanity, feeding the winde, and folly. The Ægyptian Mummies, which *Cambyses* or time hath spared, avarice now consumeth. Mummie is become Merchandise,

> *Miszraim* cures wounds, and *Pharaoh* is sold for balsoms. (V, 168)

Despite the sad subject the tone is not despondent, as it often seems when Donne, for example, considers these themes. Browne's meditation on mortality is suffused by a witty gravity and weighty exuberance that communicate his own positive, almost cheerful, poise. The generation of energy and pleasure out of such melancholy matter stamps this writing as baroque art in the fullest sense. And the vast temporal perspective of these passages serves as a catalyst to fuse ideas in their universal aspect with detail drawn from the cultural tradition. Because Browne apprehends history almost as a personal experience, the thought that grows out of it — and the process of thought growing out of history is palpably conveyed — is strengthened by the depth of feeling latent in universal ideas.

The masterful achievement of the high style in Chapter V depends upon the confluence of many specifically technical resources of style.[8] While extended treatment of Browne's technique as such is outside the scope of this study, certain

[8] Discussions of Browne's prose style outnumber any other studies. In the tradition of impressionistic appreciation, the essays on Browne in the following retain interest: Walter Pater, *Appreciations* (London, 1889); Sir Leslie Stephen, *Hours in a Library*, 4 vols. (London, 1904), II, 1–41; George Saintsbury, *A History of English Prose Rhythm* (London, 1912); Lytton Strachey, *Books and Characters* (New York, 1922); Basil Anderton, *Sketches from a Library Window* (Cambridge, 1922). More technical studies include: Norton R. Tempest, "Rhythm in the Prose of Sir Thomas Browne," *Review of English Studies*, 3 (1927): 308–18; Edward L. Parker, "The Cursus in Sir Thomas Browne," *PMLA*, 53 (1938): 1037–53; Dietrich Bischoff, *Sir Thomas Browne (1605–1682) als Stilkünstler* (Heidelberg, 1943); Michael F. Moloney, "Metre and *Cursus* in Sir Thomas Browne's Prose," *Journal of English and Germanic Philology*, 58 (1959): 60–67; William Whallon, "Hebraic Synonymy in Sir Thomas Browne," *E L H*, 28 (1961): 335–52. Morris Croll's articles are, of course, relevant and "The Baroque Style in Prose," cited above, bears specifically on Browne's use of the loose Senecan style in *Religio Medici*; see also George Williamson, *The Senecan Amble* (Chicago, 1951). More comprehensive treatments of Browne's thought in relation to his style include: F. P. Wilson, *Seven-*

features relevant to our interest in the thematic substance of Chapter V may be described apart from any underlying theory.

As we have noted, the phrases of Browne that live on in the ear and the mind bear a similarity to the aphorisms of Bacon, but are more witty, even consciously playful, and establish ampler patterns of rhythm than do Bacon's pointed counsels and *aperçus*. Elaborate schemes of sound, rejected by the proponents of Senecanism as an abuse of the Ciceronian oratorical style, are nevertheless present in Browne's ardent meditative prose. So far from abandoning "words" for "things" Browne exploits the independent associations words *qua* words can awaken both through their frame of cultural reference and their intrinsic sound values. The opening paragraph of Chapter V, for example, quoted and considered above, reinforces its ironic thematic contrast by projecting that contrast at the level of diction. The long resounding words, chiefly Latin, embody what the curt monosyllables, chiefly native, must oppose and undercut; and yet, despite the irony directed against them, their beauty enhances and confirms their value, at least imaginatively. This balancing of feeling and attitude through diction is common, of course, to all artistically effective prose, but Browne handles this oblique and delicate device with a degree of formal deliberation usually reserved to poetry. And the concentrated use of devices even more dependent upon the play of sound, such as the vibrant continuants *m* and *n*, justifies in stricter terms the label of prose-poet so frequently applied to the Browne of Chapter V of *Urn Burial.*

On the other hand, Browne's prose-poem lacks sensuously vivid imagery and also the profusion of figures and tropes recommended for the high style by classical rhetoric. The

teenth Century Prose (Berkeley, 1960), chap. 4, on *Urn Burial* and *The Garden of Cyrus*; the superlative essay by Austin Warren, "The Style of Sir Thomas Browne," *Kenyon Review*, 13 (1951): 674–87, which analyzes the various levels of style in Browne's major works as related to their subject and discursive purpose; Frank L. Huntley, *Sir Thomas Browne*, pp. 117–34, 218–22.

figures one does find tend to be great archetypal symbols ("Life is a pure flame, and we live by an invisible Sun within us" [V, 169].) and derive from the ingrained habits of thought and expression in centuries of philosophy, theology, and divine poetry rather than from any teeming power of fresh invention. The texture of Browne's high style might be better accounted for, then, by reference to patristic rhetoric than in terms of the classical-humanist tradition. Professor Huntley has shown how certain clusters of images take on symbolic value in relation to the complementary themes of *Urn Burial* and *The Garden of Cyrus*; in my estimate, he correctly does not stress these images as primary to the structure or effect of the companion pieces. Such patterns of mentioning are less the cause of unity in *Urn Burial*, still less the locus of poetic pleasure, than they are artistically consistent projections at the level of language of a thematic direction determined elsewhere. They are symptoms and confirmations of a unified inspiration and purpose in *Urn Burial* rather than the source of unity. Finally, in so far as style may be talked about as a detachable element, the unique density and power legions of readers have found in Browne's prose texture (as distinct from his music) are created primarily by a cultural contextualism in which characters, places, and events in the Bible, history, and ancient literature are invested with an emblematically rich, yet controlled, suggestiveness. Because this learned imagination is essential to the fabric of Browne's prose, the merely verbal contextualism of the New Criticism does not offer an adequate method of analysis or basis for appreciation.

What is perhaps most remarkable about Browne's sustained flight in the high style is that it is also a continuous tissue of irony. Nowhere is Browne more caught up in the mood of Christian Stoicism; yet nowhere does he summon up more fully the moving eloquence of the grand style. So far from corroding its object, the irony embellishes what the whole tenor of *Urn Burial* is exposing and rejecting. Consider this sentence, the concluding one of the paragraph beginning "There is nothing strictly immortall, but immortality," in which Browne makes his explicit declaration that "the sufficiency of Christian Immortality frustrates all earthly glory, and the quality of either state after death makes a folly of posthumous memory":

> But man is a Noble Animal, splendid in ashes, and pompous in the grave, solemnizing Nativities and Deaths with equall lustre, nor omitting Ceremonies of bravery, in the infamy of his nature. (V, 169)

The superb effect of this derives from the simultaneous elevation and undercutting of the same object. Its relation to the argument of this paragraph reveals no unconscious division of mind; nor is the praise simply an outflow of emotion, the irony purely a function of intellect. The admiration and the irony are each the response of a full play of sensibility. While Browne knows and feels *sub specie aeternitatis* the absurdity of what men have sought in burial customs, he can also see and appreciate the nobility of their motive.

Browne's irony is positive and creative and thus compatible with sublimity. It is no sharp instrument for rationalizing emotion, for confining it to the bounds of logic and casting away whatever will not fit within those limits. From the standpoint of Christian truth, "Ceremonies of bravery" are fit targets for ironic reduction. But they are also man's assertion of the value of his affective and imaginative life, an assertion that may, as *Urn Burial* demonstrates, find little support in hard fact, but which Browne instinctively and incurably respects and to which he therefore pays the tribute of the grand style. While his norm for judgment is the absolute of Christian truth, he can still maintain a stance, a sympathy, and a sense of commitment that are wholly human in a way that Donne, for example, rarely can in his funeral sermons. This is why *Urn Burial* avoids the crabbed accent and monotony of the medieval *contemptus mundi*, almost invariably associated with the theme of mortality and "vanity, vanity, all is vanity." The melancholy appropriate to Browne's theme never descends to despair, but maintains a healthy balance. This inviolable poise in the face of searchingly examined contraries — custom and nature, reason and faith, the human and divine, the relative and absolute — is an important element of continuity between *Religio Medici* and *Urn Burial.* Each work explores the intellectual and emotional certainties and ambiguities existing between such opposites; each discovers through its subject matter, theme, and action the value as well as the limits of the peculiarly human. It is hardly surprising, therefore, that Browne's profoundest ironies do not express themselves as harshly mocking thrusts at human pride, ignorance, and error by a detached and all-knowing observer. Maintaining instead a balance of detachment and affective involvement, Browne encourages us to be happy participants in the human condition.

CHAPTER VIII

THE GARDEN OF CYRUS: A PLATONIC EXERCISE

> – Quincunxes in Heaven above, Quincunxes in Earth below, & Quincunxes in the water beneath the Earth; Quincunxes in Deity, Quincunxes in the mind of man; Quincunxes in bones, in optic nerves, in Roots of Trees, in leaves, in petals, in every thing![1]
>
> SAMUEL TAYLOR COLERIDGE, 1804

THIS famous response to *The Garden of Cyrus* – a blend of astonishment, uncertain admiration, and just a shade of impatience – has doubtless been seconded by countless readers less sympathetic to Browne than Coleridge. Browne everywhere intimates that the quincunx or five-figure according to which the ancients laid out their gardens is a type of the universal mathematical principle which is the basis, subject, method, and conclusion of this treatise. Toward the close of Chapter IV, he identifies the *Timaeus* as his source for the five-pointed figure.

> Of this Figure *Plato* made choice to illustrate the motion of the soul, both of the world and man; while he delivereth that God divided the whole conjunction length-wise, according to the figure of a Greek χ, and then turning it about reflected it into a circle; By the circle implying the uniform motion of the first Orb, and by the right lines, the planetical

[1] *Coleridge on the Seventeenth Century*, ed. Brinkley, p. 449.

> and various motions within it. And this also with application unto the soul of man, which hath a double aspect, one right, whereby it beholdeth the body, and objects without; another circular and reciprocal, whereby it beholdeth it self. The circle declaring the motion of the indivisible soul, simple, according to the divinity of its nature, and returning into it self; the right lines respecting the motion pertaining unto sense, and vegetation, and the central decussation, the wondrous connexion of the severall faculties conjointly in one substance. And so conjoyned the unity and duality of the soul, and made out the three substances so much considered by him; That is, the indivisible or divine, the divisible or corporeal, and that third, which was the *Systasis* or harmony of those two, in the mystical decussation.
>
> And if that were clearly made out which *Justin Martyr* took for granted, this figure hath had the honour to characterize and notifie our blessed Saviour, as he delivereth in that borrowed expression from *Plato*; *Decussavit eum in universo,* the hint whereof he would have *Plato* derive from the figure of the brazen Serpent, and to have mistaken the Letter X for T, whereas it is not improbable, he learned these and other mystical expressions in his Learned Observations of Ægypt, where he might obviously behold the Mercurial characters, the handed crosses, and other mysteries not thoroughly understood in the sacred Letter X, which being derivative from the Stork, one of the ten sacred animals, might be originally Ægyptian, and brought into *Greece* by *Cadmus* of that Countrey. (IV, 220–21)

Throughout *The Garden of Cyrus* Browne hints at the mysterious significance of the quincunx, even in its most mundane appearances. In tracing the origin and deepest meaning of the quincunx, as well as its countless examples, Browne engages in the kind of Pythagoreanism which is an inseparable and salient part of his Platonic outlook. The habit of scanning the entire visible and invisible world for its continuous network of corresponding symbols bodying forth the one truth of religion permeates *The Garden* more completely than it does any other of Browne's works.

In this mathematical symbol Professor Huntley finds the secret of the unity of the companion pieces, the key to *Urn Burial* as well as *The Garden of Cyrus*: the relation of "the Greek theta, θ, which is *thanatos* or death to the circle [that] is God, perfection, immortality," and to "the cross, the only antidote (in Browne's Christian mind) to the opium of time." [2] Browne himself had anticipated the puzzlement that his pairing and ordering of the two treatises in the volume of 1658 might stir. In the dedicatory epistle to *The Garden*, addressed to Nicholas Bacon, he explained:

> That we conjoyn these parts of different Subjects, or that this should succeed the other; Your judgement will admit without impute of incongruity; Since the delightfull World comes after death, and Paradise succeeds the Grave. Since the verdant state of things is the Symbole of the Resurrection, and to flourish in the state of Glory, we must first be sown in corruption. Beside the ancient practise of Noble Persons, to conclude in Garden-Graves, and Urnes themselves of old, to be wrapt up in flowers and garlands. (*Works*, I, 176–77)

Professor Huntley develops the significance of Browne's remarks and shows that the complementary design of the two works is not that of companion or alternate views, but of an ascending sequence "from the lower or elemental *Urn Burial* (death) to the higher or celestial *Garden of Cyrus*, the 'numerical character' of reality (life)." [3] To spell out the details of this interpretation would require a rehearsal of Huntley's entire study; instead, I will assume that every serious reader is familiar with this now classic analysis. Since

[2] *Sir Thomas Browne*, p. 208.
[3] *Ibid.*, p. 209.

I find Huntley's analysis brilliant and altogether convincing as analysis, I do not wish to argue against it, except in one respect. I disagree with the assumption that Browne's consciously intended and discernible design must be the effect actually produced by the works themselves and, more important, that the relative roles Browne evidently envisaged for his compositions are in fact the roles they *do* play and measure the value that attaches to them. It is, then, with Huntley's assumptions and the conclusions he draws from his simultaneous analysis of the companion pieces, not with the conduct of the analysis itself, that I take issue. And in all fairness to Professor Huntley, he seems perfectly aware that he does not really touch the question of critical evaluation. For while he asserts at the outset that "Browne's scientific central chapter in *The Garden* is the heart of the whole matter . . . [and that] The design of *The Garden* . . . is primary, leading up to the very mind of the Infinite Geometrician . . . ," he recognizes that "of Browne's twin essays, readers will continue to prefer *Urn Burial*."[4] This does not mean that interpretive analysis is irrelevant to evaluation, but only that their relation is not a simple and direct proportion. And while I am interested primarily in the critical challenge posed by Huntley, it is with analysis that I must begin.

2

Browne's epistemological assumptions are more patent in *The Garden of Cyrus* than in any other of his works. The title page announces that his strategy will be to pursue his subject through the three planes of knowledge: *The Garden of Cyrus or, The Quincunciall, Lozenge, or Net-Work Plantations of the Ancients, Artificially, Naturally, Mystically Considered.* The number five, exemplified in the gardens of the ancients, functions in its guise of the quincunx as a leitmotif running through the three levels of experience and knowledge: *artificial* (human customs and arts), *natural* (natural phenomena), *mystical* (Idea, spirit, faith). The sequence of content in the five chapters corresponds exactly to the order

[4] *Ibid.*, pp. 208 and 222.

of these ascending planes of knowledge and maintains a significant symmetry. Chapters I and II are devoted to the artificial considerations; the occurrence of the quincunx in living organisms is the subject of the third and longest chapter; Chapter IV expatiates on the aesthetic delights and practical benefits of the quincuncial pattern and concludes with the explanation quoted above, that "of this Figure *Plato* made choice to illustrate the motion of the soul . . ."; Chapter V rises to the mystical consideration of five as a secret and mysterious archetypal principle, appearing in the Bible and other sacred writings, imitated in nature and also by man in various arts and customs.

As the Norfolk urns generated Browne's learned speculations and religious meditation on death, so gardens are appropriate for an excursion into the ubiquitous manifestations of the quincunx — the natural structural principle symbolic of the soul and thus of life itself. In the first paragraph of the dedication Browne makes it clear that his real subject is not actual gardens but what gardens stand for: ". . . I that was never master of any considerable garden, had not attempted this Subject. But the Earth is the Garden of Nature, and each fruitfull Countrey a Paradise" (*Works*, I, 175). The garden is thus recognized as both a natural and a traditional symbol for the fullness of the creation. It comprehends, moreover, the fusion of nature and art, since the generative force in nature, whose source is the overflowing divine love, cooperates in gardens with man's will to shape nature into accord with his own rational discipline, itself of divine origin. At the same time Browne is aware that certain aesthetic and moral tensions between nature and art are epitomized in the garden. He remarks to Nicholas Bacon in the dedication:

> You have wisely ordered your vegetable delights, beyond the reach of exception. The Turks who passt their dayes in Gardens here, will have Gardens also hereafter, and delighting in Flowers on earth, must have Lillies and Roses in Heaven. In Garden Delights 'tis not easie to hold a Mediocrity;

> that insinuating pleasure is seldome without some extremity. The Antients venially delighted in flourishing Gardens; Many were Florists that knew not the true use of a Flower; and in *Plinies* dayes none had directly treated of that Subject. Some commendably affected Plantations of venemous Vegetables, some confined their delights unto single plants, and *Cato* seemed to dote upon Cabbadge; While the Ingenuous delight of Tulipists stands saluted with hard language, even by their own Professors. (*Works*, I, 176)

Characteristically, though, Browne's stress falls upon the possibilities for typological and iconological interpretations of the quincunx:

> That the first Plantations not long after the Floud were disposed after this manner [i.e. the quincunx], the generality and antiquity of this order observed in Vineyards, and Wine plantations, affordeth some conjecture. And since from judicious enquiry, *Saturn* who divided the world between his three sonnes, who beareth a Sickle in his hand, who taught the plantations of Vines, the setting, grafting of trees, and the best part of Agriculture, is discovered to be *Noah*, whether this early dispersed Husbandry in Vineyards had not its Originall in that Patriarch, is no such Paralogicall doubt. (I, 184)

Garden plantations were thus a domain of custom not subject to the chaotic variety of burial practices. We may recall that in Chapter V of *Urn Burial* Browne speaks of "*Pyramids, Arches, Obelisks*, [as] the irregularities of vainglory, and wilde enormities of ancient magnanimity" (V, 170). From the chance-ridden architecture of these vain human monuments, Browne carries us in *The Garden of Cyrus* to a mathematical symbol for the eternal life of the soul.

Nor is the quincunx confined to man's ordering of nature;

other constructs of custom reveal the same mysterious design. In Chapter II Browne sets out to discover this figure "in sundry artificiall contrivances and manuall operations" (II, 185). Examples collected from architecture, the crowns of princes and popes, the beds and other domestic furniture of the ancients, the jeweller's craft, the battle deployments of the Romans, the plans for ancient cities, and the very stone tablets upon which God wrote the Law on Sinai testify to the continuous employment of the quincunx in all the human arts. This examination of widely diverse objects, linked by a common unifying principle to each other and to the source of all unity, places human custom in an altogether different light than in *Urn Burial*. Burial customs offer a sad history of discord, failure, and alienation from truth. The "Quincunciall" arrangement of gardens stands for and participates in the happy record of man's rational and intuitive observance of this principle of order, while in *Urn Burial* human custom is everywhere at odds with nature. Chapter III of *The Garden of Cyrus* moves on to the quincunx as a structural principle in the leaves and seminal parts of plants and stresses the harmonious link between custom and nature. And in Chapter V, where Browne carries his discourse up to the realms of religious mystery and cosmic structure, the universal harmony and epistemological optimism symbolized by the quincunx achieve their fullest resonance.

The Platonic concepts of custom, nature, and Idea as ascending planes of knowledge on the way to truth provide, then, a fundamental relation between the companion pieces. In *Urn Burial* we saw truth attained as the result of a long intellectual action which imitated the historical process of man's liberation from dependence upon futile burial customs for his preservation. By focusing upon what it is seeking to exorcise rather than upon the familiar norm of Christian truth toward which it moves, *Urn Burial* achieves an aesthetic obliqueness (not unlike that of satire) which demands and repays imaginative collaboration on the part of the reader. *The Garden of Cyrus* represents by explicit statement and in its organization the continuous presence of truth in the realms of custom, nature and Idea, as manifest in the mystical symbol of the quincunx. Instead of truth seized upon and wrested by struggle we have in *The Garden* a serene and unencumbered ascent along a path fully charted from the outset. To recognize this is, I would suggest, to recognize an important reason for the relative inferiority of the second treatise. *The Garden of Cyrus* makes a more explicit, but less significant, use of the triadic scheme of knowledge than does *Urn Burial* or *Religio Medici*, employs it, indeed, as the speculum into which the universe is organized. In *The Garden* the formal structure of the Platonic hierarchy, divested of its inherent tensions, simply frames the areas of experience through which the quincunx is to be traced. The significance of the quincunx as symbol and symptom of the harmony and unity infused from the One into the world precludes any treatment of the opposition intrinsic to the system of norms defined by the three planes of knowledge. It is therefore hardly surprising that Browne's epistemological assumptions in *The Garden of Cyrus* result in a relatively uncompelling treatment.

The Garden of Cyrus implies throughout a Timaean principle of harmony binding the three realms into a continuous and unbroken chain. Browne is as playful as he is persistent in this self-prescribed Platonic exercise. Amusing and visionary though it can often be, it also skirts dangerously close to becoming a tiresome game. For he is whimsically self-indulgent as he sports intellectually and spiritually at his ease in an epistemological utopia all too single-dimensioned and predictable. Now I do not mean to argue that the thematic center or the outcome of a work should not be evident quite early or even at once. Indeed, if the "end" is not in some sense present throughout, the author is treating his material dishonestly or, at best, with unconvincing arbitrariness. But however foreseeable its conclusion or constantly visible its thematic burden, a work of literature must invest the process of getting there with some kind of interest, that is, with conflict. Otherwise, the result cannot, in fact, be a result at all, a product coming out of something in which it is inherent but from which it is also borne as a discovery. Without a principle of tension or opposition — dramatic or intellectual or both — there can be no process, since nothing ever really begins. A static object, there from the outset, is notoriously difficult to represent satisfyingly, since literature depends upon movement and development.

3

In the previous chapter I tried to show how Browne cast his meditation on death into a mimetic essay whose potency, eloquence, and form are the authentic expression of profound tensions of thought and feeling. *The Garden of Cyrus*, I submit, is an essentially encyclopedic work. It represents a kind of discourse and invites a kind of reading more like that of *Vulgar Errors* than of *Urn Burial.* In Books II through VII of *Vulgar Errors*, Browne, having set forth the causes of error in Book I, organizes the various branches of natural phenomena and man-made works according to the accepted scientific classifications of the day. His purpose was to explain and dispel the multitude of errors that had crept into knowledge over the centuries and to restore, as fully as possible with the aid of reason, observation, and experiment, the undistorted body of truth. Similarly, Browne organizes *The Garden of Cyrus* according to the tripartite Platonic division of experience and knowledge and examines, at their appropriate levels, artificial, natural, and mysterious examples of the quincunx.

Vulgar Errors is a massive encyclopedia of the manifold vagaries of superstition and human reason; *The Garden of Cyrus* is an encyclopedic essay that traces the unity of truth in every corner of nature and the arts, heaven and earth. Because of their mechanically neat division and ordering of content, as well as their singleness of discursive purpose, both works have a readily discernible surface organization — a trait that hardly distinguishes *Urn Burial* and, still less, *Religio Medici.* But neither of these encyclopedic works is informed by structure such as signifies a process of organic creation; their form is simply a mold to facilitate a treatment in accordance with a predetermined and explicit scheme of interest.

The style, tone, and shapeliness of *The Garden of Cyrus* definitely command attention to it as a literary composition to a degree that *Vulgar Errors* does not approach. And, at the simplest level of experience of the reader, the sequence of content in *The Garden* counts a great deal for the desired effect of the work, while in *Vulgar Errors*, after Book I, or the "General Part," the sequence in which we read matters as little as it does in any reference book. *The Garden* is unmistakably the product of a literary temperament; it presents, also, more clearly and consistently, Browne's habit of Platonic interpretation of the universe, free from other infusions of thought, than do any of his three other major works. It is indispensable for understanding the mind and imagination of Sir Thomas Browne; had he not written it, our picture of him would lack clear and full delineation of a whole dimension of his temper, and indeed, of his age. The importance of *The Garden* for these reasons is well established and nothing in my own analysis is meant to detract from its significance or its beauty in these terms. But I do submit that the questions of its thematic relation to *Urn Burial*, its literary value as compared to *Urn Burial*, and its independent significance cannot all be answered in the same terms.

To insist upon the superior literary achievement of *Urn Burial* vis-à-vis its companion essay is not, of course, to do anything new; few readers and critics do not concur with this judgment. The point must nonetheless be attended to, since the interpretation of these works cannot be undertaken apart from their evaluation. Unless the primacy of value and the independence of *Urn Burial* are presupposed, it is impossible to entertain a reading such as I have offered, since to assume a mutual and equal relation is to confine the possible significance of *Urn Burial* to the range of *The Garden*. Either assumption can be no more than a provisional *modus operandi*, to be checked finally against what the analysis itself can demonstrate.

Professor Huntley, working from the questions: "Why were

these two works published together? And why in that order?" was able to show connections between *Urn Burial* and *The Garden of Cyrus* which spell out quite brilliantly Browne's own suggestive hints. But does the particular character of the thematic relation – sequential stages of the ascent from death to life, represented through motifs and images symbolizing these elemental concepts – mean that *The Garden* is aesthetically superior to *Urn Burial* and that it provides the essential key to the fullest possible understanding of that work? I think not. If, on the basis of thematic meaning, we assume at the outset or conclude after analysis a sequential, hierarchical relation, we still have given no automatically determinate critical answer such as Professor Huntley implies. One has only to refer to companion poems like *L'Allegro* and *Il Penseroso* or Donne's two *Anniversaries* to see that the degree of ethical approval or positive value attaching to the subject matter of the "celestial" members of such pairs is scarcely relevant to their relative aesthetic value and humanistic interest. We may assume that Milton was more profoundly attracted to the contemplative mode of existence under the aegis of Melancholy than to Mirth, and some critics have accordingly argued that the themes of the two poems are related as a hierarchical ascent rather than as alternative choices. But does this mean that *L'Allegro* is inferior as a poem to *Il Penseroso*? Does such a thematic reading even undercut the ethical appeal and validity of the images of pastoral pleasure in *L'Allegro*? With Donne's *Anniversaries*, where a companionate ethical relation is out of the question, the anatomizing of a dying world in a *contempus mundi* followed by an ascent to the joys of heaven does not in itself speak one way or the other to the interest or value of these poems. And to recall the great *locus classicus* of this critical issue, that Dante represents heaven as an infinitely (and literally so!) better and happier *place* than hell is axiomatic; but that the *Paradiso* is a better, more interesting, or more essential work of poetry – or part of the *Commedia* – than the *Inferno* is, to put it mildly, another question.

All this is obvious enough. What is crucial is that *Urn Burial*, so far from depending, as Huntley insists, upon *The Garden of Cyrus* for a full interpretation, is actually impoverished of much of its meaning and effect if we limit it to what a mutual relation of theme and symbols with its sequel can reveal.[5] For if we confine our response to the general subject of mortality, seen simply as the opposite of what *The Garden* deals with, we preclude appreciation of the work's unique richness. The particular vision of *Urn Burial*, like all visions of the human condition, has its alternatives and its complements, but I think we have seen that it cannot be considered partial or incomplete in the sense that Professor Huntley's analysis implies. Certainly, it does not need to be redeemed or put into just perspective by *The Garden of Cyrus*. For its melancholy is unallied to crippling despair and issues in an effect of wholeness and balanced acceptance. Its sequel, though designed for the joyous themes of life and resurrection, remains depthless. Since the kind of joyousness *The Garden of Cyrus* strives for is basically serious, it is not conveyed convincingly or satisfyingly in an extended Timaean exercise, bordering on jest, however gracefully sustained.

[5] Though Milton's epics are quite disproportionate to each other in size, scope, and genre, they can serve as a pointed, if extreme, illustration of my argument. The entire treatment of the Fall in *Paradise Lost* as well as Michael's prophecy to Adam in Book XII foreshadows that the central action in a poem dealing with Paradise regained would be Chirst's withstanding the temptations offered by Satan rather than the atonement on the Cross. And in reading *Paradise Regained* we often discover illuminating parallels and contrasts of detail, action, character and theme with the earlier poem. But such continuities as exist between the two works, as well as the explicit relation of their subjects, are superficial compared to what the integral relation of elements within *Paradise Lost* reveals. The demonstration of the richness and subtlety of Milton's great epic during the past two decades would certainly have been precluded by the critical assumption that *Paradise Regained* provides an adequate key for the analysis and comprehension of *Paradise Lost*. Indeed, recent critcism, in showing how the theme "Paradise regained" is worked from first to last into the poetic fabric and dramatic structure of the epic, implies a treatment of that theme in *Paradise Lost* more significant and more moving than in the poem which bears that subject as its title.

4

I have employed Sir Thomas Browne's Platonic epistemology to illuminate both the material and the formal structure of his major compositions. This approach reveals, I believe, some pertinent continuities of mind and art among his works. Yet, what is finally most important is the distinctive achievement of the individual writings – what, strictly speaking, we may call their originality. We have seen that the kind and degree of thematic and formal unity varies among Browne's works. In *Religio Medici*, the Christian and Platonic paradigm of knowledge gives rise to the norms which endow the treatment of religious, philosophic, and scientific issues with a structure of thought – a structure largely unrelated to discursive organization. Accordingly, the *Religio* requires chiefly material analysis, the application of the history of ideas to render its heterogeneous observations and opinions intelligible within the framework of their relevant intellectual outlook. In *Urn Burial*, the formal purpose of the work absorbs and shapes the particular data and reflections with a completeness that signifies an organically conceived and highly finished literary creation. As in a fictive work, it is the sequaciousness and self-coherence of *Urn Burial* that are decisive for its thematic and formal wholeness, while the extrinsic reference of its content is of subordinate importance. *The Garden of Cyrus*, invested with an a priori unity of thought and organization, beautifully expatiates its stated theme as represented in the pervasive figure of the quincunx, but fails, for this reader at least, to generate the kind of significant form and the quality of interest we discover in these other works. Though not to the same degree, *The Garden* is, like *Vulgar Errors*, more akin to encyclopedic than to mimetic form.

This primarily analytic and interpretive study leads us, then, to evaluative conclusions, though scarcely to revolutionary ones. The judgment of Browne's many perceptive and sensitive readers, past and present, is pretty much in agreement about the peculiar eminence of *Religio Medici* and *Urn Burial* among the entire corpus of this author's work. To say that this is so because of their greater stylistic interest and merit is perfectly true, but such a statement also begs the question—the very question that this study, operating on the assumption that style is an effect and not the cause of excellence, ultimately addresses itself to. For Browne could not engage us as he does merely through the independent appeal of his literary surface, but only through a potency of style borne of potency of vision. This engagement of thought and feeling is most markedly present in *Religio Medici* and in *Urn Burial*, each of which represents in a unique way the disproportion among the human, the phenomenal, and the divine and the poignancy of the sustained opposition among these divided levels of truth.

APPENDIX

APPENDIX

A Chronology of the Life and Literary Career of Sir Thomas Browne

1605, October 19	Birth in Cheapside, London, son of Thomas Browne, a mercer, and his wife Anne Garroway
1613	Death of Browne's father
1614(?)	Marriage of Browne's mother to Sir Thomas Dutton
1616, August 20	Admission to Winchester College
1616–23	Student at Winchester until age of eighteen
1623, December 5	Matriculation at Broadgates Hall, Oxford
1624, August 5	Delivery of Latin oration in ceremonies inaugurating Broadgates Hall as Pembroke College
1626, June 31	Admission to the degree of B.A. at Oxford
1629, June 11	Admission to the degree of M.A. at Oxford
Summer(?)	Visit to Ireland with his step-father
1629(?)–33	Medical studies at Montpellier, Padua, and Leyden
1633, December 21	Admission to M.D. degree at Leyden
1634–37	Medical apprenticeship at Oxfordshire and Yorkshire(?)
1634–35	Composition of first draft of *Religio Medici*
1637, July 11	Admission to M.D. degree at Oxford
1637	Establishment in medical practice at Norwich – Browne's home for the rest of his life
1641	Marriage to Dorothy Mileham, who bore him twelve children
1642	*Religio Medici*, two unauthorized editions published

1642, December 21–22	Sir Kenelm Digby reads *Religio Medici* and writes his "Observations" to the Earl of Dorset
1643	*Religio Medici*, authorized edition published. Digby's Observations on *Religio Medici* published
1644	Publication of Latin translation of *Religio Medici* by John Merryweather
1646	*Pseudodoxia Epidemica (Vulgar Errors)* published
1650	Expanded and revised edition of *Vulgar Errors* published
1656(?)	Composition of *A Letter to a Friend* Composition of *Hydriotaphia, Urn Burial*
1658	*Urn Burial* and *The Garden of Cyrus* published in the same volume
1664	Testifies at Bury St. Edmunds in witchcraft trial of Amy Duny and Rose Cullender, who were convicted and hanged
1667	Composition of *Brampton Urns*
1671, September	Knighted by Charles II during royal visit to Norwich
1672	Publication of sixth edition (last in Browne's life), corrected and enlarged, of *Vulgar Errors*
1682, October 19	Death on seventy-seventh anniversary of his birth
1683	*Certain Miscellany Tracts* (edited by Archbishop Tenison) published
1690	*A Letter to a Friend* published
1712	*Posthumous Works* with John Whitefoot's *Minutes for the Life of Sir Thomas Browne* published
1716	*Christian Morals* (edited by Browne's daughter, Mrs. Elizabeth Lyttleton, and by John Jeffery, Archdeacon of Norwich) published at Cambridge

BIBLIOGRAPHY

BIBLIOGRAPHY

Agrippa, Henry Cornelius. *Three Books of Occult Philosophy*, trans. J. F. London, 1651.

———. *The Vanity of Arts and Sciences.* London, 1676.

Anderson, Fulton H. *Francis Bacon.* Los Angeles, 1962.

Anderton, Basil. *Sketches from a Library Window.* Cambridge, 1922.

Andrewes, Lancelot. *Ninety-six Sermons*, ed. J. P. Wilson. 5 vols. Oxford, 1841–43.

Apuleius, Lucius. *Works.* London: Bohn's Classical Library, 1878.

Aquinas, Thomas. *Summa theologica*, trans. Fathers of the English Dominican Province. 2d ed. 22 vols. London, 1917–27.

Aristotle. *Works*, trans. under the editorship of W. D. Ross. 11 vols. Oxford, 1908–31.

Augustine, Bishop of Hippo. *The City of God*, trans. John Healey (1610), 3 vols. London: Temple Classics, 1903.

———. *The City of God*, trans. John Healey with notes by Lodovico Vives. 2d ed. London, 1620.

———. *Writings of Saint Augustine.* 17 vols. New York, 1947–59.

Bacon, Francis. *Bacon*, ed. R. F. Jones. New York, 1937.

———. *Works*, ed. J. Spedding and R. L. Ellis. 7 vols. London, 1857–59.

Baker, Herschel. *The Dignity of Man.* Cambridge, Mass., 1947.

———. *The Wars of Truth.* Cambridge, Mass., 1952.

Bellarmine, Robert. *The Ascent of the Mind to God by a Ladder of Things Created* (Douay, 1616). London, 1928.

Bennett, Joan. *Sir Thomas Browne*. Cambridge, 1962.

Bischoff, Dietrich. *Sir Thomas Browne (1605–1682) als Stilkünstler*. Heidelberg, 1943.

Blau, Joseph L. "Browne's Interest in Cabalism," *PMLA*, 49 (1934): 963–64.

———. *The Christian Interpretation of the Cabala in the Renaissance*. New York, 1944.

Bonaventura, St. *The Mind's Road to God*, trans. George Boas. New York: The Library of Liberal Arts, 1953.

Bottrall, Margaret. *Every Man a Phoenix: Studies in Seventeenth-Century Autobiography*. London, 1958.

Bréhier, Emile. *The Philosophy of Plotinus*, trans. J. Thomas. Chicago, 1958.

Brinkley, Roberta F. (ed.). *Coleridge on the Seventeenth Century*. Durham, N.C., 1955.

Browne, Sir Thomas. *Works*, ed. Simon Wilkin. 4 vols. London, 1835–36.

———. *Works*, ed. Sir Geoffrey Keynes. 2d ed. 4 vols. Chicago, 1964.

———. *Religio Medici*, ed. W. A. Greenhill. London, 1881.

———. *Religio Medici and other Works*, ed. L. C. Martin. Oxford, 1964.

Burton, Robert. *The Anatomy of Melancholy*, ed. Floyd Dell and Paul Jordan-Smith. New York, 1951.

Burtt, E. A. *The Metaphysical Foundations of Modern Physical Science*. Rev. ed. London, 1932.

Bush, Douglas. *English Literature in the Earlier Seventeenth Century*. Rev. ed. Oxford, 1962.

Calvin, John. *Institutes of the Christian Religion*, trans. John Allen. 6th ed. 2 vols. Philadelphia, 1921.

Campagnac, E. T. (ed.). *The Cambridge Platonists*. Oxford, 1901.

Casaubon, Meric. *A Treatise of Use and Custome*. London, 1638.

Cassirer, Ernst. "Giovanni Pico della Mirandola," *Journal of the History of Ideas*, 3 (1942): 123–44, 319–46.

———. *The Platonic Renaissance in England*, trans. James P. Pettegrove. Austin, 1953.

Cassirer, Ernst, Paul O. Kristeller, and J. H. Randall, Jr. (eds.). *The Renaissance Philosophy of Man.* Chicago, 1948.

Catalogue of the Libraries of the Learned Sir Thomas Brown, and Dr. Edward Brown, his son. London, 1710–11.

Cawley, Robert R. "Sir Thomas Browne and His Reading," *PMLA*, 48 (1933): 426–70.

Chalmers, Gordon K. "Hieroglyphs and Sir Thomas Browne," *Virginia Quarterly Review*, 11 (1935): 547–60.

———. "Sir Thomas Browne, True Scientist," *Osiris*, 2 (1936): 28–79.

———. "'That Universal and Publick Manuscript,'" *Virginia Quarterly Review*, 26 (1950): 414–30.

Chastel, A. *Marsile Ficin et l'art.* Paris, 1954.

Cheynell, Francis. *Chillingworthi novissima.* London, 1644.

Chillingworth, William. *Works.* 3 vols. London, 1820.

Clement of Alexandria, trans. G. W. Butterworth. London and New York: Loeb Classical Library, 1919.

Cline, J. M. "*Hydriotaphia*," *Five Studies in Literature, University of California Publications in English*, 8 (1940): 73–100.

Collingwood, R. G. *The Idea of Nature.* New York, 1960.

Cornford, Francis M. *Plato and Parmenides.* London, 1939.

———. *Plato's Theory of Knowledge.* London, 1935.

Croll, Morris. "Attic Prose in the Seventeenth Century," *Studies in Philology*, 18 (1921): 79–128.

———. "Attic Prose: Lipsius, Montaigne, Bacon," *Schelling Anniversary Papers*, pp. 117–50. New York, 1923.

———. "The Baroque Style in Prose," *Studies in English Philology: A Miscellany in Honor of Frederick Klaeber*, ed. K. Malone and M. B. Ruud, pp. 427–56. Minneapolis, 1929.

Cudworth, Ralph. *The True Intellectual System of the Universe*, ed. J. Harrison, 3 vols. London, 1845.

Curtius, E. R. *European Literature and the Latin Middle Ages*, trans. W. Trask. New York, 1953.

Descartes, René. *Discours de la méthode.* Paris, 1946.

———. *A Discourse of a Method for the Wel-guiding of*

Reason, and the Discovery of Truth in the Sciences. London, 1649.

Digby, Sir Kenelm. *Observations upon Religio Medici.* London, 1643.

Dionysius the Areopagite. *Works*, trans. John Parker. London, 1897.

———. *On the Divine Names* and *The Mystical Theology*, trans. C. E. Rolt. London and New York, 1920.

Donne, John. *Poems*, ed. H. J. C. Grierson. 2 vols. Oxford, 1912.

———. *The Sermons of John Donne*, ed. G. R. Potter and E. M. Simpson. 10 vols. Berkeley, 1953–62.

Dréano, Maturin. *La Pensée religieuse de Montaigne.* Paris, 1936.

Dunn, W. P. *Sir Thomas Browne: A Study in Religious Philosophy.* Minneapolis, 1950.

Ellmann, Richard. *The Identity of Yeats.* New York, 1954.

Ellrodt, Robert. *Neoplatonism in the Poetry of Spenser.* Geneva, 1960.

Festugière, A. -J. *Contemplation et vie contemplative selon Platon.* Paris, 1950.

———. *La Philosophie de l'amour de Marsile Ficin et son influence sur la littérature Française au XVIe siècle.* Paris 1941.

———. *La Révélation d'Hermès Trismégiste.* 4 vols. Paris, 1944–54.

Ficino, Marsilio. *Commentary on Plato's Symposium*, ed. and trans. Sears Jayne. University of Missouri Studies, Vol. XIX, No. 1; Columbia, 1944.

———. *Opera omnia*, ed. M. Sancipriano and P. O. Kristeller. 2 vols. (1576). Turin, 1959.

———. *Platonic Theology*, trans. in part Josephine L. Burroughs, *Journal of the History of Ideas*, 5 (1944): 227–39.

Finch, Jeremiah S. "Sir Thomas Browne and the Quincunx," *Studies in Philology*, 37 (1940): 274–82.

———. *Sir Thomas Browne: A Doctor's Life of Science and Faith.* New York, 1950.

First Book of Common Prayer (1549). London: Everyman's Library, 1910.

Francis of Sales. *An Introduction to a Devoute Life,* [trans. John Yakesley]. 3d ed. Rouen, 1614.

Fuller, Thomas. *The Holy State and the Profane State,* ed. M. G. Walten. 2 vols. New York, 1938.

Garin, Eugenio. *Giovanni Pico della Mirandola.* Florence, 1937.

Gilson, Étienne. *The Christian Philosophy of Saint Augustine,* trans. L. E. M. Lynch. New York, 1960.

———. *History of Christian Philosophy in the Middle Ages.* New York, 1955.

———. *The Philosophy of St. Bonaventura,* trans. I. Trethowan and F. J. Sheed. New York, 1938.

Glanvill, Joseph. *The Vanity of Dogmatizing.* London, 1661.

Gosse, Edmund. *Sir Thomas Browne.* London, 1905.

Guitton, J. *Le Temps et l'éternité chez Platon et Saint Augustin.* Paris, 1933.

Hales, John. *Tract Concerning Schisme and Schismaticks.* London, 1642.

Harris, Victor. *All Coherence Gone.* Chicago, 1949.

Harrison, John Smith. *Platonism in English Poetry of the Sixteenth and Seventeenth Centuries.* New York, 1903.

Hazlitt, William. *Complete Works,* ed. P. P. Howe. 21 vols. London, 1930–33.

Heideman, Margaret A. "*Hydriotaphia* and *The Garden of Cyrus*: A Paradox and a Cosmic Vision," *University of Toronto Quarterly,* 19 (1950): 235–46.

Herbert, George. *Works,* ed. F. E. Hutchinson. Oxford, 1953.

"Hermes Trismegistus." *Corpus Hermeticum,* ed. A. D. Nock and trans. into French A. -J. Festugière. 4 vols. Paris, 1945–54.

———. *Hermetica,* ed. and trans. Walter Scott. 4 vols. Oxford, 1924–36.

Hobbes, Thomas. *Leviathan,* ed. M. Oakeshott. Oxford, 1946.

Hooker, Richard. *Of The Laws of Ecclesiastical Polity.* 2 vols. London: Everyman's Library, 1907.

Hoopes, Robert. *Right Reason in the English Renaissance.* Cambridge, Mass., 1962.

Huntley, Frank L. "The Publication and Immediate Reception of *Religio Medici*," *The Library Quarterly*, 25 (1955): 203–18.

———. "Sir Thomas Browne and the Metaphor of the Circle," *Journal of the History of Ideas*, 14 (1953): 353–64.

———. *Sir Thomas Browne: A Biographical and Critical Study*. Ann Arbor, 1962.

———. "Sir Thomas Browne: The Relationship of *Urn Burial* and *The Garden of Cyrus*," *Studies in Philology*, 53 (1956): 204–19.

Inge, William R. *The Philosophy of Plotinus*. 2 vols. London, 1918.

Jaeger, Werner. *Aristotle: Fundamentals of the History of His Development*, trans. R. Robinson. Oxford, 1934.

Jayne, Sears. "Ficino and the Platonism of the English Renaissance," *Comparative Literature*, 4 (1952): 214–36.

———. *John Colet and Marsilio Ficino*. Oxford, 1963.

Jordan, Wilbur K. *The Development of Religious Toleration in England*. 4 vols. Cambridge, Mass., 1932–40.

Keynes, Geoffrey. *A Bibliography of Sir Thomas Browne*. Cambridge, 1924.

Klibansky, Raymond. *The Continuity of the Platonic Tradition during the Middle Ages*. London, 1939.

Kocher, Paul H. *Science and Religion in Elizabethan England*. San Marino, Calif., 1953.

Kristeller, Paul O. *The Philosophy of Marsilio Ficino*, trans. Virginia Conant. New York, 1943.

———. *Renaissance Thought*. New York, 1961.

Laud, William. *Works*, ed. W. Scott and J. Bliss. 7 vols. Oxford, 1847–60.

Leroy, Olivier. *Le Chevalier Thomas Browne (1605–1682), médecin, styliste, & métaphysicien*. Paris, 1931.

Lovejoy, Arthur O. *The Great Chain of Being*. Cambridge, Mass., 1936.

Lovejoy, Arthur O. and George Boas. *Primitivism and Related Ideas in Antiquity*. Baltimore, 1935.

McGinn, Donald J. *The Admonition Controversy*. New Brunswick, N. J., 1949.

Macrobius. *Commentary on the Dream of Scipio*, trans. William H. Stahl. New York, 1952.

Martz, Louis L. *The Paradise Within*. New Haven and London, 1964.

———. *The Poetry of Meditation*. New Haven, 1954.

Marvell, Andrew. *Poems and Letters*, ed. H. M. Margoliouth. 2d ed. 2 vols. Oxford, 1952.

Merton, Egon S. *Science and Imagination in Sir Thomas Browne*. New York, 1949.

Migne, J. P. (ed.). *Patrologia Latina*, 221 vols. Paris, 1844–65.

Milton, John. *Complete Poems and Major Prose*, ed. Merritt Y. Hughes. New York, 1957.

———. *Complete Prose Works*, ed. Don M. Wolfe *et al.* 8 vols. New Haven, 1953– .

Mitchell, W. Fraser. *English Pulpit Oratory from Andrewes to Tillotson*. London, 1932.

Moloney, Michael F. "Metre and *Cursus* in Sir Thomas Browne's Prose," *Journal of English and Germanic Philology*, 58 (1959): 60–67.

Montaigne, Michel Eyquem de. *The Essayes of Michael Lord of Montaigne*, trans. John Florio (1603). 3 vols. London: Everyman's Library, 1928.

Morainvillier, Louis de. *Examen philosophiae Platonicae*. St. Malo, 1650.

More, Henry. *A Collection of Several Philosophical Writings of Dr. Henry More*. 2d ed. Cambridge, 1662.

Nelson, John C. *Renaissance Theory of Love*. New York, 1958.

Nicolson, Marjorie H. *The Breaking of the Circle*. Evanston, Ill., 1950.

———. Review of Lynn Thorndike's *A History of Magic and Experimental Science*, Vols. VII and VIII, *The Seventeenth Century* (New York, 1958), *Philological Quarterly*, 38 (1959): 282–85.

Origen. *Writings*, trans. Frederick Crombie. 2 vols. Edinburgh: Antenicene Christian Library, 1869.

Panofsky, Erwin. *Studies in Iconology: Humanistic Themes in the Art of the Renaissance*. New York, 1939.

Parker, Edward L. "The Cursus in Sir Thomas Browne," *PMLA*, 53 (1938): 1037–53.

Pascal, Blaise. *Les Pensées et oeuvres choisies*, ed. J. Dedieu. Paris, 1937.

———. *Pensées*, trans. W. F. Trotter. New York, 1958.

Pater, Walter. *Appreciations*. London, 1889.

Philo Judaeus. *Works*, trans. C. D. Yonge. 4 vols. London: The Bohn Library, 1890.

Plato. *The Dialogues*, trans. B. Jowett. 4 vols. Oxford, 1953.

Plotinus. *The Enneads*, trans. Stephen MacKenna. 2d ed., rev. B. S. Page. London, 1956.

Proclus. *The Elements of Theology*, ed. and trans. E. R. Dodds. Oxford, 1933.

Robb, Nesca A. *Neoplatonism of the Italian Renaissance*. London, 1935.

Rosán, Laurence J. *The Philosophy of Proclus*. New York, 1949.

Ross, Alexander. *Arcana microcosmi*. London, 1652.

———. *Medicus medicatus*. London, 1645.

———. *The New Planet no Planet*. London, 1646.

———. *The Philosophicall Touch-Stone*. London, 1645.

Røstvig, Marie-Sofie. *The Happy Man*. Oslo, 1954.

Saintsbury, George. *A History of English Prose Rhythm*. London, 1912.

Schultz, Howard. *Milton and Forbidden Knowledge*. New York, 1955.

Secret, F. *Les Kabbalistes Chrétiens de la Renaissance*. Paris, 1964.

Sencourt, Robert. *Outflying Philosophy*. London, 1923.

Shorey, Paul. *Platonism Ancient and Modern*. Berkeley, 1938.

———. "Platonism and the History of Science," *Proceedings of the American Philosophical Society*, 66 (1927): 159–82.

———. *What Plato Said*. Chicago, 1933.

Smith, John. *Select Discourses*. London, 1660.

Stephen, Sir Leslie. *Hours in a Library*. 4 vols. London, 1904.

Strachey, Lytton. *Books and Characters*. New York, 1922.

Taylor, A. E. *A Commentary on Plato's Timaeus*. Oxford, 1928.

Taylor, Jeremy. *Works*, ed. R. Heber and C. P. Eden. 10 vols. London, 1847–54.

Tempest, Norton. "Rhythm in the Prose of Sir Thomas Browne," *Review of English Studies*, 3 (1927): 308–18.

Thorndike, Lynn. *A History of Magic and Experimental Science.* Vols. VII and VIII, *The Seventeenth Century*. New York, 1958.

Timaeus a Calcidio translatus commentarioque instructus, ed. J. H. Waszink. London, 1962.

Traherne, Thomas. *Centuries, Poems, and Thanksgivings*, ed. H. M. Margoliouth. 2 vols. Oxford, 1958.

Tulloch, John. *Rational Theology and Christian Philosophy in England in the Seventeenth Century*. 2 vols. Rev. ed. London, 1874.

Tuve, Rosemond. *Elizabethan and Metaphysical Imagery*. Chicago, 1947.

———. *A Reading of George Herbert*. London, 1952.

Vaughan, Henry. *Works*, ed. L. C. Martin. 2d ed. Oxford, 1957.

Vaughan, Thomas. *Anima magica abscondita*. London, 1650.

———. *Anthroposophia theomagica*. London, 1650.

———. *A Hermeticall Banquet Drest by a Spagiricall Cook*. London, 1652.

Villey, Pierre. *Les Sources & l'évolution des essais de Montaigne*. 2d ed. 2 vols. Paris, 1933.

Wallerstein, Ruth. *Studies in Seventeenth-Century Poetic*. Madison, Wisc., 1950.

Warren, Austin. "The Style of Sir Thomas Browne," *Kenyon Review*, 13 (1951): 674–87.

Webber, Joan. *Contrary Music: The Prose Style of John Donne*. Madison, Wisc., 1963.

Westfall, Richard S. *Science and Religion in Seventeenth-Century England*. New Haven, 1958.

Whallon, William. "Hebraic Synonymy in Sir Thomas Browne," *E L H*, 28 (1961): 335–52.

Whichcote, Benjamin. *Moral and Religious Aphorisms*, ed. W. R. Inge. London, 1930.

———. *Works*. 4 vols. Aberdeen, 1751.

White, Helen C. *English Devotional Literature [Prose] 1600–1640*. Madison, Wisc., 1931.

———. *The Tudor Books of Private Devotion.* Madison, Wisc., 1951.

Whitehead, Alfred N. *Science and the Modern World.* London, 1925.

Whittaker, Thomas. *The Neo-Platonists: A Study in the History of Hellenism.* 2d ed. Cambridge, 1918.

Willey, Basil. *The Seventeenth Century Background.* New York, 1953.

Williamson, George. "The Purple of *Urn Burial*," *Modern Philology*, 62 (1964): 110–17.

———. *The Senecan Amble.* Chicago, 1951.

Wilson, F. P. *Seventeenth Century Prose.* Berkeley, 1960.

Wind, Edgar. *Pagan Mysteries in the Renaissance.* New Haven, 1958.

Windelband, Wilhelm. *A History of Philosophy*, trans. James H. Tufts. 2d ed. New York, 1958.

Wolfson, Harry A. *Philo.* Rev. printing. 2 vols. Cambridge, Mass., 1948.

Zeitlin, Jacob. "Development of Bacon's Essays," *Journal of English and Germanic Philology*, 27 (1928): 496–519.

Ziegler, Dewey K. *In Divided and Distinguished Worlds.* Cambridge, Mass., 1943.

INDEX

INDEX